GRA

PHY

APPLIED TYPOGRAPHY 10

edited by Japan Typography Association ©2000

published by Graphic-sha Publishing Co,. Ltd

ISBN4-7661-1157-5   331580   686.22 JAP

First Edition 2000

Graphic-sha Publishing Co., Ltd.

1-9-12 Kudan-kita, Chiyoda-ku,

Tokyo 102-0073 Japan

Phone. 3-3263-4318

Fax. 3-3263-5297

Printed in Japan

University
for the
Creative Arts

Ashley Road
Epsom
Surrey
KT18 5BE

Tel: 01372 202461
E-mail: libraryepsm@uca.ac.uk

A P P L I E D **10**
T Y P O G R A P H Y
J A P A N
T Y P O G R A P H Y
A S S O C I A T I O N

目次 Contents

編集・制作スタッフ
Editorial creative staff

| 年鑑編集長 | Editor in Chief |
| 篠原 榮太 | Eita Shinohara |

| 出版委員長 | Chairman of Publishing Committee |
| 山田 正彦 | Masahiko Yamada |

出版委員	Member of Publishing Committee
味岡 伸太郎	Shintaro Ajioka
石山 俊郎	Toshiro Ishiyama
河井 義則	Yoshinori Kawai
七種 泰史	Yasushi Saikusa
坂元 良弘	Yoshihiro Sakamoto
新谷 秀実	Hidemi Shingai
高田 雄吉	Yukichi Takada
深井 宏	Hiroshi Fukai
藤田 隆	Takashi Fujita
宮坂 克己	Katsumi Miyasaka

| ブックデザイン | Book Design |
| 七種 泰史 | Yasushi Saikusa |

デザイン	Design
七種 泰史	Yasushi Saikusa
武井 真由美	Mayumi Takei
土屋 美恵	Mie Tsuchiya
(株)デザインシグナル	Design Signal Inc.

| 編集・進行 | Editorial Director |
| 山田 信彦 [グラフィック社] | Nobuhiko Yamada [Graphic-sha] |

撮影	Photographer
木原 勝幸 [スタジオ点]	Katsuyuki Kihara [Studio Ten]
田村 尚行 [スタジオ点]	Naoyuki Tamura [Studio Ten]
大谷 昌基 [スタジオ点]	Masaki Otani [Studio Ten]

| 翻訳 | Transrator |
| (株)バベル | Babel Inc. |

| 事務局 | Excutive Office |
| 石井 万里子 | Mariko Ishii |

凡例	AD	アートディレクター	art director
	CD	クリエイティブディレクター	creative director
	DE	デザイナー	designer
	CW	コピーライター	copywriter
	PR	プログラマー	programmer
	PD	プロデューサー	producer
	CG	コンピュータグラフィックス	computer graphics
	WR	ライター	writer
	IL	イラストレーター	illustrator
	PH	フォトグラファー	photographer
	CL	クライアント	client

日本
タイ
ポ
グラ
フィ
年鑑
2000
APPLIED
TYPOGRAPHY 10
JAPAN
TYPOGRAPHY
ASSOCIATION

VISUAL IDENTITY
LOGOTYPES, SYMBOLS, MARKS
TYPEFACES
PICTOGRAMS & DIAGRAMS
GRAPHICS
EDITORIAL
PACKAGING
DISPLAY & ENVIRONMENT
VISUAL & DIGITAL MEDIA
RESEARCH & INVESTIGATION

Shinohara Eita, Editor in Chief

Applied Typography 10 is the 21st installment in this series, which waslaunched back in 1969. The publication, which originally appeared every other year, eventually became an annual, and there have been many vicissitudes and a good deal of trial and error along the way. As I look back today, I think it is worth taking stock of the exact significance of bringing out a publication such as this every year. As is the case with every edition of Applied Typography, one crucial consideration in the choice of pieces to include is deciding what role the publication is to play in the field of typographic design. Our editorial policy has been to give pride of place to works that reflect the trends of the day without losing sight of standard typography. The open-competition format, the limited number of works that can be selected for inclusion, and the physical confines of the book itself all inevitably result in discrepancies with typography as actually practiced -- a perpetual dilemma that will probably always be with us. Nonetheless, I do believe that we have succeeded in raising certain questions on the subject of typography that should provide food for thought about the exact nature of the art. And we have refined our instincts in the process, which should ensure this   publication continues to serve as a source of typographical information well into the future. It is now a century since metal type was first developed in Japan. How has typography grappled with the challenges of modernization in the intervening hundred years? How has it adapted to contemporary society, especially the advent of electronics? The appearance of the Year 2000 edition of Applied Typography is as good a time as any to stop and reflect on these questions. At the same time, one cannot help but wonder how typography will have evolved by 2100, a further hundred years on —though that is a task beyond even the most fertile imagination.

年鑑編集長 篠原 榮太

この日本タイポグラフィ年鑑2000は、1969年に第1号を発刊してから21号目となるものである。当時は隔年刊行だったのを、途中から毎年刊行としたのであるが、その間、紆余曲折と試行錯誤の連続だったような気がする。今、その経過を振り返って、年鑑というものの意味をあらためて自問自答している。毎号のことではあるが、作品の収録では、タイポグラフィックデザインの状況にどんな役割を果たそうとしているのかが重要なポイントになる。その編集方針では、時代を反映しているものを主としながらも、スタンダードなタイポグラフィも見失わないようはかられてきた。公募という形式、そして選考による掲載作品数の限界、更に本という構造では、実作品との差異に矛盾を感じざるを得ないが、これは永遠につづくジレンマとして残るのであろう。しかし、タイポグラフィへのある種の問題提起をしているのは事実だと思うし、その存在の意味を問うものであり、また問われるものでもあろう。今後もその感性を磨きつつ、タイポグラフィ情報を持続させていきたいものである。金属活字が日本で開発されて、およそ100年が経過したが、この100年の間に、タイポグラフィが近代化にどう対峙し、また、エレクトロニクスの発達で、いかに現代社会に対応してきたのか、この2000年号をむかえたことは意義深いものがある。これからの100年、つまり2100年のタイポグラフィは想像もつかないが、それでもなお、2100年のタイポグラフィに想いを馳せるものである。

審査委員長 **工藤 強勝**

グラフィックの核を形成するタイポグラフィ

この一年余りの間、タイポグラフィに関する大変興味深い展覧会の開催と出版物の刊行があった。一つは、1999年2月に『日本のタイポグラフィック1946−95』展がギンザ・グラフィック・ギャラリーで開催、併せて作品集も刊行され、10月には『装幀時代』（臼田捷治著）が発刊した。いずれも共通としているテクストは近代から現在までのモダンタイポグラフィの系譜をタイポグラフィというファクターを中心に縦横に明らかにしている点である。この二つのドキュメントから浮上してくるものはタイポグラフィがいかにグラフィックデザインの核を形成し、受容しているかを明察できることである。さて今年鑑では、設定以来初めて大賞受賞作なしという結果になった。過去の大賞をパースペクティブに眺望しながら議論し、表現への新しい取組み、厚み、密度、完成度など多面的観点から予兆が感じられる該当作品がなく見送ることになった。田中一光による「人間と文字」CD-ROMについては、15年間、世界各地の文字遺産を渉猟し、カレンダーで発表し続けてきた集大成を電子出版化した活動に対しては、何らかの賞に値するのではないかとも話題になった。このようなムーヴメントは長期に携わるので、一年間というスパンで評価することは難しい。今後は数年にわたる活動にも光をあてることも考慮しながら、年鑑の持つポテンシャルをさらに高め、日本だけでなく海外にも広めていきたい。

Kudo Tsuyokatsu Chairman, Screening Committee

Typography : The Core of Graphic Design

The past year or so has seen several extremely interesting events and publications relating to typography. One was the exhibition "The Transition of Modern Typography in Japan 1946-95," held at the Ginza Graphic Gallery in February 1999, and the catalog of works produced to accompany it. This was followed in October by the appearance of Usuda Shoji's Sotei Jidai ("The Age of Bookbinding"). The two publications share a common thread: they skillfully trace the evolution of modern typography down to the present day as an art in its own right. In the process they demonstrate convincingly how typography has always been at the core of graphic design. This year the Applied Typography Grand Prize has not been awarded for the first time since its institution. After much discussion, none of the pieces submitted was found to display the boldness in experimenting with new forms of expression, depth, density, polish and overall promise shown by past winners. It was suggested that Tanaka Ikko's CD-ROM "Man and Writing" deserved some type of commendation. That work is a digital compendium of written texts gathered from every corner of the globe and published in calendar form over the course of fifteen years. However, given its long-term nature, recognizing an endeavor such as this with an annual prize presents some difficulty. Broadening our horizons to take account of projects with a span of years will be one of the tasks that faces us as we strive more fully to harness the potential an annual like this offers. We hope also to expand our readership beyond Japan to other climes.

応募・収録作品点数	カテゴリー	Category	Entered	Selected
Number of Works	ビジュアル・アイデンティティ	VI Systems	86	29
Entered & Selected	ロゴタイプ・シンボルマーク	Logotypes, Symbols, Marks	641	177
	タイプフェイス	Typefaces	17	11
	ピクトグラム	Pictograms	7	4
	ダイヤグラム	Diagrams	5	4
	グラフィック	Graphics	224	70
	エディトリアル	Editorial	77	27
	パッケージ	Packaging	61	14
	環境・立体	Display & Environment	15	7
	映像・デジタルメディア	Visual & Digital Media	3	1
	研究・実験	Research & Investigation	60	18
	合計	Grand Total	1196	362

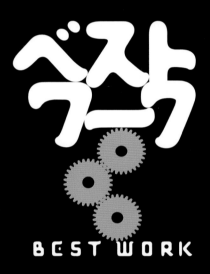

BEST WORK

イサムノグチ
庭園美術館
The Isamu Noguchi Garden Museum Japan

The Isamu Noguchi Garden Museum Japan

3519, Mure, Mure-cho, Kita-gun,
Kagawa, 761-0121, Japan
Phone:087-870-1500 Fax:087-845-0505
イサム・ノグチ庭園美術館
〒761-0121 香川県木田郡牟礼町牟礼3519

イサムノグチ
The Isamu Noguchi Garden Museum Japan
庭園美術館

財団法人イサム・ノグチ日本財団

Curatorial Advisor
Ryu Niimi

事務局長
新見 隆

The Isamu Noguchi Garden Museum Japan.
3519 Mure, Mure-cho, Kita-gun,
Kagawa 761-0121, Japan
Tel:087-870-1500
Fax:087-845-0505
mail:isamuya@mocha.ocn.ne.jp

〒761-0121 香川県木田郡牟礼町牟礼3524-1
電話:美術館087-870-1500 財団087-845-1757
ファックス:087-845-6777
E-mail:isamuya@mocha.ocn.ne.jp

BEST
WORK

001
AD 田中 一光
   IKKO TANAKA
DE 田中 一光
   IKKO TANAKA
   緒方 裕子
   YUKO OGATA
CL イサムノグチ庭園美術館

イサムノグチ庭園美術館　〒761-0121　香川県木田郡牟礼町牟礼3519　Phone:087-870-1500　Fax:087-845-0505

イサム ノグチ
The Isamu Noguchi Garden Museum Japan
庭園美術館

The Isamu Noguchi Garden Museum Japan
3519, Mure, Mure-cho, Kita-gun,
Kagawa, 761-0121, Japan
Phone:087-870-1500　Fax:087-845-0505

イサム ノグチ
The Isamu Noguchi Garden Museum Japan
庭園美術館

The Isamu Noguchi Garden Museum Japan
3519, Mure, Mure-cho, Kita-gun,
Kagawa, 761-0121, Japan
Phone:087-870-1500　Fax:087-845-0505

001

スカパー！だらけの1999年。
SKY PerfecTV!

AD　長谷川 羊介
　　YOSUKE HASEGAWA

DE　長谷川 羊介
　　YOSUKE HASEGAWA

CL　日本デジタル放送サービス

SKY PerfecTV!

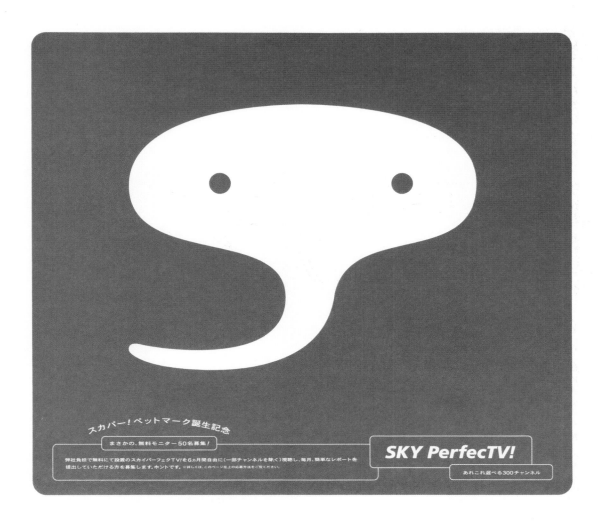

002

11

003

003

AD 味岡 伸太郎
SHINTARO AJIOKA

DE 味岡 伸太郎
SHINTARO AJIOKA

CL 日本タイポグラフィ協会

004

BEST
WORK

004

AD 中川 憲造
KENZO NAKAGAWA

DE 延山 博保
HIROYASU NOBUYAMA

CL 明治製菓

珈琲
CLUB

COFFEE IS THE BEST OF ALL MEDICINES.
IT'S SAVORY AROMA IS OUR PLEASURE.

005

BEST
WORK

005

AD 森沢 博之
   HIROYUKI MORISAWA

DE 森沢 博之
   HIROYUKI MORISAWA

CL 珈琲 CLUB

タカキング

BEST
WORK

006
AD 高原 新一
   SHINICHI TAKAHARA
DE 高原 新一
   SHINICHI TAKAHARA
CL たかデザインプロダクション

書体名：タカキング

あいうえおかきくけこ
さしすせそたちってと
なにぬねのはひふへほ
まみむめもやゝゆよん
アイウエオカキクケコ
サシスセソタチツテト

変梭或嬰壱液駅悦謁榎
援演擲庵欧我画改獲角
耭較鎧侃乾寒勧巻基畿
欺蟻座峡恭弩極欣筋緊
形畦込此墾社爵釈若譲
擾殖森粗創爽凋喋帳暢

BEST
WORK

006

AD 高原 新一
    SHINICHI TAKAHARA

DE 高原 新一
    SHINICHI TAKAHARA

CL たかデザインプロダクション

森の妖精たち
料理とお酒を堪能
笑顔の花嫁さん

夢講座　祝賀
陶創作展
権利者

アズ明朝体W5

あいうえおかきくけこ
さしすせそたちつてと
なにぬねのはひふへほ
まみむめもやゆよらり
るれろわをんゐゑーー

アイウエオカキクケコ
サシスセソタチツテト
ナニヌネノハヒフヘホ
マミムメモヤユヨラリ
ルレロワヲンヰヱーー

BEST WORK

007

AD 東幸央
YUKIO AZUMA

DE 東幸央
YUKIO AZUMA

CL 白水社

海から吹きよせる風は
銀色に輝く都市の上空で
ゆっくりと旋回し、
言葉のぬけがらを拾いあつめ
北をめざして去ろうとしていた。

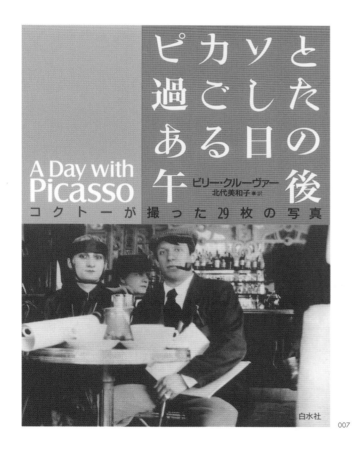

ピカソと
過ごした
ある日の
午後
A Day with
Picasso
コクトーが
撮った 29 枚の写真

ビリー・クルーヴァー
北代美和子＊訳

白水社
007

海から吹きよせる風は
銀色に輝く都市の上空で
ゆっくりと旋回し、
言葉のぬけがらを拾いあつめ
北をめざして去ろうとしていた。

書体名：アズ明朝体W5（カナ書体）

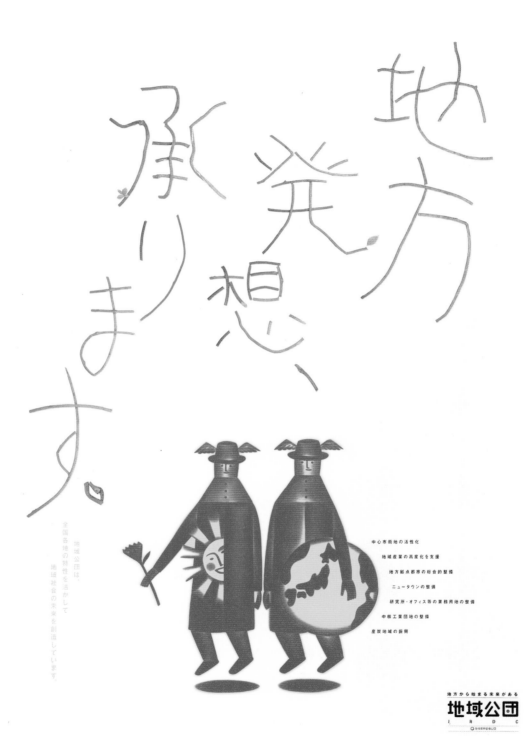

地方発想、承ります。

地域公団は、全国各地の特質を活かして、地球社会の未来を創造しています。

中心市街地の活性化
地域産業の高度化を支援
地方拠点都市の総合的整備
ニュータウンの整備
研究所・オフィス等の業務用地の整備
中核工業団地の整備
産炭地域の振興

地方から始まる未来がある
地域公団
J R D C
地域振興整備公団

BEST
WORK

008

AD 樋口 清孝
   KIYOTAKA HIGUCHI

DE 樋口 清孝
   KIYOTAKA HIGUCHI

CW 丸山 暁美
   AKEMI MARUYAMA

PH 樋口 清孝
   KIYOTAKA HIGUCHI

IL ネモト 円筆
   ENPITSU NEMOTO

CL 地域振興整備公団

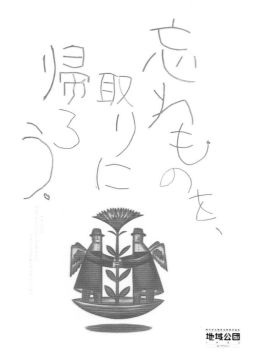

忘れものを、取りに帰ろう。

東京って、誰のふるさとなんだろう。

地域公団

活気が街にやって来る。

地域公団

緑黄色を摂ると、会社も元気になる。

地域公団

008

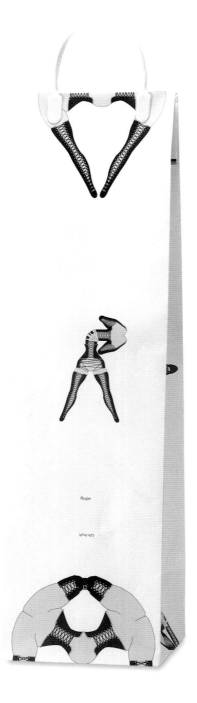

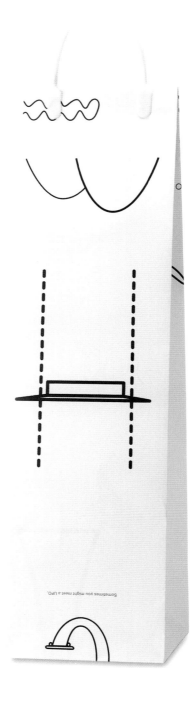

Rope

Uh-huh

letters

Sometimes you might meet a UFO.

BEST
WORK

009

AD 奥村 昭夫
AKIO OKUMURA

DE 奥村 昭夫
AKIO OKUMURA

吉倉 隆之
TAKAYUKI YOSHIKURA

CL インターメディウム研究所

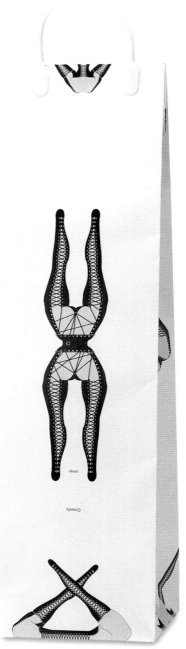

Don't worry. Just make a phone call home.

Heel

Greedy

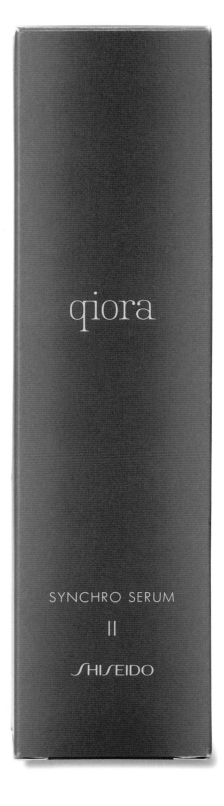

BEST WORK

010

AD 池田 修一
SHUICHI IKEDA

工藤 青石
AOSHI KUDO

DE 平野 敬子
KEIKO HIRANO

工藤 青石
AOSHI KUDO

松本 泉
IZUMI MATSUMOTO

菊池 泰輔
TAISUKE KIKUCHI

池谷 潤子
JUNKO IKEGAYA

CD 池田 修一
SHUICHI IKEDA

CL 資生堂

010

25

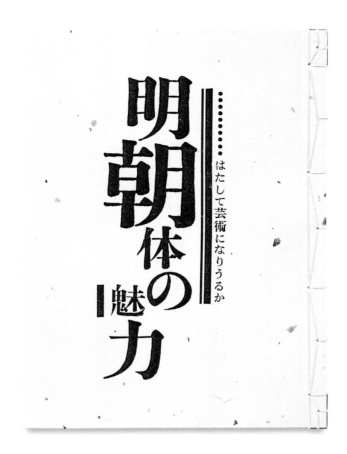

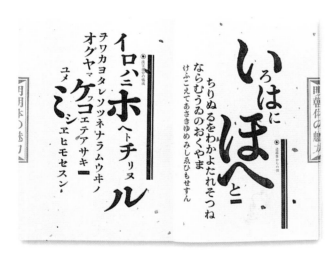

011
AD 篠原 榮太
EITA SHINOHARA

DE 篠原 榮太
EITA SHINOHARA

CL レターハウス

011

27

スケールを作る

care of　Press Book 1

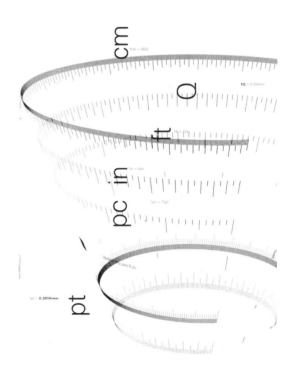

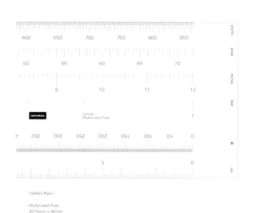

Yukihiro Kanzi

Multiscaled Rule
357.5mm x 90mm

BEST WORK

353

AD 山口 信博
NOBUHIRO YAMAGUCHI

DE 斎藤 広介
KOSUKE SAITO

斎藤 亜季子
AKIKO SAITO

CL 山口デザイン事務所

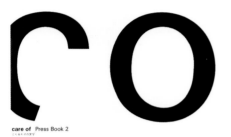

care of Press Book 2
とりあわせの文字

Hiro Sugiyama

写真と空間のとりあわせ
Photo: Irving Penn

Yoshihiro Saito

写真と言葉の組み合わせ
によるタイポグラフィの
タイトル・試行
Photo: Raquel Dompierre

Trippen

trippen

Nobuhiko Yamaguchi

写真と空間のとりあわせ
Photo: Irving Penn

care of Press Book 2

Yoshihiro Saito

Kosuke Saito

Akiko Saito

中国語

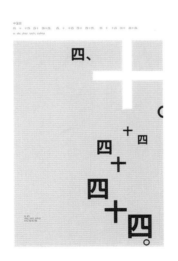

ドイツ語

イタリア語

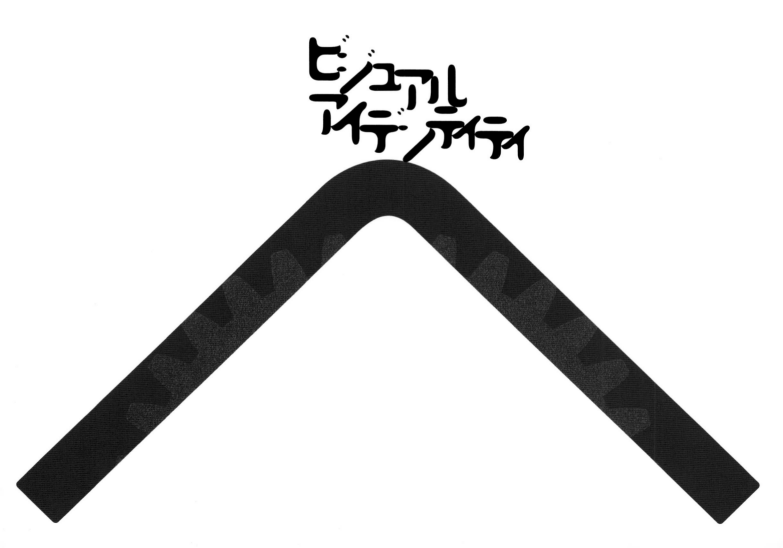

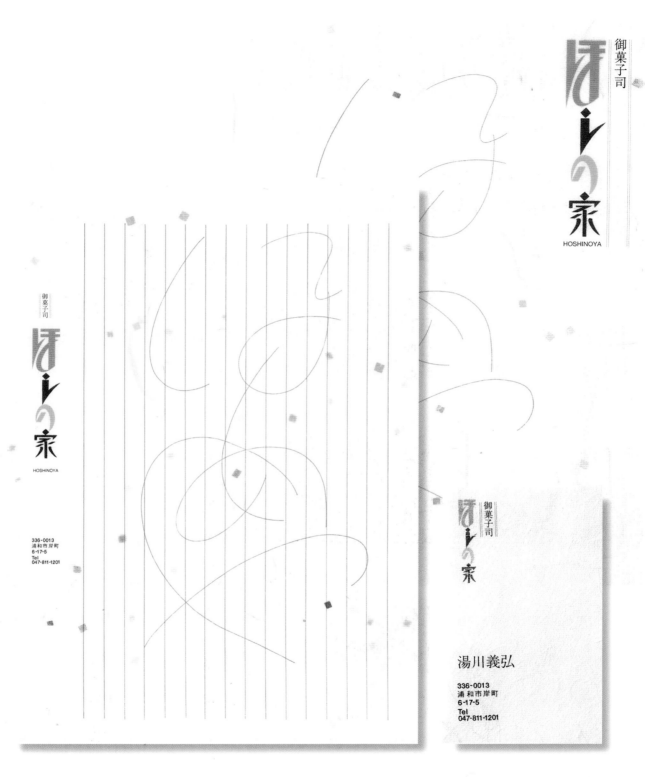

012

AD 篠原 榮太
EITA SHINOHARA

DE 篠原 榮太
EITA SHINOHARA

CL ほしの家

imi
nen
tds
eit
rui
mt
u
te

Inter Medium Institute Graduate School
(IMI GS)
Public Relations

Ai Yamakawa
e-mail : yamakawa@iminet.ac.jp

Inter Medium Institute (IMI)
Box100 21F World Trade Center Bldg,
1-14-16, Nankokita, Suminoe-ku, Osaka
559-0034 JAPAN
phone +81-6-6615-6390   fax +81-6-6615-6391
URL: http://www.iminet.ac.jp/

imi
nen
tds
eit
rui
mt
u
te

インターメディウム研究所 (IMI)　〒559-0034 大阪市住之江区南港北1-14-16 大阪WTCビル21階 メールボックス100番　phone 06-6615-6390　fax 06-6615-6391

imi
nen
tds
eit
rui
mt
u
te

インターメディウム研究所 (IMI)
〒559-0034 大阪市住之江区南港北1-14-16 大阪WTCビル21階 メールボックス100番
phone 06-6615-6390　fax 06-6615-6391

013

AD　奥村 昭夫
　　AKIO　OKUMURA

DE　時本 知広
　　TOMOHIRO　TOKIMOTO

CL　インターメディウム研究所

013

World Environment Day
Global 500 Roll of Honour
グローバル500賞

5 June, 1999   Tokyo, Japan

World Environment Day
Commemorative Symposium

World Environment Day
Celebrations
世界環境デー記念行事

5 June, 1999 Tokyo

INVITATION
ご招待券

World Environment Day
Ceremony of Global 500 Award
記念式典

平成11年6月5日(土)
東京プリンスホテル「鳳凰の間」
Saturday, 5 June, 1999
Ho-O-no-Ma, The Tokyo Prince Hotel

014
AD 三木 健
KEN MIKI

DE 三木 健
KEN MIKI

酒井田 成之
SHIGEYUKI SAKAIDA

高橋 佐和
SAWA TAKAHASHI

CL United Nations
Environment Programme

014

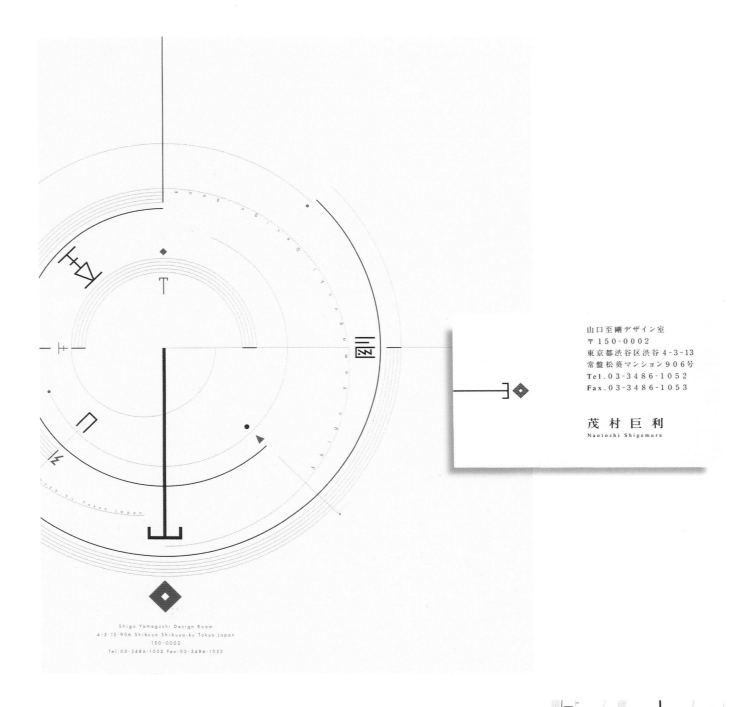

山口至剛デザイン室
〒150-0002
東京都渋谷区渋谷4-3-13
常盤松葵マンション906号
Tel.03-3486-1052
Fax.03-3486-1053

茂村巨利
Naotoshi Shigemura

Shigo Yamaguchi Design Room
4-3-13-906 Shibuya Shibuya-ku Tokyo Japan
150-0002
Tel 03-3486-1052 Fax 03-3486-1053

015

AD 山口 至剛
SHIGO YAMAGUCHI

DE 茂村 巨利
NAOTOSHI SHIGEMURA

CL 山口至剛デザイン室

015

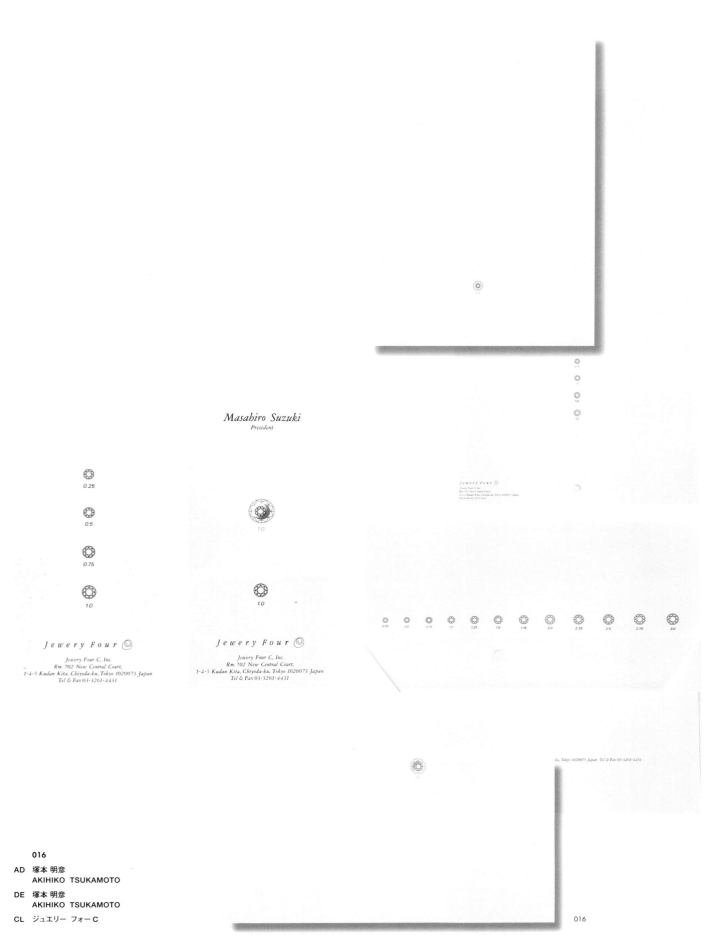

016

AD 塚本 明彦
　　AKIHIKO TSUKAMOTO

DE 塚本 明彦
　　AKIHIKO TSUKAMOTO

CL ジュエリー フォーC

017

AD　立花 幹也
　　MIKIYA TACHIBANA

DE　イエロードッグスタジオ
　　YELLOW DOG STUDIO

CL　クレヨン

Mobile Land

Mobile Land

018

018

AD 奥村 昭夫
AKIO OKUMURA

DE 福本 泰代
YASUYO FUKUMOTO

CL ジャパンブリッジ

2000年度〈第五期〉研究生募集中
説明会・入試日程はお問い合わせください。

マルチメディア時代の新しい価値を創造するために

Inter Medium Institute Graduate School

マルチメディア時代の新しい価値を創造するために

Inter Medium Institute Graduate School

019

AD 奥村 昭夫
AKIO OKUMURA

DE 福本 泰代
YASUYO FUKUMOTO

CL インターメディウム研究所

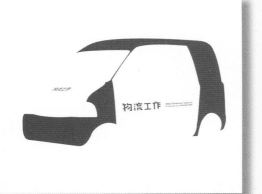

物流工作

020

AD 奥村 昭夫
AKIO OKUMURA

DE 福本 泰代
YASUYO FUKUMOTO

CL ジャパンブリッジ

AD 飯守 恪太郎
    KAKUTARO IIMORI

DE 飯守 恪太郎
    KAKUTARO IIMORI

    小林 珠美
    TAMAMI KOBAYASHI

PD 平島 節夫
    SETSUO HIRASHIMA

CW 酒井 千尋
    CHIHIRO SAKAI

CL インフォマティクス

021

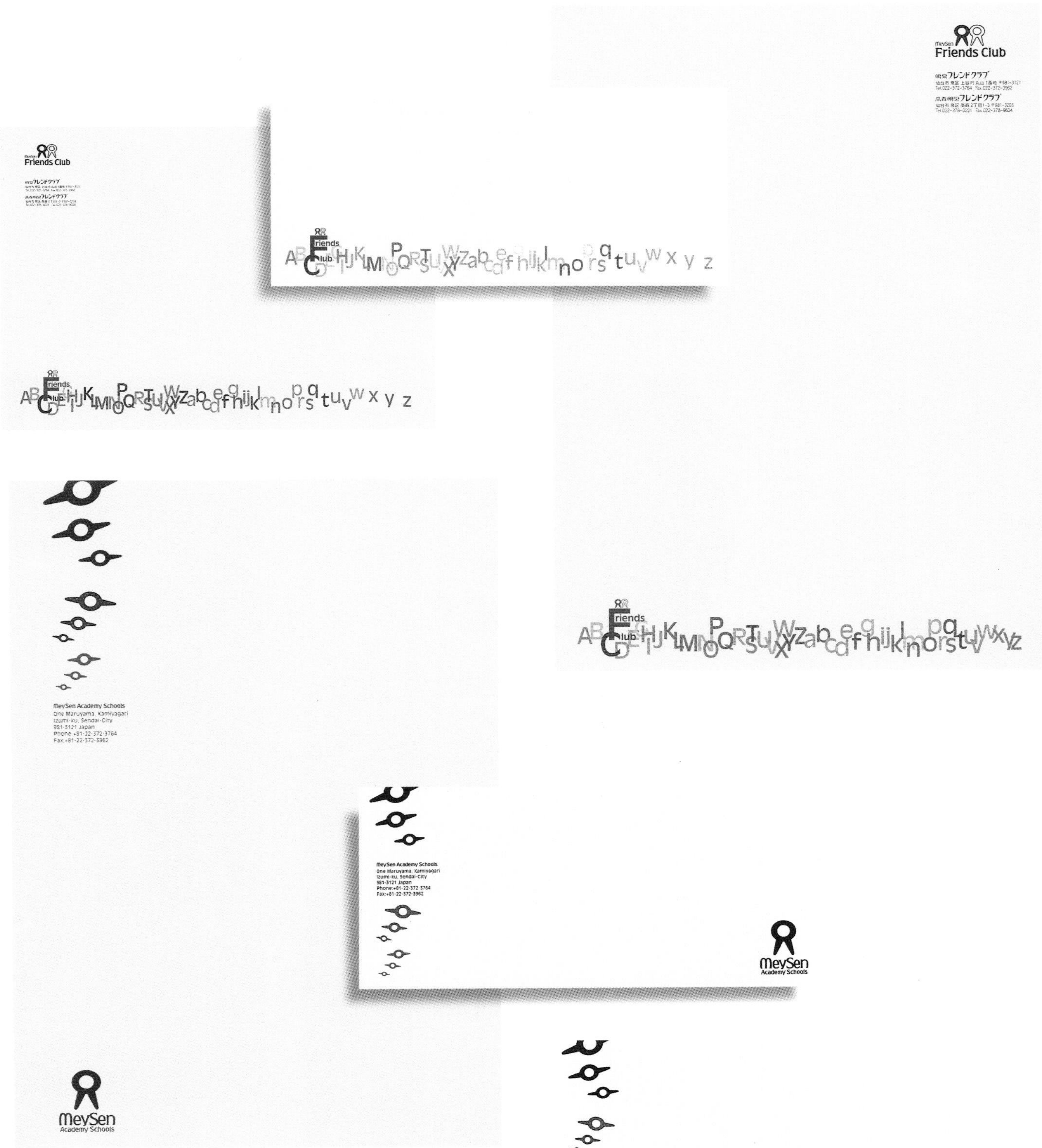

022

AD 飯守 恪太郎
KAKUTARO IIMORI

DE 飯守 恪太郎
KAKUTARO IIMORI

小林 珠美
TAMAMI KOBAYASHI

CW 酒井 千尋
CHIHIRO SAKAI

CL 宮城明泉学園

022

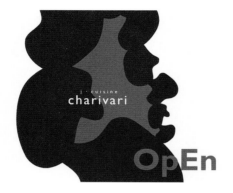

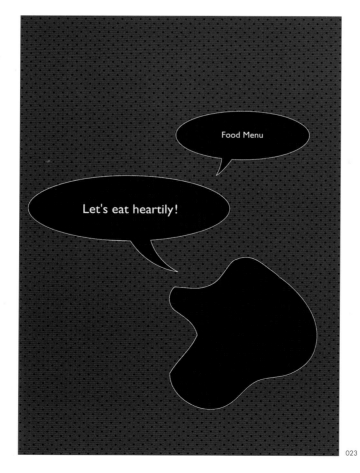

023
AD シマダ タモツ
   TAMOTSU SHIMADA
DE シマダ タモツ
   TAMOTSU SHIMADA
CW 上村 慎也
   SHINYA KAMIMURA
CL せつ

add co.,ltd.

企画営業部・プロデューサー
津 好 京 子

株式会社アッド
〒556-0014大阪市浪速区
大国2丁目17番9号
tel:06 6641 2626 fax:06 6641 2636
http://ss4.inet-osaka.or.jp/~addco/
E-mail:addco@mbox.inet-osaka.or.jp

add co.,ltd.

2-17-9
Daikoku Naniwa-ku
Osaka Japan

add co.,ltd.

2-17-9
Daikoku Naniwa-ku
Osaka Japan

024

024

AD   シマダ タモツ
    TAMOTSU SHIMADA

DE   シマダ タモツ
    TAMOTSU SHIMADA

CL   アッド

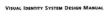

神戸国際会館
KOBE INTERNATIONAL HOUSE

神戸国際会館
KOBE INTERNATIONAL HOUSE

株式会社 神戸国際会館
神戸市中央区御幸通 8丁目1番6号　〒651-0087
Tel: 078-231-8161 (代表)　Fax: 078-231-8120

KOBE INTERNATIONAL HOUSE CO.,LTD.
8-1-6, Goko-dori, Chuo-ku, KOBE 651-0087, Japan
Tel: +81-(0)78-231-8161　Fax: +81-(0)78-231-8120

神戸国際会館
KOBE INTERNATIONAL HOUSE

株式会社 神戸国際会館
神戸市中央区御幸通 8丁目1番6号　〒651-0087
Tel: 078-231-8161 (代表)　Fax: 078-231-8120

KOBE INTERNATIONAL HOUSE CO.,LTD.
8-1-6, Goko-dori, Chuo-ku, KOBE 651-0087, Japan
Tel: +81-(0)78-231-8161　Fax: +81-(0)78-231-8120

025

025

AD　藤脇 慎吾
　　SHINGO FUJIWAKI

DE　中川 亮
　　RYO NAKAGAWA

　　西村 真一
　　SHINICHI NISHIMURA

CL　神戸国際会館

有限会社ニード
457-0066
名古屋市南区鳴尾2-104
Telephone 052-613-2525
Facsimile 052-613-2525

NEED Inc.
2-104 Naruo Minamiku Nagoya
457-0066 Japan
Telephone 8152-613-2525
Facsimile 8152-613-2525

有限会社ニード
457-0066
名古屋市南区鳴尾2-104
Telephone 052-613-2525
Facsimile 052-613-2525

NEED Inc.
2-104 Naruo Minamiku Nagoya
457-0066 Japan
Telephone 8152-613-2525
Facsimile 8152-613-2525

有限会社ニード
457-0066
名古屋市南区鳴尾2-104
Telephone 052-613-2525
Facsimile 052-613-2525

新海　掌
クリエイティブディレクター

026
AD　山田 正彦
　　MASAHIKO　YAMADA
DE　山田 正彦
　　MASAHIKO　YAMADA
CL　ニード

026

office

office

プロデューサー
紀田 寛

株式会社 オフィス カン
〒107-0061 東京都港区北青山3-10-8 北条ビル4F
TEL・FAX:03-3499-8488
本社:〒410-0815 静岡県沼津市南本郷町8-31
TEL:0559-33-5075 FAX:0559-33-6121

office

027

027

AD 井川 啓
　 KEI IKAWA

DE 井川 啓
　 KEI IKAWA

CL オフィス カン

taki corporation

営業部

松本さおり

株式会社 タキコーポレーション
〒151-0051
東京都渋谷区千駄ヶ谷3-7-4 アカデミービル3F
tel.03-3478-8022　fax.03-3478-8023
taki-pic@tc4.so-net.ne.jp

sales dept.

saori matsumoto

taki corporation inc.
academy bldg. 3f, 3-7-4, sendagaya,
shibuya-ku, tokyo, 151-0051 japan
tel. 81-3-3478-8022　fax. 81-3-3478-8023
taki-pic@tc4.so-net.ne.jp

taki corporation

taki corporation

taki corporation inc.
academy bldg. 3f, 3-7-4, sendagaya, shibuya-ku, tokyo, 151-0051 japan tel. 81-3-3478-8022 fax. 81-3-3478-8023 taki-pic@tc4.so-net.ne.jp

028

AD　海老名 淳
　　ATZSHI EVINA

DE　海老名 淳
　　ATZSHI EVINA

CL　タキコーポレーション

028

有限会社 キキ・コンサルティング
東京都 新宿区 西新宿 1-26-2 新宿野村ビル 36階 〒163-0553
KIKI CONSULTING CO.,LTD.
Shinjyuku Nomura Bldg.36F 26-2,Nishi-Shinjyuku, 1-chome,Shinjyuku-ku,Tokyo 163-0553

Phone: 03-5325-6590   Facsimile: 03-5325-6591

KIKI
CONSULTING
CO.,LTD.

代表取締役
石田 由紀子

有限会社 キキ・コンサルティング
東京都新宿区西新宿 1-26-2
新宿野村ビル 36階 〒163-0553
Phone：03-5325-6590
Facsimile：03-5325-6591

AIU保険会社 代理店

Director
Yukiko Ishida

KIKI CONSULTING CO.,LTD.
Shinjyuku Nomura Bldg.36F
26-2,Nishi-Shinjyuku, 1-chome,
Shinjyuku-ku,Tokyo163-0553
Phone：03-5325-6590
Facsimile：03-5325-6591

24時間緊急サービス
（AIGカスタマーサポート）
フリーダイヤル：0120-01-9016

KIKI
CONSULTING
CO.,LTD.

029

AD 寒河江 亘太
    KOTA SAGAE

DE 寒河江 亘太
    KOTA SAGAE

CD 岡本 欣也
    KINYA OKAMOTO

CW 岡本 欣也
    KINYA OKAMOTO

CL キキ・コンサルティング

029

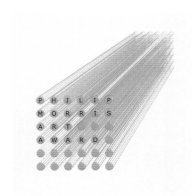

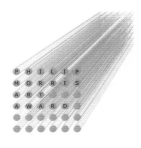

PHILIP MORRIS ART AWARD
Aoyama Tower Bldg. 9F, 2-24-15, Minamiaoyama, Minato-ku, Tokyo 107-0062, Japan
Phone:03-3405-8332 Fax:03-3405-5417 Home Page:www.pm-artaward.net

PHILIP MORRIS ART AWARD
Aoyama Tower Bldg. 9F, 2-24-15, Minamiaoyama, Minato-ku, Tokyo 107-0062, Japan
Phone:03-3405-8332 Fax:03-3405-5417 Home Page:www.pm-artaward.net

030

030

AD 寒河江 亘太
　　KOTA SAGAE

DE 寒河江 亘太
　　KOTA SAGAE

CD 浅野 豊久
　　TOYOHISA ASANO

CL フィリップモリス

デザイン神田屋
京都府相楽郡精華町光台7-2-2-5-404
〒619-0237
Tel. & Fax.0774-94-5802

031
AD 神田 浩
HIROSHI KANDA

DE 神田 浩
HIROSHI KANDA

CL デザイン神田屋

031

ひめじウェルカム21実行委員会
姫路市記念事業推進室

〒670-8501
姫路市安田四丁目1番地
Tel.0792-21-2101
Fax.0792-21-2834
URL/http://www.welcome21.co.jp
E-mail/info@welcome21.co.jp

032

AD　平野 敬子
　　KEIKO HIRANO

DE　平野 敬子
　　KEIKO HIRANO

CL　ひめじウェルカム21実行委員会

032

tatsuya Satoh

a   j   r
h   a
              i   m

佐 藤 辰 哉

770-0911 徳島市東船場1丁目13番地 TiOビルNew-3F
tel/fax:088-655-4058　予約ダイヤル0120-405-877

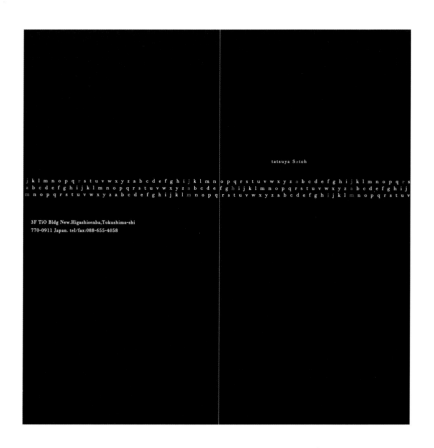

tatsuya Satoh

jklmnopqrstuvwxyzabcdefghijklmnopqrstuvwxyzabcdefghijklmnopqrs
abcdefghijklmnopqrstuvwxyzabcdefghijklmnopqrstuvwxyzabcdefghij
mnopqrstuvwxyzabcdefghijklmnopqrstuvwxyzabcdefghijklmnopqrstuv

3F TiO Bldg New.Higashisenba,Tokushima-shi
770-0911 Japan. tel/fax:088-655-4058

Certificate of Guarantee

tatsuya Satoh

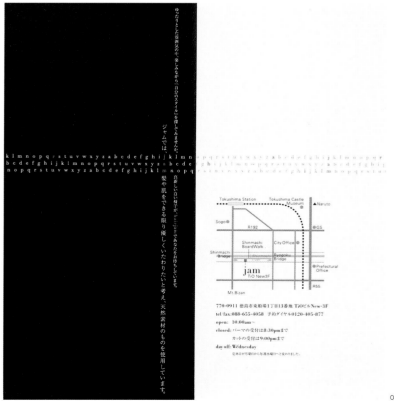

jam
TiO New-3F

770-0911 徳島市東船場1丁目13番地 TiOビルNew-3F
tel/fax:088-655-4058　予約ダイヤル0120-405-877
open: 10:00am〜
closed: パーマの受付は8:30pmまで
　　　カットの受付は9:00pmまで
day off: Wednesday
定休日が月曜日から与週水曜日へと変わりました。

033

AD　藤本 孝明
　　TAKAAKI FUJIMOTO

DE　藤本 孝明
　　TAKAAKI FUJIMOTO

CL　ヘア・ジャム

033

M.Y.K NORIKO
DESIGN OFFICE：107-0062 東京都港区南青山5-3-27 裕実生御南青山ビル90F作　Tel.03-5464-0343 Fax.03-5464-0342
SHOP：107-0062 東京都港区南青山5-3-10 フロムファーストビルB1　Tel.03-5464-2410 Fax.03-5464-2411

デザイナー
福島 紀子

M.Y.K. NORIKO
ショップ：107-0062 東京都港区南青山5-3-10 フロムファーストビルB1
Tel.03-5464-2410 Fax.03-5464-2411

034

AD　田中 一光
　　IKKO　TANAKA

DE　田中 一光
　　IKKO　TANAKA

　　大内 修
　　OSAMU　OUCHI

CL　御幸毛織

034

TETSUYA OHTA

TEL: 03-3479-3697 FAX: 03-3479-6434
Sun Minami-Aoyama 303
3-14-14 Minami-Aoyama Minato-ku
TOKYO 107-0062 JAPAN

TETSUYA OHTA DESIGN STUDIO

TETSUYA OHTA DESIGN STUDIO

TETSUYA OHTA
TEL: 03-3479-3697 FAX: 03-3479-6434
Sun Minami-Aoyama 303
3-14-14 Minami-Aoyama Minato-ku
TOKYO 107-0062 JAPAN

TETSUYA OHTA DESIGN STUDIO

TETSUYA OHTA
TEL: 03-3479-3697 FAX: 03-3479-6434
Sun Minami-Aoyama 303
3-14-14 Minami-Aoyama Minato-ku
TOKYO 107-0062 JAPAN

TETSUYA OHTA DESIGN STUDIO

TETSUYA OHTA
TEL: 03-3479-3697 FAX: 03-3479-6434
Sun Minami-Aoyama 303
3-14-14 Minami-Aoyama Minato-ku
TOKYO 107-0062 JAPAN

035
AD 太田 徹也
　　TETSUYA OHTA

DE 太田 徹也
　　TETSUYA OHTA

CL 太田徹也デザイン室

035

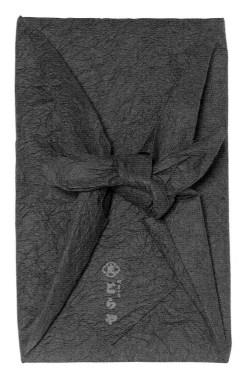

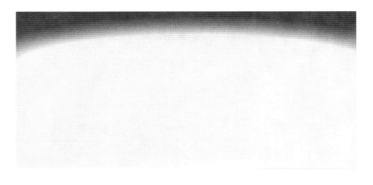

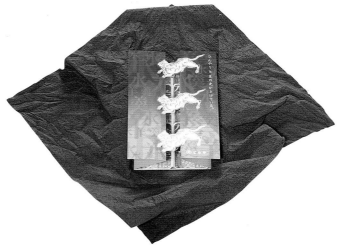

036

AD 鈴木 善博
ZEMPAKU SUZUKI

DE 鈴木 善博
ZEMPAKU SUZUKI

近馬 朋子
TOMOKO KONMA

CW 松塚 しのぶ
SHINOBU MATSUZUKA

CL 虎屋

036

カトリック大阪大司教区
補佐司教
松浦 悟郎
〒540-0004　大阪市中央区玉造 2 - 24 - 22
Tel.06・6941・9700　Fax.06・6946・1345

Auxiliary Bishop
Michael Goro Matsuura
Archbishop's Residence
24 - 22, 2-chome, Tamatukuri, Chuo-ku, Osaka,
540 - 0004 Japan.
Tel.06 - 6941 - 9700　Fax.06 - 6946 - 1345

037

AD　関 和廣
　　KAZUHIRO SEKI

DE　関 和廣
　　KAZUHIRO SEKI

CW　松浦 悟郎
　　GORO MATSUURA

CL　松浦悟郎

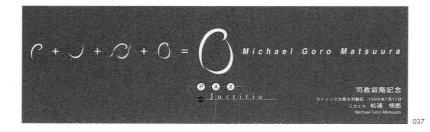

037

038

AD　ソニーデザインセンター
　　SONY CORPORATION
　　DESIGN CENTER

DE　尾村 匡昭
　　MASAAKI OMURA

　　福原 寛重
　　HIROSHIGE FUKUHARA

　　中山 禎之
　　YOSHIYUKI NAKAYAMA

CL　ソニー

038

AD 8vo
8vo

DE 8vo
8vo

CL USP Arts

14-29 August 1998
Queen's Hall Jaffa Cake

Flux

Live new music at the Edinburgh Festival Fringe

Nick Cave, Spiritualized, PJ Harvey, The Jesus and Mary Chain, Asian Dub Foundation, Ken Kesey, David Thomas, John Zorn
and much more

Edinburgh Fringe, Aug 98

Flux

@Jaffa Cake
Grassmarket
Sun 16/Mon 17 The Jesus & Mary Chain. Tue 18 Je t'aime Gainsbourg. Thu 20 Roddy Frame. Fri 21 The Bathers, Pearl Fishers. The Swiss Family Orbison. Sat 22 Arab Strap & The Nectarine No 9. Sun 23 David Thomas & Yo La Tengo. Tue 25 P J Harvey. Thu 27 Asian Dub Foundation.
All doors 8pm
Tickets from £8
Box Office 0131 667 7776
A USP Arts Presentation

Edinburgh Fringe, Aug 98

Flux

@Queen's Hall
Clerk Street
Fri 14/Sat 15 Spiritualized & Steve Martland. Sun 16 Ken Kesey & Ken Babbs. Fri 21 Sat 22 Nick Cave. Fri 28 John Zorn. Sat 29 The Creatures.
All doors 8pm
Tickets from £10
Box Office 0131 667 7776
A USP Arts Presentation

Edinburgh Fringe, Aug 98

Flux

@Queen's Hall Clerk Street
Fri 14/Sat 15 Spiritualized & Steve Martland. Sun 16 Ken Kesey & Ken Babbs. Fri 21 Sat 22 Nick Cave. Fri 28 John Zorn. Sat 29 The Creatures.
@Jaffa Cake Grassmarket
Sun 16/Mon 17 The Jesus & Mary Chain. Tue 18 Je t'aime Gainsbourg. Thu 20 Roddy Frame. Fri 21 The Bathers, Pearl Fishers. The Swiss Family Orbison. Sat 22 Arab Strap & The Nectarine No 9. Sun 23 David Thomas & Yo La Tengo. Tue 25 P J Harvey. Thu 27 Asian Dub Foundation.
All doors 8pm
Tickets from £8
Box Office 0131 667 7776
A USP Arts Presentation

040

040

AD 8vo
    8vo

DE 8vo
    8vo

CL USP Arts

A USP ARTS PRESENTATION

EDINBURGH FESTIVAL
13-30 AUGUST 1999
QUEEN'S HALL
ROSS BANDSTAND

FLUX

ORBITAL

KEN KESEY, * WITH THE MAGIC BUS

SPIRITUALIZED
NICK CAVE
JOHN CALE*
MARC ALMOND
THE FALL
IVOR CUTLER*
TINDERSTICKS
DAVID THOMAS
HITCHCOCK'S THE LODGER**

LIVE SCORE BY DIVINE COMEDY'S JOBY TALBOT
PERFORMED BY THE MATRIX ENSEMBLE
TICKETS 0870 90 70 999
0131 220 4349/0131 668 2019
WWW.FLUXFESTIVAL.COM

*IN ASSOCIATION WITH THE EDINBURGH INTERNATIONAL BOOK FESTIVAL
**IN ASSOCIATION WITH THE EDINBURGH INTERNATIONAL FILM FESTIVAL

FESTIVAL REVUE   8vo   W   blue sky ❄   elfi

FLUX
EDINBURGH FESTIVAL
AUGUST 99

INCLUDING OPEN AIR AT
PRINCES STREET GARDENS...

ORBITAL,
NICK CAVE
& MORE...

FESTIVAL REVUE   LEVI'S

PERFECT LATE-NIGHT SETTING.

ROSS BANSTAND, PRINCES ST. GARDENS
FRI 27TH AUG, 8PM, £12.50/£10
NICK CAVE
THE WORLD'S COOLEST MAN MAKES A TRIUMPHAL
RETURN WITH A NEW SHOW FOR THIS FLUX EXCLUSIVE –
ACCOMPANIED BY A HAND-PICKED BAND OF MUSICIANS.
CAVE PRESENTS AN EVENING OF NEW SONGS WITH NEW
ARRANGEMENTS OF OLD FAVOURITES.
IN ASSOCIATION WITH FESTIVAL REVUE

ROSS BANSTAND, PRINCES ST. GARDENS
SAT 28TH AUG, 8PM, £12.50
KEN KESEY
AND THE MAGIC BUS
KEN KESEY RETURNS TO FLUX WITH THE MAGIC BUS,
THE ORIGINAL PRANKSTERS AND SPECIAL GUESTS.
HIS 60'S 'ACID TEST' LAUNCHED THE GRATEFUL DEAD,
THE ACID EXPLOSION AND THE SUMMER OF LOVE.
PRANKSTERISM TURNED WOODSTOCK INTO A FREE
FESTIVAL AND MORE RECENTLY WAS THE INSPIRATION
FOR THE RAVE GENERATION. DON'T MISS THIS UNIQUE,
OPEN AIR, PSYCHEDELIC TRIP.
IN ASSOCIATION WITH FESTIVAL REVUE AND THE EDINBURGH
INTERNATIONAL BOOK FESTIVAL

QUEEN'S HALL
MON 30TH AUG, 8PM. (FINISH 10.45PM) £11
TINDERSTICKS
THE HIPPEST BAND IN THE WORLD ARE BACK WITH A
BRAND NEW SHOW LAUNCHING A BRAND NEW ALBUM.
CLASS ACTS COME NO CLASSIER THAN THIS. "ONE OF
THE MOST EAGERLY AWAITED APPEARANCES OF THE
EDINBURGH FESTIVAL", THE SCOTSMAN

041

041

AD 8vo
    8vo

DE 8vo
    8vo

CL USP Arts

ロゴタイプ
シンボルマーク

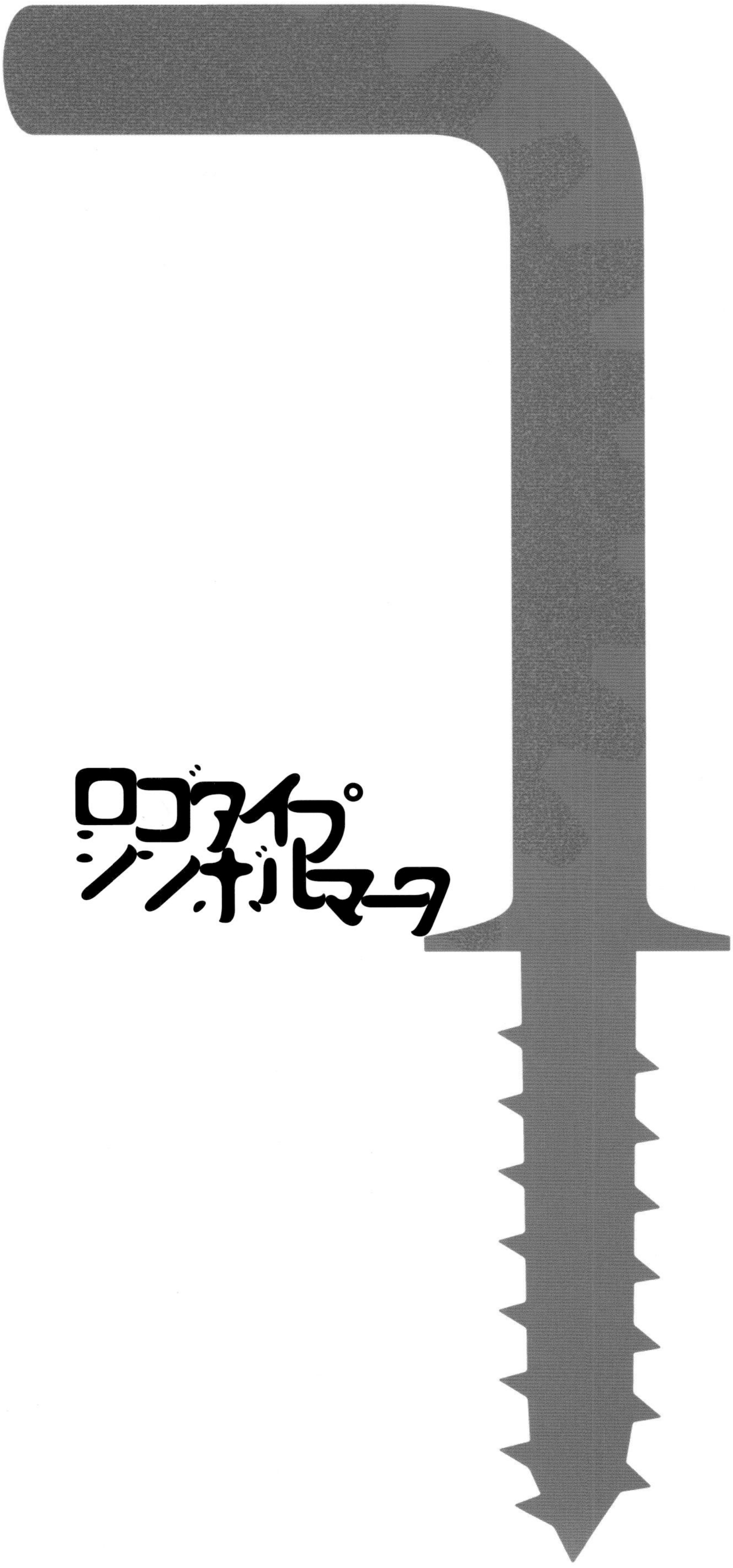

LOGOTYPES,
SYMBOLS, MARKS

042

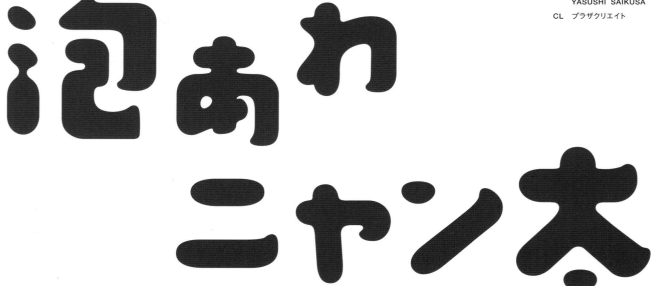

043

042

AD 七種 泰史
YASUSHI SAIKUSA

DE 七種 泰史
YASUSHI SAIKUSA

CL プラザクリエイト

043

AD 七種 泰史
YASUSHI SAIKUSA

DE 七種 泰史
YASUSHI SAIKUSA

CL プラザクリエイト

044

物流工作

045

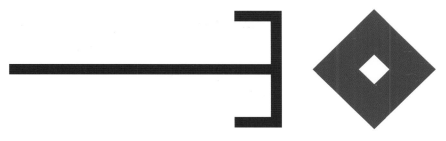

046

044

AD 平澤 卓
TAKU HIRASAWA

DE 青木 陸祐
MICHISUKE AOKI

平澤 卓
TAKU HIRASAWA

CL 愛媛新聞社

045

AD 奥村 昭夫
AKIO OKUMURA

DE 福本 泰代
YASUYO FUKUMOTO

CL ジャパンブリッジ

046

AD 山口 至剛
SHIGO YAMAGUCHI

DE 茂村 巨利
NAOTOSHI SHIGEMURA

CL 山口至剛デザイン室

あなた次第

047

047

AD　本谷 一也
　　 KAZUYA MOTOTANI

　　 片岡 悦郎
　　 ETSUROH KATAOKA

DE　坂元 良弘
　　 YOSHIHIRO SAKAMOTO

CL　エジソン生命

048

AD　高橋 善丸
　　 YOSHIMARU TAKAHASHI

DE　高橋 善丸
　　 YOSHIMARU TAKAHASHI

CL　詩遊社

049

AD　アラン・チャン
　　 ALAN CHAN

DE　アラン・チャン
　　 ALAN CHAN

　　 アルビン・チャン
　　 ALVIN CHAN

　　 マン・ソー・ファン
　　 MAN SO FAN

CL　夢美術館

048

夢美術館
YUME MUSEUM
CANAL CITY

049

050

051

PAPER STUDIO

052

050

AD 七種 泰史
YASUSHI SAIKUSA

DE 土屋 美恵
MIE TSUCHIYA

CL プラザクリエイト

051

AD 濱島 達也
TATSUYA HAMAJIMA

寒河江 亘太
KOTA SAGAE

DE 寒河江 亘太
KOTA SAGAE

CL サントリー

052

AD 三木 健
KEN MIKI

DE 三木 健
KEN MIKI

CL 平和紙業

053

AD 中川 憲造
KENZO NAKAGAWA

DE 延山 博保
HIROYASU NOBUYAMA

CL タワーショップ

054

AD 中川 憲造
KENZO NAKAGAWA

DE 延山 博保
HIROYASU NOBUYAMA

CL 明治製菓

055

AD 中川 憲造
KENZO NAKAGAWA

DE 延山 博保
HIROYASU NOBUYAMA

CL 明治製菓

056

AD 中川 憲造
KENZO NAKAGAWA

DE 延山 博保
HIROYASU NOBUYAMA

　清水 証
AKIRA SHIMIZU

CL タワーショップ

横浜
紅茶

053

054

給食のカレー

055

056

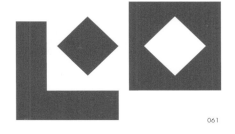

057

060

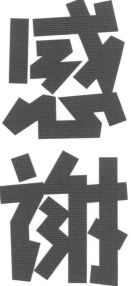

058

061

059

057

AD 山田 正彦
MASAHIKO YAMADA

DE 山田 正彦
MASAHIKO YAMADA

CL DESIGN BOX

058

AD 山田 正彦
MASAHIKO YAMADA

DE 山田 正彦
MASAHIKO YAMADA

CL ジャック

059

AD 山田 正彦
MASAHIKO YAMADA

DE 山田 正彦
MASAHIKO YAMADA

CL ジャック

060

AD 坂元 良弘
YOSHIHIRO SAKAMOTO

DE 坂元 良弘
YOSHIHIRO SAKAMOTO

CL 京王百貨店

061

AD 山口 至剛
SHIGO YAMAGUCHI

DE 島内 泰弘
YASUHIRO SHIMAUCHI

CL デイリー・ヒロ音楽出版社

062

AD 田中 一光
IKKO TANAKA

DE 田中 一光
IKKO TANAKA

緒方 裕子
YUKO OGATA

CL イサムノグチ庭園美術館

063

AD 平澤 卓
TAKU HIRASAWA

DE 青木 陸祐
MICHISUKE AOKI

CL オフィス空間騎行

064

AD 竹智 淳
JUN TAKECHI

DE 竹智 淳
JUN TAKECHI

CG 藤田 裕一
YUICHI FUJITA

CL ミディ

065

AD 青木 陸祐
MICHISUKE AOKI

DE 青木 陸祐
MICHISUKE AOKI

平澤 卓
TAKU HIRASAWA

CL 川田三郎

066

AD 高田 雄吉
YUKICHI TAKADA

DE 高田 雄吉
YUKICHI TAKADA

CL 川崎製鉄、阪急電鉄、
近鉄不動産

062

063

064

065

066

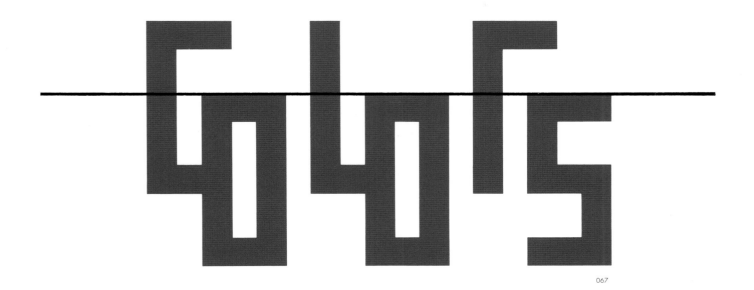

067

068

067

AD 太田 徹也
TETSUYA OHTA

DE 太田 徹也
TETSUYA OHTA

CL カラーズ

068

AD 青葉 益輝
MASUTERU AOBA

DE 赤嶺 知美
TOMOMI AKAMINE

藤井 功
ISAO FUJII

CL リクルート

069

AD 七種 泰史
　　YASUSHI SAIKUSA

DE 七種 泰史
　　YASUSHI SAIKUSA

CL プラザクリエイト

Palette Collection

We love to try them on

069

COMPASS

070

070

AD 七種 泰史
　　YASUSHI SAIKUSA

DE 七種 泰史
　　YASUSHI SAIKUSA

CL 富士薬品

artlist
INTERNATIONAL
C/O. YUBIDO INC. 7-4-2 ATRIUM AOYAMA B1
MINAMI-AOYAMA MINATO-KU TOKYO JAPAN

071

NTT-DO

072

071
AD 三浦 滉平
    KOHEI MIURA

DE 三浦 滉平
    KOHEI MIURA

CL 遊美堂

072
AD 太田 徹也
    TETSUYA OHTA

DE 太田 徹也
    TETSUYA OHTA

CL エヌ・ティ・ティ・ドゥ

073
AD 吉延 高明
    TAKAAKI YOSHINOBU

DE 吉延 高明
    TAKAAKI YOSHINOBU

CL スイートスリープ

073

taiwa

KYOTO PATISSERIE COLLEGE

074

074

AD 奥村 昭夫
AKIO OKUMURA

DE 上野 光生
MITSUO UENO

CL 大和学園

075

AD 橋本 謙次郎
KENJIRO HASHIMOTO

DE 橋本 謙次郎
KENJIRO HASHIMOTO

CL STILL

076

AD 奥村 昭夫
AKIO OKUMURA

DE 福本 泰代
YASUYO FUKUMOTO

CL ジャパンブリッジ

077

AD 藤本 孝明
TAKAAKI FUJIMOTO

DE 藤本 孝明
TAKAAKI FUJIMOTO

CL 東新町一丁目商店街組合

still
STYLISH
SALON

075

076

Shin machi
ATRIUM 1st

077

70

multi-form

078

079

MAIHAMA

080

078

AD 工藤 強勝
TSUYOKATSU KUDO

DE 工藤 強勝
TSUYOKATSU KUDO

安田 真奈己
MANAMI YASUDA

CL ヤギコーポレーション

079

AD 伊藤 勝一
KATSUICHI ITO

DE 伊藤 勝一
KATSUICHI ITO

藤原 俊哉
TOSHIYA FUJIWARA

CL ディジタルビデオ

080

AD 北山 郁夫
IKUO KITAYAMA

DE 伊藤 勝一
KATSUICHI ITO

藤原 俊哉
TOSHIYA FUJIWARA

CL イクスピアリ

081

AD 山田 正彦
MASAHIKO YAMADA

DE 山田 正彦
MASAHIKO YAMADA

CL ニード

082

AD 山口 至剛
SHIGO YAMAGUCHI

DE 島内 泰弘
YASUHIRO SHIMAUCHI

CL デイリー・ヒロ音楽出版社

083

AD 工藤 強勝
TSUYOKATSU KUDO

DE 工藤 強勝
TSUYOKATSU KUDO

CL 佐倉市立美術館

084

AD 海老名 淳
ATZSHI EVINA

DE 海老名 淳
ATZSHI EVINA

CL シティ出版

081

082

083

084

085

086

088

087

089

090

085

AD 寺島 佐知子
SACHIKO TERAJIMA

DE 寺島 佐知子
SACHIKO TERAJIMA

CL ガールスカウト東京第33団

086

AD 野上 周一
SHUICHI NOGAMI

DE 野上 周一
SHUICHI NOGAMI

CL イースト

087

AD 池上 貴文
TAKAFUMI IKEGAMI

DE 池上 貴文
TAKAFUMI IKEGAMI

CL プラザクリエイト

088

AD シャープ総合デザイン本部／
情報システム事業本部
デザインセンター
SHARP CORPORATE
DESIGN CENTER

DE シャープ総合デザイン本部／
情報システム事業本部
デザインセンター
SHARP CORPORATE
DESIGN CENTER

CL シャープ

089

AD ソニーデザインセンター
SONY CORPORATION
DESIGN CENTER

DE 尾村 匡昭
MASAAKI OMURA

中山 禎之
YOSHIYUKI NAKAYAMA

CL ソニー

090

AD 山口 至剛
SHIGO YAMAGUCHI

DE 茂村 巨利
NAOTOSHI SHIGEMURA

CL カルピス

091

AD 井川 啓
 KEI IKAWA

DE 井川 啓
 KEI IKAWA

CL オフィス　カン

092

AD 柏 実
 MINORU KASHIWA

DE 菱田 浩一
 KOICHI HISHIDA

CL ユー・アイ・シー・テレコムジャパン

093

AD 杉本 通規
 MICHINORI SUGIMOTO

DE 杉本 通規
 MICHINORI SUGIMOTO

CL イングス

094

AD 片山 宏明
 HIROAKI KATAYAMA

DE 片山 宏明
 HIROAKI KATAYAMA

CL イージーネット

095

AD 関 和廣
 KAZUHIRO SEKI

DE 関 和廣
 KAZUHIRO SEKI

CL ダブル・クロック

096

AD 関 和廣
 KAZUHIRO SEKI

DE 関 和廣
 KAZUHIRO SEKI

CL ダブル・クロック

091

092

093

094

095

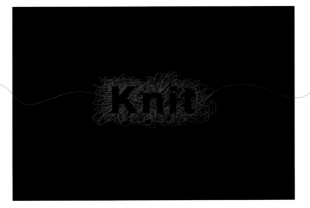

096

097

AD 寒河江 亘太
KOTA SAGAE

DE 寒河江 亘太
KOTA SAGAE

CL プレジャー

097

KIKI
CONSULTING
CO.,LTD.

098

098

AD 岡本 欣也
KINYA OKAMOTO

寒河江 亘太
KOTA SAGAE

DE 寒河江 亘太
KOTA SAGAE

CL キキ・コンサルティング

j · cuisine
charivari

099

ASIAN MODERN STYLE

LOIS CAFE

100

099

AD　シマダ タモツ
　　TAMOTSU SHIMADA

DE　シマダ タモツ
　　TAMOTSU SHIMADA

CL　せつ

100

AD　立花 幹也
　　MIKIYA TACHIBANA

DE　イエロードッグ スタジオ
　　YELLOW DOG STUDIO

CL　クレヨン

101

AD　奥村 昭夫
　　AKIO OKUMURA

DE　桶本 尚子
　　TAKAKO OKEMOTO

CL　アイリーンアーカイブ

102

AD　寒河江 亘太
　　KOTA SAGAE

DE　寒河江 亘太
　　KOTA SAGAE

CL　ナイーブ

Aileen

Archive 101

naive

102

OFFICE
SAIKAKU
event produce & planning

103

104

Dream
Together with Kids
toward the Bright Future

105

106

CAR TERRACE

107

103

AD 佐藤 雅知
MASATOMO SATO

DE 伊藤 勝一
KATSUICHI ITO

藤原 俊哉
TOSHIYA FUJIWARA

CL ロイズファーム

104

AD 大平 弘
HIROSHI OHIRA

DE 大平 弘
HIROSHI OHIRA

福井 博章
HIROAKI FUKUI

CL おふぃす西鶴

105

AD 太田 徹也
TETSUYA OHTA

DE 太田 徹也
TETSUYA OHTA

CL セゾンファンデックス

106

AD 石山 俊郎
TOSHIRO ISHIYAMA

DE イクス
ICS

CL トミー

107

AD 荒木 義信
YOSHINOBU ARAKI

DE 内藤 正比呂
MASAHIRO NAITO

CL 東京トヨペット

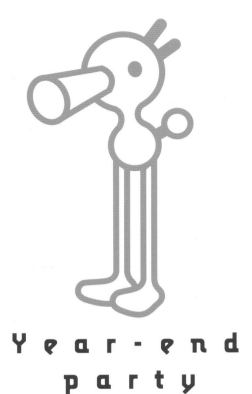

Year-end party

108

TAKOYAKI DAICHAN

109

hisako

110

Victorian Gardening

111

otari

112

BRASSERIE
Mahogany

113

108
AD　平澤 卓
　　TAKU HIRASAWA

DE　青木 陸祐
　　MICHISUKE AOKI

CL　パンプキン　キング

109
AD　中沢 定幸
　　SADAYUKI NAKAZAWA

DE　中沢 定幸
　　SADAYUKI NAKAZAWA

CL　長野飲食ビジネス開発

110
AD　高田 雄吉
　　YUKICHI TAKADA

DE　高田 雄吉
　　YUKICHI TAKADA

CL　ヒサコネイル

111
AD　大崎 淳治
　　JUNJI OSAKI

DE　大崎 淳治
　　JUNJI OSAKI

CL　早川造園

112
AD　渡辺 みつお
　　MITSUO WATANABE

DE　渡辺 みつお
　　MITSUO WATANABE

CL　小谷村

113
AD　森沢 博之
　　HIROYUKI MORISAWA

DE　森沢 博之
　　HIROYUKI MORISAWA

CL　マホガニー

a b b i t

114

informatix
SPACE-TIME DESIGNING

115

116

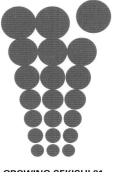

GROWING SEKISUI 21

117

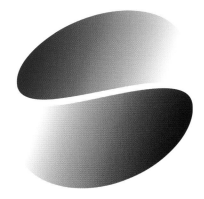

Sony Assurance

118

114

AD 関 和廣
KAZUHIRO SEKI

DE 関 和廣
KAZUHIRO SEKI

CL デザインルーム・アオイ

115

AD 飯守 恪太郎
KAKUTARO IIMORI

DE 飯守 恪太郎
KAKUTARO IIMORI

小林 珠美
TAMAMI KOBAYASHI

CL インフォマティクス

116

AD 奥村 昭夫
AKIO OKUMURA

DE 福本 泰代
YASUYO FUKUMOTO

CL インターメディウム研究所

117

AD 奥村 昭夫
AKIO OKUMURA

DE 東 恵子
KEIKO HIGASHI

CL セキスイマーケティングセンター

118

AD ソニーデザインセンター
SONY CORPORATION
DESIGN CENTER

DE 尾村 匡昭
MASAAKI OMURA

山口 幸紀
KOKI YAMAGUCHI

福原 寛重
HIROSHIGE FUKUHARA

CL ソニー損害保険

APERIOS

119

120

119

AD ソニーデザインセンター
SONY CORPORATION
DESIGN CENTER

DE 尾村 匡昭
MASAAKI OMURA

CL ソニー

120

AD ソニーデザインセンター
SONY CORPORATION
DESIGN CENTER

DE 尾村 匡昭
MASAAKI OMURA

中山 禎之
YOSHIYUKI NAKAYAMA

CL ソニー

121

AD 中川 憲造
KENZO NAKAGAWA

DE 森上 暁
SATOSHI MORIKAMI

CL 中川ケミカル

122

AD 竹内 オサム
OSAMU TAKEUCHI

藤田 誠
MAKOTO FUJITA

DE 竹内 オサム
OSAMU TAKEUCHI

CL ランドネットDD

123

AD 藤本 孝明
TAKAAKI FUJIMOTO

DE 藤本 孝明
TAKAAKI FUJIMOTO

CL ヘア・ジャム

124

AD 仲 経晴
TSUNEHARU NAKA

DE 仲 将晴
MASAHARU NAKA

CL ジャパンメイクアップアーティスト
ネットワーク

Windee
Collection

121

Randnet

122

qrstuvwxyzabcdefghijklmnopqr
hijklmnopqrstuvwxyzabcdefghij
tuvwxyzabcdefghijklmnopqrstu

123

メイクの日
May9

124

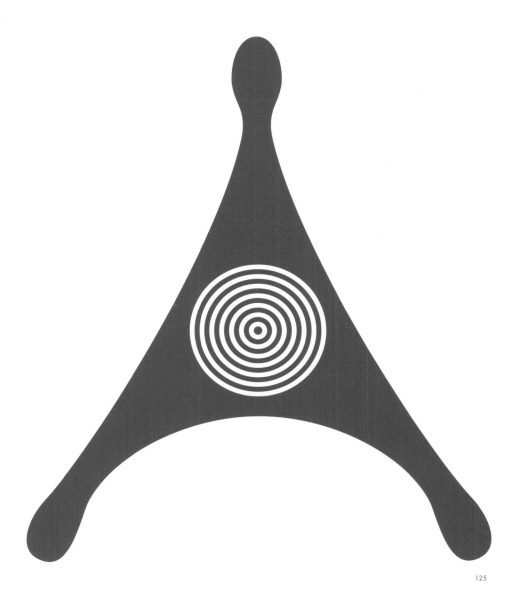

125

126

125
AD 大崎 淳治
　　JUNJI OSAKI

DE 大崎 淳治
　　JUNJI OSAKI

CL 国際美学会議組織委員会

126
AD 森沢 博之
　　HIROYUKI MORISAWA

DE 森沢 博之
　　HIROYUKI MORISAWA

CL とりくった

127

AD 坂元 良弘
YOSHIHIRO SAKAMOTO

DE 日下部 昌子
MASAKO KUSAKABE

CL 埼玉学園大学

127

128

128

AD 七種 泰史
YASUSHI SAIKUSA

DE 七種 泰史
YASUSHI SAIKUSA

CL キューブロダクツ

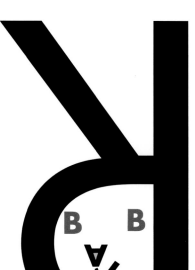

129

AD 伊藤 勝一
KATSUICHI ITO

DE 伊藤 勝一
KATSUICHI ITO

CL 王子製紙

129

130

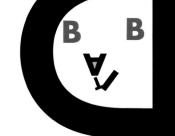

131

130

AD 太田 徹也
TETSUYA OHTA

DE 太田 徹也
TETSUYA OHTA

CL ユーミー

131

AD 青木 陸祐
MICHISUKE AOKI

DE 青木 陸祐
MICHISUKE AOKI

平澤 卓
TAKU HIRASAWA

CL Seiko Saeki

132

132

AD 関 和廣
KAZUHIRO SEKI

DE 関 和廣
KAZUHIRO SEKI

CL GGGG

133

AD 平野 敬子
KEIKO HIRANO

DE 平野 敬子
KEIKO HIRANO

CL ひめじウエルカム21実行委員会

134

AD 青木 陸祐
MICHISUKE AOKI

DE 青木 陸祐
MICHISUKE AOKI

平澤 卓
TAKU HIRASAWA

CL デザイン考房

135

AD 平田 博
HIROSHI HIRATA

DE 伊藤 勝一
KATSUICHI ITO

CL 北村心臓血管クリニック

136

AD 伊藤 勝一
KATSUICHI ITO

DE 伊藤 勝一
KATSUICHI ITO

CL 東京グラフィックサービス工業会

137

AD 高田 雄吉
YUKICHI TAKADA

DE 高田 雄吉
YUKICHI TAKADA

CL 知恵のわ

138

AD 井川 啓
KEI IKAWA

DE 井川 啓
KEI IKAWA

CL 文化庁

133

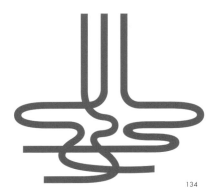

134

135

136

137

138

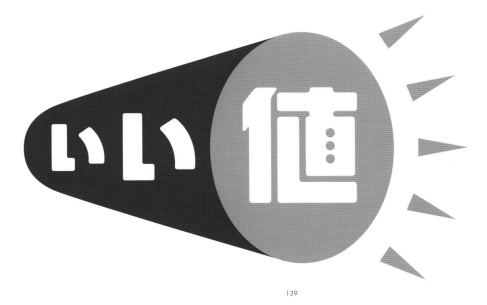

139

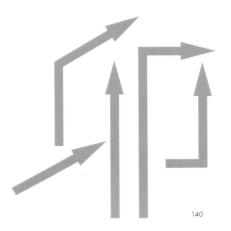

140

141

国際クリエィティブ・コミュニケーションズ
International Creative Communications

142

143

坂元 良弘
YOSHIHIRO SAKAMOTO

139
AD 坂元 良弘
YOSHIHIRO SAKAMOTO

DE 坂元 良弘
YOSHIHIRO SAKAMOTO

CL 京王百貨店

140
AD 南部 俊安
TOSHIYASU NANBU

DE 南部 俊安
TOSHIYASU NANBU

CL Taste Inc.

141
AD 七種 泰史
YASUSHI SAIKUSA

DE 七種 泰史
YASUSHI SAIKUSA

CL プラザクリエイト

142
AD 徐 明
JOMEI

DE 徐 明
JOMEI

徐 珂
JOKA

CL ICC

143
AD 奥村 昭夫
AKIO OKUMURA

DE 上野 光生
MITSUO UENO

CL 国際デザイン交流協会

Otsuka-Tei

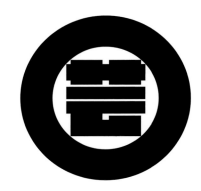

144

145

146

147

148

144

AD 中沢 定幸
SADAYUKI NAKAZAWA

DE 中沢 定幸
SADAYUKI NAKAZAWA

CL 大塚亭

145

AD 棚瀬 伸司
SHINJI TANASE

タナセ カツジ
KATSU TANASE a.k.a. TANASEX

DE 棚瀬 伸司
SHINJI TANASE

CL グランドキャニオンエンタテインメント

146

AD 坂元 良弘
YOSHIHIRO SAKAMOTO

DE 日下部 昌子
MASAKO KUSAKABE

CL カゴメ

147

AD 坪内 祝義
TOKIYOSHI TSUBOUCHI

DE 坪内 祝義
TOKIYOSHI TSUBOUCHI

CL エンゼルランド　ふくい

148

AD 奥村 昭夫
AKIO OKUMURA

DE 福本 泰代
YASUYO FUKUMOTO

CL ジャパンブリッジ

Fun Run Together

Reebok

149

150

152

151

It beats

153

149

AD　新谷 秀実
　　HIDEMI SHINGAI

DE　倉地 亜紀子
　　AKIKO KURACHI

CD　法月 俊夫
　　TOSHIO NORIZUKI

CL　リーボック　ジャパン

150

AD　竹智 淳
　　JUN TAKECHI

DE　竹智 淳
　　JUN TAKECHI

CL　Ruby in the Soda

151

AD　竹智 淳
　　JUN TAKECHI

DE　竹智 淳
　　JUN TAKECHI

CL　Ruby in the Soda

152

AD　竹智 淳
　　JUN TAKECHI

DE　竹智 淳
　　JUN TAKECHI

CL　Ruby in the Soda

153

AD　工藤 俊之
　　TOSHIYUKI KUDO

DE　工藤 俊之
　　TOSHIYUKI KUDO

CL　金沢美術工芸大学

ololololololol

V.SON1C

154

Ruby in the Soda

NO MENTION SHALL BE MADE OF CORAL, OR OF PEARL : FOR THE PRICE OF WISDOM IS ABOVE RUBIE.

155

156

154

AD 山岸 正美
MASAMI YAMAGISHI

DE 西澤 弘真
HIROMASA NISHIZAWA

CL ヴィ・ソニック

155

AD 竹智 淳
JUN TAKECHI

DE 竹智 淳
JUN TAKECHI

CL Ruby in the Soda

156

AD 味岡 伸太郎
SHINTARO AJIOKA

DE 味岡 伸太郎
SHINTARO AJIOKA

CL 入河屋

劇団 ザックバラン

157

VIN LIVIN
LIVIN LIV
VIN LIVIN
LIVIN LIV
VIN LIVIN

158

NORIKO

159

FONT 1000

160

157

AD シマダ タモツ
TAMOTSU SHIMADA

DE シマダ タモツ
TAMOTSU SHIMADA

CL パラフィールド

158

AD 田中 一光
IKKO TANAKA

DE 田中 一光
IKKO TANAKA

山本 寛
KAN YAMAMOTO

CL 西友

159

AD 田中 一光
IKKO TANAKA

DE 田中 一光
IKKO TANAKA

大内 修
OSAMU OUCHI

CL 御幸毛織

160

AD 味岡 伸太郎
SHINTARO AJIOKA

DE 味岡 伸太郎
SHINTARO AJIOKA

CL FONT1000

161

AD 高田 雄吉
YUKICHI TAKADA

DE 高田 雄吉
YUKICHI TAKADA

CL 関西フィルハーモニーオーケストラ

161

162

AD 平野 敬子
KEIKO HIRANO

DE 平野 敬子
KEIKO HIRANO

CD 池田 修一
SHUICHI IKEDA

工藤 青石
AOSHI KUDO

CL 資生堂

162

163

AD 阿部 芳一
YOSHIKAZU ABE

DE 阿部 芳一
YOSHIKAZU ABE

CL QUEST PLUS Inc.

163

164

164

AD 山口 至剛
SHIGO YAMAGUCHI

DE 茂村 巨利
NAOTOSHI SHIGEMURA

CL スイングジャーナル社

eNOKI OPTICIAN

165

165

AD 塚本 明彦
AKIHIKO TSUKAMOTO

DE 塚本 明彦
AKIHIKO TSUKAMOTO

CL 榎眼鏡商

166

AD 太田 徹也
TETSUYA OHTA

DE 太田 徹也
TETSUYA OHTA

CL ツー

166

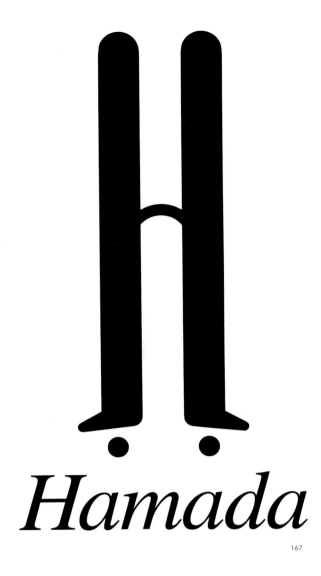

Hamada

167

imi nen tds eit rui mt u t e

168

add co.,ltd.

169

167

AD 渡部 孝一
KOICHI WATANABE

DE 渡部 孝一
KOICHI WATANABE

CL 濱田貴久美

168

AD 奥村 昭夫
AKIO OKUMURA

DE 時本 知広
TOMOHIRO TOKIMOTO

CL インターメディウム研究所

169

AD シマダ タモツ
TAMOTSU SHIMADA

DE シマダ タモツ
TAMOTSU SHIMADA

CL アッド

170

AD 味岡 伸太郎
SHINTARO AJIOKA

DE 味岡 伸太郎
SHINTARO AJIOKA

CL 星野昌彦

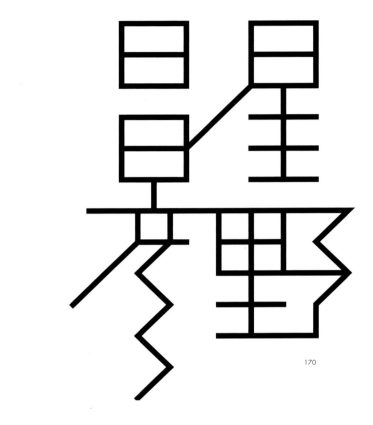

170

171

AD 味岡 伸太郎
SHINTARO AJIOKA

DE 味岡 伸太郎
SHINTARO AJIOKA

CL 入河屋

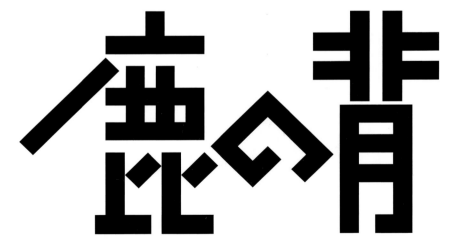

171

172

AD 味岡 伸太郎
SHINTARO AJIOKA

DE 味岡 伸太郎
SHINTARO AJIOKA

CL 入河屋

173

AD 味岡 伸太郎
SHINTARO AJIOKA

DE 味岡 伸太郎
SHINTARO AJIOKA

CL 星野昌彦

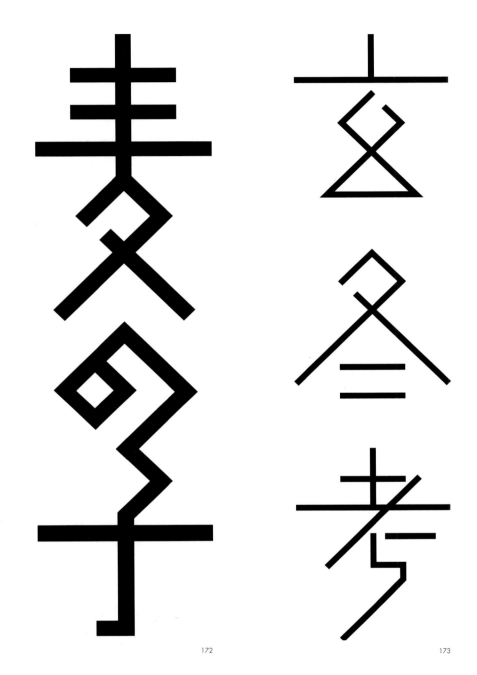

172

173

174

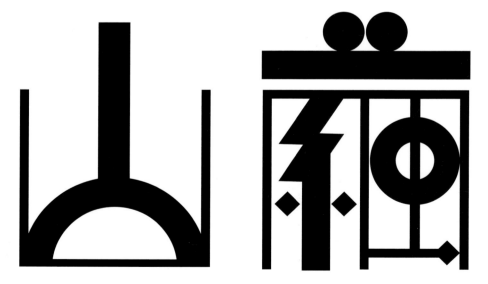

Restaurant YAMAMAYU

175

174
AD 篠原 榮太
　　EITA SHINOHARA
DE 篠原 榮太
　　EITA SHINOHARA
CL 千尋ファッション

175
AD 篠原 榮太
　　EITA SHINOHARA
DE 篠原 榮太
　　EITA SHINOHARA
CL レストラン山繭

向日葵

176

玉の緒

177

時の達人

178

176
AD 篠原 榮太
 EITA SHINOHARA
DE 篠原 榮太
 EITA SHINOHARA
CL フラワー彩

177
AD 篠原 榮太
 EITA SHINOHARA
DE 篠原 榮太
 EITA SHINOHARA
C 玉の緒

178
AD 木下 勝弘
 KATSUHIRO KINOSHITA
DE 木下 勝弘
 KATSUHIRO KINOSHITA
CL 日本経済新聞

179

AD 木下 勝弘
KATSUHIRO KINOSHITA

DE 木下 勝弘
KATSUHIRO KINOSHITA

CL ORANGE

179

180

180

AD 中川 憲造
KENZO NAKAGAWA

DE 延山 博保
HIROYASU NOBUYAMA

CL 明治製菓

181

181

AD 奥村 昭夫
AKIO OKUMURA

DE 楠本 尚子
TAKAKO OKEMOTO

CL 日本パッケージデザイン協会

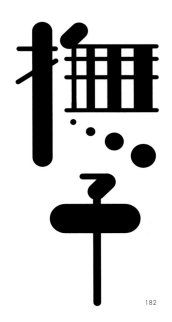

183

AD 味岡 伸太郎
SHINTARO AJIOKA

DE 味岡 伸太郎
SHINTARO AJIOKA

CL 八南新聞店

183

182

182

AD 篠原 榮太
EITA SHINOHARA

DE 篠原 榮太
EITA SHINOHARA

CL フラワー彩

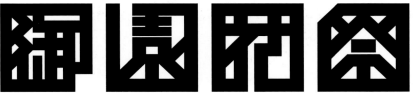

184

AD 味岡 伸太郎
SHINTARO AJIOKA

DE 味岡 伸太郎
SHINTARO AJIOKA

CL 御園花祭保存会

184

185

185

AD 杉崎 真之助
SHINNOSKE SUGISAKI

DE 奥野 千明
CHIAKI OKUNO

CL 中島らも事務所

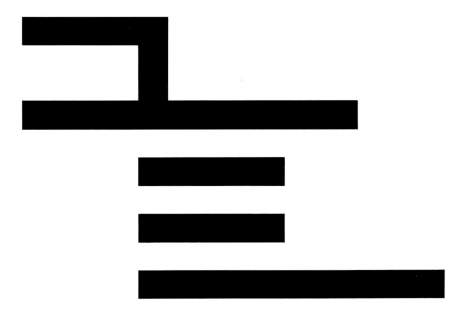

186

AD　太田 徹也
　　TETSUYA OHTA

DE　太田 徹也
　　TETSUYA OHTA

CL　ユーミー

187

AD　伊藤 勝一
　　KATSUICHI ITO

DE　伊藤 勝一
　　KATSUICHI ITO

CL　神奈川県中小企業経営センター

テ゛サ゛インかながわ

187

188

「揚きう魚」たち 189

190

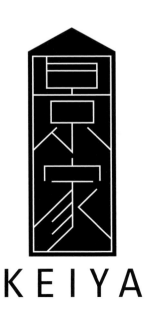

KEIYA 191

188

AD 山田 正彦
　　MASAHIKO YAMADA

DE 山田 正彦
　　MASAHIKO YAMADA

CL DESIGN BOX

189

AD 守先 正
　　TADASHI MORISAKI

　　竹智 こずえ
　　KOZUE TAKECHI

DE 竹智 こずえ
　　KOZUE TAKECHI

CL 小学館

190

AD 片山 宏明
　　HIROAKI KATAYAMA

DE 片山 宏明
　　HIROAKI KATAYAMA

CL 石橋プロダクション

191

AD うちきば がんた
　　GANTA UCHIKIBA

　　柳澤 豊
　　YUTAKA YANAGISAWA

DE うちきば がんた
　　GANTA UCHIKIBA

CL 景家

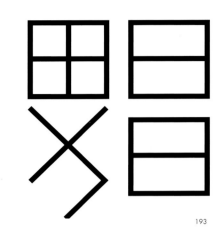

192

AD　味岡 伸太郎
　　SHINTARO AJIOKA

DE　味岡 伸太郎
　　SHINTARO AJIOKA

CL　御園花祭保存会

193

AD　味岡 伸太郎
　　SHINTARO AJIOKA

DE　味岡 伸太郎
　　SHINTARO AJIOKA

CL　山本昌男

194

AD　中川 憲造
　　KENZO NAKAGAWA

DE　延山 博保
　　HIROYASU NOBUYAMA

CL　明治製菓

195

AD　守先 正
　　TADASHI MORISAKI

　　竹智 こずえ
　　KOZUE TAKECHI

DE　竹智 こずえ
　　KOZUE TAKECHI

CL　小学館

192

193

銀座スキート

194

はじめに
料理壺の中の鰻
洪水を起こす水霊
大地を支える神々
恋する鰻とヤシ椰子
人食い大蛇の腹は宝の山
聖なる鰻は祖先の魂
鮫と竜をめぐる伝承
海から訪れる神の贈物
海上他界と海霊の系譜
おわりに
引用・参考文献

195

100

あま甘藷

196

有限会社 八南新聞店

197

酢黒里

198

瓣花

199

年賀状 いいね 写真が

200

196
AD 味岡 伸太郎
　　SHINTARO AJIOKA
DE 味岡 伸太郎
　　SHINTARO AJIOKA
CL 入河屋

197
AD 味岡 伸太郎
　　SHINTARO AJIOKA
DE 味岡 伸太郎
　　SHINTARO AJIOKA
CL 八南新聞店

198
AD 那須 潤子
　　JUNKO NASU
DE 那須 潤子
　　JUNKO NASU
CL クロレラライト本社

199
AD 久米 亜紀子
　　AKIKO KUME
DE 久米 亜紀子
　　AKIKO KUME
CL マーナ

200
AD 七種 泰史
　　YASUSHI SAIKUSA
DE 土屋 美恵
　　MIE TSUCHIYA
CL プラザクリエイト

カモン！エブリボディ

201

じんもんこん :-) 1999

202

鶴姫の館

203

朝里川温泉郷

204

湘栄建設(株)

205

201

AD　加藤 哲志
　　SATOSHI KATO

DE　坂元 良弘
　　YOSHIHIRO SAKAMOTO

CL　エグザス

202

AD　谷 卓司
　　TAKUSHI TANI

DE　谷 卓司
　　TAKUSHI TANI

CL　情報処理学会人文科学と
　　コンピュータ研究会

203

AD　正木 茂
　　SHIGERU MASAKI

DE　正木 茂
　　SHIGERU MASAKI

CL　野迫川村

204

AD　高原 新一
　　SHINICHI TAKAHARA

DE　高原 新一
　　SHINICHI TAKAHARA

CL　朝里川温泉組合

205

AD　彦根 正
　　TADASHI HIKONE

DE　彦根 正
　　TADASHI HIKONE

CL　湘栄建設

一番しぼり 206

天涯の花 207

ふしぎ草紙 208

206
AD 篠原 榮太
EITA SHINOHARA

DE 篠原 榮太
EITA SHINOHARA

CL 伊勢丹・吉原製油

207
AD 篠原 榮太
EITA SHINOHARA

DE 篠原 榮太
EITA SHINOHARA

CL 松竹・新橋演舞場

208
AD 篠原 榮太
EITA SHINOHARA

DE 篠原 榮太
EITA SHINOHARA

CL 松竹・新橋演舞場

KAITO
Amazing fresh taste
sea-man

209

210

209
AD 大平 弘
HIROSHI OOHIRA

DE 大平 弘
HIROSHI OOHIRA

西川 博信
HIRONOBU NISHIKAWA

CL SEA-MAN 鮮魚・食品販売

210
AD 石江 延勝
NOBUKATU ISHIE

DE 浦辺 映子
EIKO URABE

CL 天ぷら・和食の店「かわず」

211
AD 安彦 伸一
SHINICHI ABIKO

CL 草場武敏

211

212

AD 森沢 博之
HIROYUKI MORISAWA

DE 森沢 博之
HIROYUKI MORISAWA

CL 水口酒造

213

AD 宮崎 利一
TOSHIKAZU MIYAZAKI

DE 宮崎 利一
TOSHIKAZU MIYAZAKI

CL 大阪学院大学

214

AD 小林 正美
MASAMI KOBAYASHI

DE 神田 友美
TOMOMI KANDA

CL 神戸ベイシェラトン
ホテルアンドタワーズ、シプス

215

AD 大谷 博洋
HIROYOSHI OTANI

DE 大谷 博洋
HIROYOSHI OTANI

CL 浅田屋

道後蔵酒

This sake is produced using the same
traditional techniques as were used in
Dogo over one hundred years ago.

大辛口

212

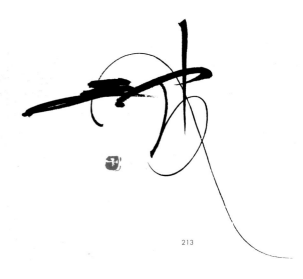

213

寿司処
sushi bar ISONO

日本料理「松風」

214

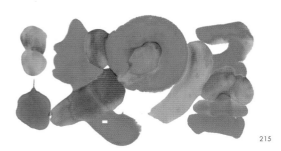

215

アイプフェイス

TYPEFACES

VIBE RED
Bold

AΛBCDEFGHhIJ
KLMNOPQRSTU
VWXYZ*!?&@@

abcdefghijklmn
opqrstuvwxyz.,,,

0123456789%$

http://www.vibe.co.jp/

Hello Japan typography annual!!
Hello music new generation!!
More than just music, More than just tv.

This "vibe red bold" is the original font of vibe to
use in all the programs of vibe and graphics,
the inside of the web site.

216

AD 甲谷 一
HAJIME KABUTOYA

DE 甲谷 一
HAJIME KABUTOYA

CD 寺井 弘典
HIRONORI TERAI

日比野 緑
MIDORI HIBINO

CL VIBEミュージックチャンネル

VIBE RED
Medium

AΛBCDEFGHhIJ
KLMNOPQRSTU
VWXYZ*!?&@@
abcdeſghijklmn
opqrstuvwxyz.,„
0123456789%$

http://www.vibe.co.jp/

Hello Japan typography annual!!
Hello music new generation!!
More than just music, More than just tv.

This "vibe red medium" is the original ſont oſ vibe to
use in all the programs oſ vibe and graphics,
the inside oſ the web site.

216

WHITE

ABCDEFGHIJKL
MNOPQRSTUV
WXYZ*!?&@~/
abcdeffçhijklmn
opqrstuvwxyz.,„
0123456789%$

http://www.vibe.co.jp/

Hello Japan typography annual!!
Hello music new generation!!
More than just music, More than just tv.

This "vibe white bold" is the original font of vibe to
use in all the programs of vibe and graphics,
the inside of the web site.

216
AD 甲谷 一
HAJIME KABUTOYA
DE 甲谷 一
HAJIME KABUTOYA
CD 寺井 弘典
HIRONORI TERAI
日比野 緑
MIDORI HIBINO
CL VIBEミュージックチャンネル

VIBE WHITE
Medium

ABCDEFGHIJKL
MNOPQRSTUV
WXYZ*!?&@~/
abcdeffçhijklmn
opqrstuvwxyz.,„
0123456789%$

http://www.vibe.co.jp/

Hello Japan typography annual!!
Hello music new generation!!
More than just music, More than just tv.

This "vibe white medium" is the original font of vibe
to use in all the programs of vibe and graphics,
the inside of the web site.

216

Direction
Line

A B C D E F G H I J
K L M N O P Q R S
T U V W X Y Z ? %
a b c d e f g h i j k l m n
o p q r s t u v w x y z . ,
0 1 2 3 4 5 6 7 8 9

Everyone now unde

Everyone now understands that the world
of computers can only exist on the basis
of language. Typography is an act which

Everyone now understands that the world of computers
can only exist on the basis of language. Typography is
an act which visualizes the concept of letters and words.

217

AD 南部 俊安
TOSHIYASU NANBU

DE 南部 俊安
TOSHIYASU NANBU

Direction Line (Method-2)

Direction Line (Method-1)

217

XY-Z

ABCDEFGHIJ
KLMNOPQRS
TUVWXYZ/!?

abcdefghijklmn
opqrstuvwxyz.,

1234567890

THANK YOU!!

ENERGY/HAPPY AND POSITIVE
GRATITUDE/COURAGE/WORDS
ALLOWED TO LIVE/WHISPERE

This font name is "XY-Z".
As for the inquiry about this font, to this.
e-mail:ciel@wc4.so-net.ne.jp

218
AD 甲谷一
HAJIME KABUTOYA
DE 甲谷一
HAJIME KABUTOYA
CL XY

218

atonic

a b c d e f g h i j
k l m n o p q r s
t u v w x y z ?.:,;!

0123456789

it's a simple process

it's a simple process. as
we said before,each live
cyliths is inherently
sensitive to one of

it's a simple process. as we said
before,each live cyliths is
inherently sensitive to one of three
wavelengths of light red,green, or

219

AD タナセ カツジ
KATSU TANASE
A. K. A. TANASEX

DE タナセ カツジ
KATSU TANASE
A. K. A. TANASEX

CD 棚瀬 伸司
SHINJI TANASE

219

雅楽-L

あいうえおかきくけこ
さしすせそたちつてと
なにぬねのはひふへほ
アイウエオカキクケコ
サシスセソタチツテト
ナニヌネノハヒフヘホ
亜唖娃阿哀愛挨姶逢葵
茜穐悪握渥旭葦芦鯵梓
圧斡扱宛姐虻飴絢綾鮎
或粟袷安庵按暗案闇鞍

芸術作品を通して、心が通い合う
ことほど神聖なものはありません。
芸術を愛する者は、ある作品と出

芸術作品を通して、心が通い合うことほど神聖なものはありません。
芸術を愛する者は、ある作品と出会った瞬間、自己を超越するので
す。その時、自分自身でありながら、自分自身ではなく、無限を

220
AD 鈴木 正広
MASAHIRO SUZUKI

DE 鈴木 正広
MASAHIRO SUZUKI

雅楽-M

あいうえおかきくけこ
さしすせそたちつてと
なにぬねのはひふへほ
アイウエオカキクケコ
サシスセソタチツテト
ナニヌネノハヒフヘホ
亜唖娃阿哀愛挨姶逢葵
茜穐悪握渥旭葦芦鯵梓
圧斡扱宛姐虻飴絢綾鮎
或粟袷安庵按暗案闇鞍

芸術作品を通して、心が通い合う
ことほど神聖なものはありません。
芸術を愛する者は、ある作品と出

芸術作品を通して、心が通い合うことほど神聖なものはありません。
芸術を愛する者は、ある作品と出会った瞬間、自己を超越するの
です。その時、自分自身でありながら、自分自身ではなく、無限を ₂₂₀

雅楽-B

あいうえおかきくけこ
さしすせそたちつてと
なにぬねのはひふへほ
アイウエオカキクケコ
サシスセソタチツテト
ナニヌネノハヒフヘホ
亜唖娃阿哀愛挨姶逢葵
茜穐悪握渥旭葦芦鯵梓
圧斡扱宛姐虻飴絢綾鮎
或粟袷安庵按暗案闇鞍

芸術作品を通して、心が通い合う
ことほど神聖なものはありません。
芸術を愛する者は、ある作品と出

芸術作品を通して、心が通い合うことほど神聖なものはありません。
芸術を愛する者は、ある作品と出会った瞬間、自己を超越するの
です。その時、自分自身でありながら、自分自身ではなく、無限を

220
AD 鈴木 正広
MASAHIRO SUZUKI

DE 鈴木 正広
MASAHIRO SUZUKI

220

ラスベガス

あいうえおかきくけこ
さしすせそたちつてと
なにぬねのはひふへほ
まみむめもやゆよらり
るれろわをんあいうえ
アイウエオカキクケコ
サシスセソタチツテト
ナニヌネノハヒフヘホ
マミムメモヤユヨラリ
ルレロワヲンアイウエ

エヌディーシーグラフィックス
はひととひと、ひとともの、ひ
ととかんきょうのあいだにある

エヌディーシーグラフィックスはひととひと、ひととものの、ひ
ととかんきょうのあいだにあるいろいろなもんだいを、デザイ
ンによってかいけつし、きもちのいいせいかつをじつげんする

221
AD 中川 憲造
KENZO NAKAGAWA

DE 森上 暁
SATOSHI MORIKAMI

印田 裕之
HIROYUKI INDA

CL 横浜みなとみらい21

221

アヴァロン

アイウエオカキクケコ
サシスセソタチツテト
ナニヌネノハヒフヘホ
マミムメモヤユヨラリ
ルレロワヲン？！

アヴァロン
ボールド

アイウエオカキクケコ
サシスセソタチツテト
ナニヌネノハヒフヘホ
マミムメモヤユヨラリ

スクーター
プロトタイプ
クリエイション

スクーター
プロトタイプ
クリエイション

222

AD 後藤 隆哉
TAKAYA GOTO

DE 小沼 孝至
TAKASHI KONUMA

CL オキシジェン

フーチャリスティックス
フォーホイールヴィークル
エレクトリックライトマジック

フーチャリスティックス
フォーホイールヴィークル
エレクトリックライトマジック

ホームメイド

アイウエオカキクケコ
サシスセソタチツテト
ナニヌネノハヒフヘホ
マミムメモヤユヨラリ
ルレロワヲン？！、。

**ホームメイド
ラフ**

アイウエオカキクケコ
サシスセソタチツテト
ナニヌネノハヒフヘホ
マミムメモヤユヨラリ

カスタード　　　　　カスタード
ピーナツバター　　　ピーナツバター
クイックレシピ　　　クイックレシピ

フレッシュフルーツジュース　　フレッシュフルーツジュース
スウィートホイップクリーム　　スウィートホイップクリーム
ベイクトチョコチップクッキー　ベイクトチョコチップクッキー

223
AD　後藤 隆哉
　　TAKAYA GOTO
DE　小沼 孝至
　　TAKASHI KONUMA
CL　オキシジェン

223

ロボテック
インライン

アイウエオカキクケコ
アサシスセソタチツテト
アナニヌネノハヒフヘホ
マミムメモヤユヨラリ
ルレロワヲン？！，．

ロボテック
アウトライン

アイウエオカキクケコ
アサシスセソタチツテト
アナニヌネノハヒフヘホ
マミムメモヤユヨラリ

ファインゴール
タッチダウンパス
サヨナラホームラン

ファインゴール
タッチダウンパス
サヨナラホームラン

224

AD　後藤 隆哉
　　TAKAYA GOTO

DE　小沼 孝至
　　TAKASHI KONUMA

CL　オキシジェン

シューティングガード　パワーゲーム
チャンピオンシップポイント
ファウル　アクシデンタルオフサイド

シューティングガード　パワーゲーム
チャンピオンシップポイント
ファウル　アクシデンタルオフサイド

PICTOGRAMS
&
DIAGRAMS

ピクトグラム
ダイヤグラム

BASEBALL

SOCCER

TENNIS

VOLLEYBALL

FIELD AND TRACK

HORSE RACE

GYMNAS-TICS

SWIMMING

AMERICAN FOOTBALL

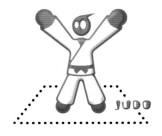

JUDO

SUMO

SPEED SKATE

SKI

FIGURE SKATE

SKI JUMP

225

AD 竹智 淳
   JUN TAKECHI

DE 竹智 淳
   JUN TAKECHI

CD 笹川 堅志
   KENSHI SASAGAWA

CL 日本テレビ放送網

225

お手洗・男

スペースシアター

コミュニティールーム

お手洗・女

ファンタジーエッグ

電話

お手洗・身障者

コンピュータルーム

ベビールーム

喫煙コーナー

サイエンス・ラボ

幼児コーナー

レストラン

クラフトルーム

ものしりコーナー

226

AD 坪内 祝義
TOKIYOSHI TSUBOUCHI

DE 坪内 祝義
TOKIYOSHI TSUBOUCHI

CL エンゼルランド ふくい

226

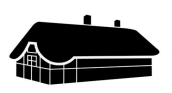

Mexico

Burkina Faso

India

Iran

Namibia

Indonesia

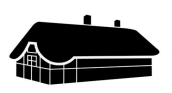

Denmark

Iran

Madagascal

227

AD 南部 俊安
TOSHIYASU NANBU

吉田 州宏
KUNIHIRO YOSHIDA

DE 南部 俊安
TOSHIYASU NANBU

CD 杉野 壮
TSUYOSHI SUGINO

CL 松下電工

China

Colombia

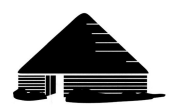

New Caledonia

227

228

AD 荒井 幸子
   SACHIKO ARAI

DE 川上 鮎美
   AYUMI KAWAKAMI

CL 日本海コンサルタント

228

229

AD 太田 徹也
TETSUYA OHTA

DE 太田 徹也
TETSUYA OHTA

CL 良品計画

NATIONWIDE EXPANSION
無印良品の海外店舗展開

[RYOHIN KEIKAKU ANNUAL REPORT]

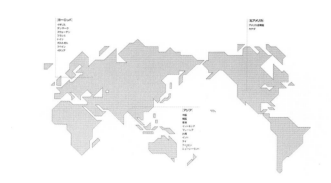

229

DISTRIBUTION CENTER AND NETWORK
流通センター及び配送ネットワーク 良品計画

[RYOHIN KEIKAKU ANNUAL REPORT]

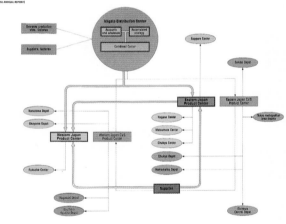

230

AD 太田 徹也
TETSUYA OHTA

DE 太田 徹也
TETSUYA OHTA

CL 良品計画

230

STATISTICS OF NIPPON PAPER INDUSTRIES
数字でみる日本製紙 売上高構成

[NIPPON PAPER INDUSTRIES ANNUAL REPORT]

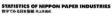
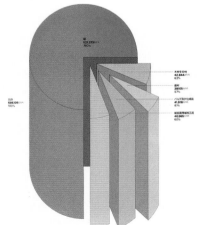

231

AD 太田 徹也
TETSUYA OHTA

DE 太田 徹也
TETSUYA OHTA

CL 日本製紙

231

RECYCLED PAPER NOW
再生紙の現在 環境問題とリサイクル モリサワ

[MITSUMI YOKOGUMI]

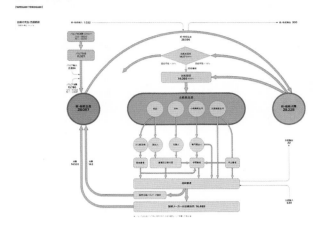

232

TAKENAKA CORPORATE GROUP
グループで創造する都市・人間環境 竹中工務店

[TAKENAKA REAL ESTATE CORPORATE BROCHURE]

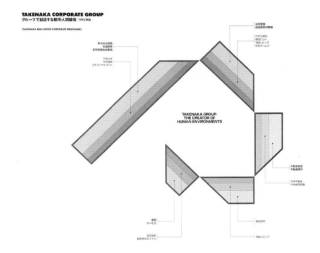

TAKENAKA GROUP:
THE CREATOR OF
HUMAN ENVIRONMENTS

233

JAPANESE SOCIETY, PRESENT AND IN THE COMING CENTURY
現在と21世紀の日本社会 くもんこども研究所

[IMALAZA]

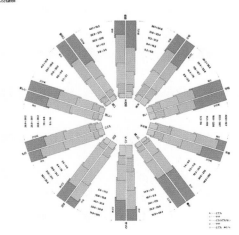

232

AD　太田 徹也
　　TETSUYA OHTA

DE　太田 徹也
　　TETSUYA OHTA

CL　モリサワ

233

AD　太田 徹也
　　TETSUYA OHTA

DE　太田 徹也
　　TETSUYA OHTA

CL　竹中工務店

234

AD　太田 徹也
　　TETSUYA OHTA

DE　太田 徹也
　　TETSUYA OHTA

CL　くもん こども研究所

235

AD 中川 憲造
KENZO NAKAGAWA

DE 森上 暁
SATOSHI MORIKAMI

中山 典科
NORIKA NAKAYAMA

IL 延山 博保
HIROYASU NOBUYAMA

CL 国際技能振興財団

ものづくり 人づくり

財団法人 国際技能振興財団

技能五輪国際大会における日本の順位の推移

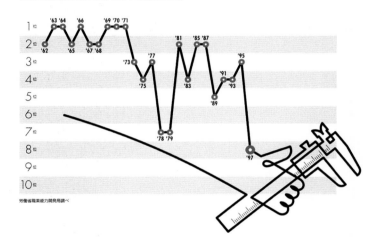

労働省職業能力開発局調べ

235

236

AD 中川 憲造
KENZO NAKAGAWA

DE 森上 暁
SATOSHI MORIKAMI

中山 典科
NORIKA NAKAYAMA

IL 延山 博保
HIROYASU NOBUYAMA

CL 国際技能振興財団

236

グラフィック

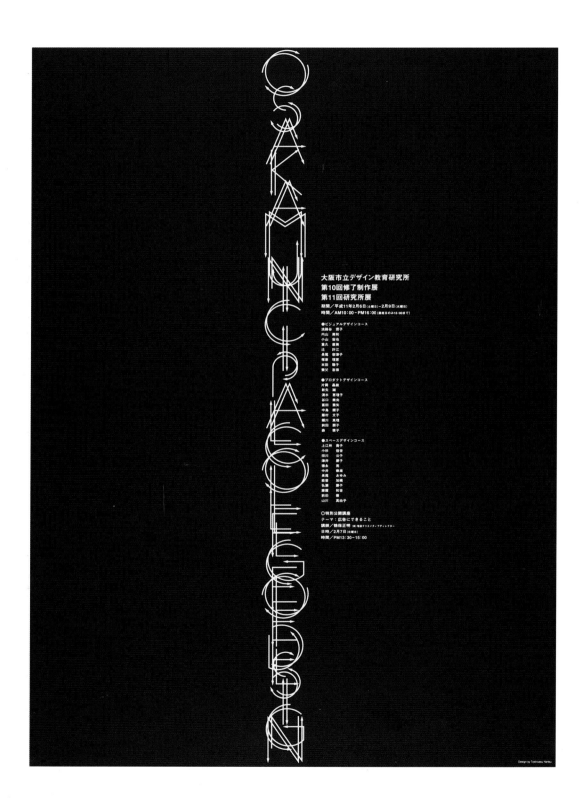

237
AD 南部 俊安
   TOSHIYASU NANBU

DE 南部 俊安
   TOSHIYASU NANBU

CL 大阪市立デザイン研究所

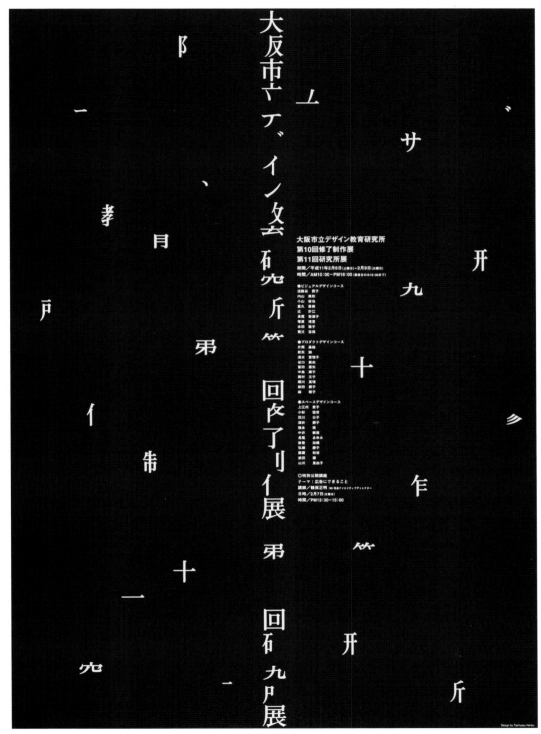

大阪市立デザイン教育研究所
第10回修了制作展
第11回研究所展
期間／平成11年2月6日(土曜日)～2月9日(火曜日)
時間／AM10:00～PM16:00 (最終日のみ15:00まで)

●ビジュアルデザインコース
濱路谷　哲子
内山　美和
小山　宏也
重丸　貴典
辻　計江
長嶋　奈津子
塚原　理恵子
本田　睦子
鞍父　忠修

●プロダクトデザインコース
片岡　昌紘
新矢　薫
清水　里理子
谷口　美央
富田　直矢
中島　直子
藤村　文子
細川　高理
刻田　睦子
森　麻子

●スペースデザインコース
上江洲　貴世
小杉　佳世
田川　公子
津井　鯖子
舘本　亮
中井　根緒
長尾　あゆみ
数吉　加織
薩羅　聡子
前田　知俊
山川　真由子

○特別公開講座
テーマ：広告にできること
講師／鶴保正明 (株)電通クリエイティブディレクター
日時／2月7日(日曜日)
時間／PM13:30～15:00

Design by Toshinobu Kanbai

Everyone now understands that the world of computers can only exist on the basis of language. Typography is an act which visualizes the concept of letters and words. Both computers and typography are a main current of your times. I think that the key to successful creation now is to understand the kind of relationships through which the linguistic world of computers and typography is converted into the visual world.

238

AD 南部 俊安
TOSHIYASU NANBU

DE 南部 俊安
TOSHIYASU NANBU

CL TASTE INC.

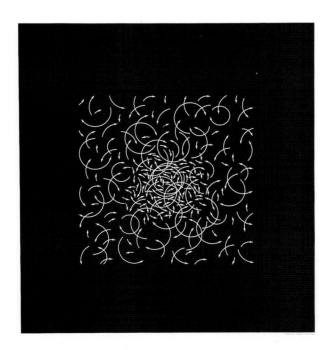

Everyone now understands that the world of computers can only exist on the basis of language. Typography is an art which visualizes the concept of letters and words. Both computers and typography are a main current of your times. I think that the key to successful creation now is to understand the kind of relationships through which the linguistic world of computers and typography is converted into the visual world.

Everyone now understands that the world of computers can only exist on the basis of language. Typography is an art which visualizes the concept of letters and words. Both computers and typography are a main current of your times. I think that the key to successful creation now is to understand the kind of relationships through which the linguistic world of computers and typography is converted into the visual world.

238

Everyone now understands that the world of computers can only exist on the basis of language. Typography is an art which visualizes the concept of letters and words. Both computers and typography are a main current of your times. I think that the key to successful creation now is to understand the kind of relationships through which the linguistic world of computers and typography is converted into the visual world.

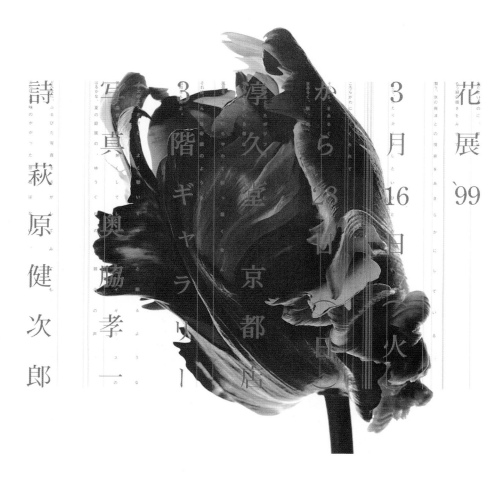

花展 '99

3月16日（火）から28日（日）まで

淳久堂京都店 3階ギャラリー

写真 奥脇孝一

詩 萩原健次郎

239

AD 高橋 善丸
    YOSHIMARU TAKAHASHI

DE 高橋 善丸
    YOSHIMARU TAKAHASHI

CW 萩原 健次郎
    KENJIRO HAGIWARA

PH 奥脇 孝一
    KOICHI OKUWAKI

CL じゅんく堂書店

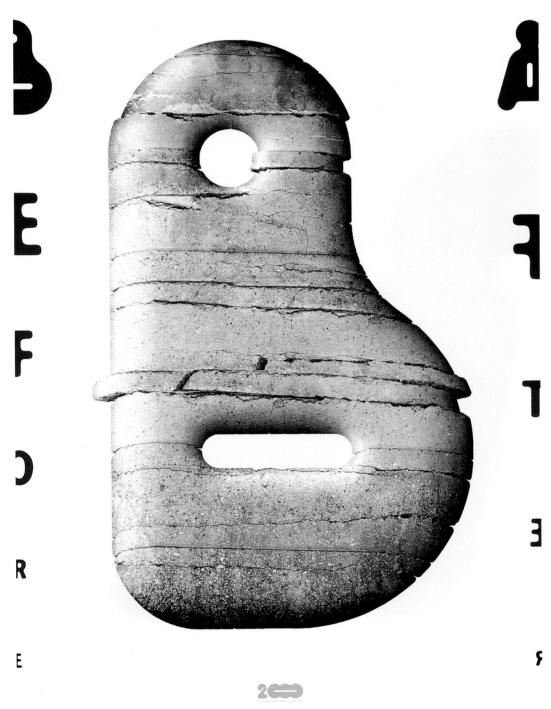

240

240

AD　高橋 善丸
　　YOSHIMARU TAKAHASHI

DE　高橋 善丸
　　YOSHIMARU TAKAHASHI

CL　日本グラフィックデザイナー協会

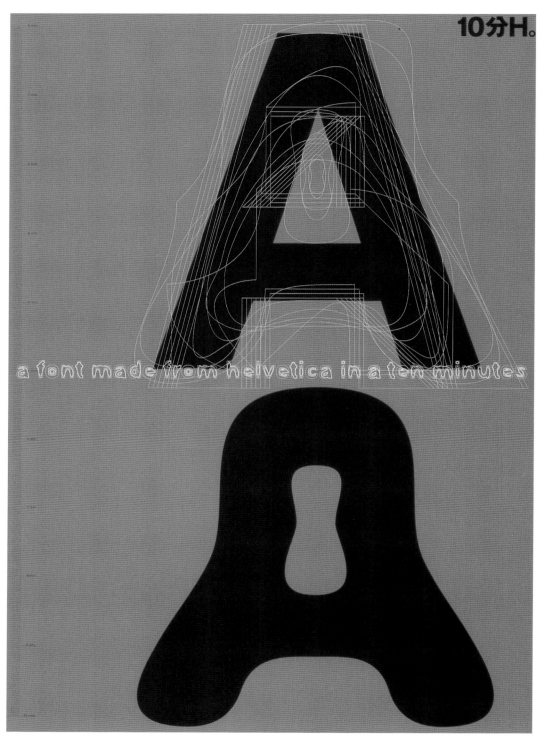

241

241

AD 杉崎 真之助
　　SHINNOSKE　SUGISAKI

DE 杉崎 真之助
　　SHINNOSKE　SUGISAKI

CL 日本タイポグラフィ協会

モリサワ・タイポグラフィ・スペース 第15回企画展
Man and Writing CD-ROM Exhibition

1999年6月3日(木)—8月10日(火)
10:00—18:00 日曜・祝日休館／入場無料

人間と文字

CD ROM

展

MOTS
MORISAWA TYPOGRAPHY SPACE
〒162-0802 新宿区下宮比町2-27モリサワビル4F
TEL : 03-3267-1233 ／ FAX : 03-3267-1536
http://www.morisawa.co.jp/gallery/MOTS-mots.html

Design by Ikko Tanaka

242

242

AD　田中 一光
　　IKKO TANAKA

DE　田中 一光
　　IKKO TANAKA

　　大内 修
　　OSAMU OUCHI

CL　モリサワ

色で失敗したことありませんか
コーセーは、今日の気持ちで選べる487色

243

243

AD 青葉 益輝
MASUTERU AOBA

DE 金井 庄一
SHOICHI KANAI

藤井 功
ISAO FUJII

PH 高井 哲郎
TETSURO TAKAI

CL コーセー

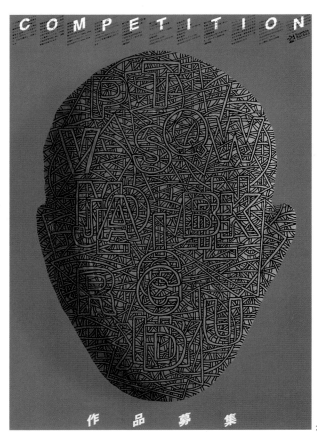

244

AD 青葉 益輝
MASUTERU AOBA

DE 藤井 功
ISAO FUJII

赤嶺 知美
TOMOMI AKAMINE

CL ガーディアン・ガーデン

244

INVITATION

アジアの風'99

'99アジアコレクション「幕張大賞」

1999年9月22日(水) 18:00開演

幕張メッセイベントホール

ASIA COLLECTION
MAKUHARI
GRAND PRIX

ASIA
COLLE
CTION
MAKUHARI
GRAND
PRIX

245

245

AD　大杉 学
　　MANABU OSUGI

DE　須永 英司
　　EIJI SUNAGA

CD　村瀬 秀明
　　SHUMEI MURASE

CL　アジアコレクション実行委員会

MUSA PAPER LAND
eco

ムーサペーパーランド［エコ］
古紙配合100%しかもファンシーな30色の "OK エコジャパン"
豊かな風合いと印刷適性をもちしかもエコロジーをプラスしたファ
ンシーペーパー "OK エコプラス"。ポスター・パッケージ・エ
ディトリアルに紙の表情が生きています。245名のデザイナー・
イラストレーターが自由にデザインしたタッグシールも OK エ
コプラス。ぜひご覧ください。
6月2日(水) 3日(木) 4日(金) 10：00AM ～ 7：00PM
TBホール 大阪市中央区東心斎橋 2-1-1 TEL：06-6213-3192
主催：ムーサ株式会社 後援：王子製紙株式会社 日本紙パルプ商事株式会社

246

246

AD 奥村 昭夫
　　AKIO OKUMURA

DE 福本 泰代
　　YASUYO FUKUMOTO

CL ムーサ

International Design Exhibition Osaka '99
the 9th international design festival, Osaka

Date : Oct. 9th (sat.) –13th (wed.), 1999 10:00 – 18:00

Place : Asia and Pacific Trade Center / ATC Hall O's Building South Wing B2F 2·1·10, Nanko-kita, Suminoe-ku, Osaka

Promoter : JAPAN DESIGN FOUNDATION 3-1-800 Umeda 1-chome, Kitaku, Osaka, 530-0001 Japan Phone : + 81 6 6346-2611 Fax : + 81 6 6346-2615

第9回 国際デザイン・フェスティバル

国際デザイン展'99

会期：1999年10月9日（土）－10月13日（水）10:00－18:00　会場：アジア太平洋トレードセンター／ATCホール　大阪市住之江区南港北 2·1·10

入場料金：大人1,000円（800円）／学生700円（500円）（ ）内は前売券　■前売券発売所　ローソンチケット　■問い合わせ先　財団法人 国際デザイン交流協会 フェスティバル事業部　TEL 06-6346-2612

展示内容：■第9回国際デザイン・アオード受賞者業績展示　■第6回国際デザイン・コンペティション作品展示　テーマ［編む-intertextuality］—未知なる可能性を求めて—　■協会企画展　テーマ "21世紀へ生かすーデザインの知恵"　■国際交流展　■イベント＆ショップ

併催：■アジア太平洋デザイン交流会議'99　10月12日（火）13日（水）2日間

主催：■ 財団法人 国際デザイン交流協会　〒530-0001　大阪市北区梅田1丁目3-1-800 大阪駅前第一ビル8階　TEL 06-6346-2611(代表) FAX 06-6346-2615

後援：通商産業省、外務省、文化庁、大阪府、大阪市、大阪府教育委員会、大阪市教育委員会、大阪商工会議所、財団法人大阪21世紀協会、アジア太平洋トレードセンター株式会社

このポスターは、補助の事業を受けて製作しました。 This poster was submitted the Japan Keirin Association through its Promoter funds from KEIRIN RACE

247

247

AD 奥村 昭夫
AKIO OKUMURA

DE 上野 光生
MITSUO UENO

CL 国際デザイン交流協会

4

248
AD 塚本 明彦
　　AKIHIKO TSUKAMOTO

DE 塚本 明彦
　　AKIHIKO TSUKAMOTO

CL ディグトーキョー コーポレーション

248

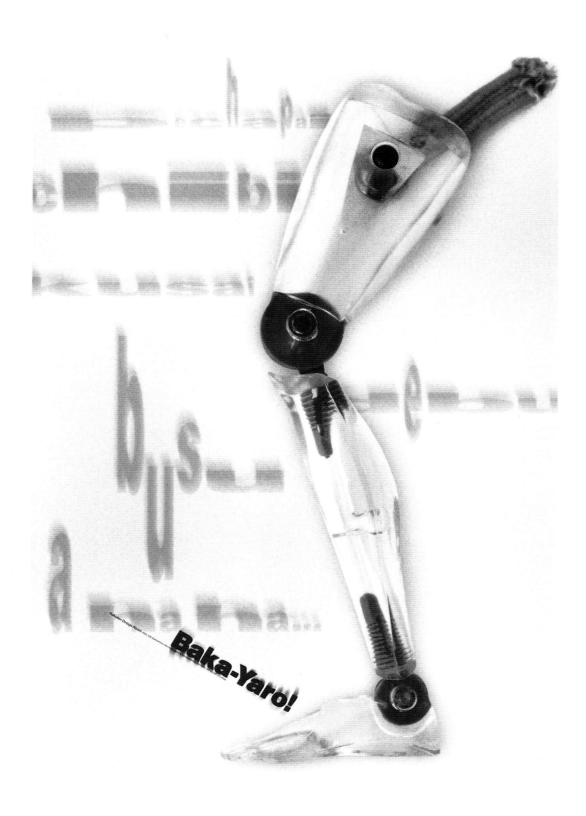

249

AD 木村 経典
    KYOTEN KIMURA

DE 木村 経典
    KYOTEN KIMURA

    柳島 眞樹
    MAKI YANAGISHIMA

PH 泊 昭雄
    AKIO TOMARI

CL 楽天デザイン室

250

AD 井川 啓
KEI IKAWA

DE 井川 啓
KEI IKAWA

CL 伊勢丹

fortunate
the man
who,
at the
right
moment,
meets
the right
friend;
fortunate
also the
man who,
at the
right
moment,
meets
the right
enemy.

t.s.eliot

hans-ruedi lutz
mit emil ruder begann unser erlebnis typographie
durch emil ruder entstand unsere freundschaft
dank emil ruder bleibt typographie unser endloser kontakt

hans-ruedi
deine typographie ist inzwischen sichtbar
ich bin noch an der arbeit

helmut schmid

design is attitude

251

252

AD 南部 俊安
   TOSHIYASU NANBU

DE 南部 俊安
   TOSHIYASU NANBU

CL ダブル・クロック・デザインギャラリー

252

253

253

AD 田中 一光
IKKO TANAKA

DE 田中 一光
IKKO TANAKA

大内 修
OSAMU OUCHI

CL サンパウロ現代美術館

254

254

AD 田中 一光
IKKO TANAKA

DE 田中 一光
IKKO TANAKA

緒方 裕子
YUKO OGATA

PH 坂田 栄一郎
EIICHIRO SAKATA

CL 高山右近実行委員会

255

255

AD 奥村 昭夫
   AKIO OKUMURA

DE 東 恵子
   KEIKO HIGASHI

CL インターメディウム研究所

256

256

AD カン・タイクン
   KAN TAI-KEUNG

DE カン・タイクン
   KAN TAI-KEUNG

   ラム・ワイハン
   LAM WAI HUNG

PH C. K. ワン
   C. K. WONG

CG NG・チャクボン
   NG CHEUK BONG

CL Department of Fine Arts
   The Taiwan University Associates

靳

Kan

埭

Tai-

強

Keung

设

Design

展

Show

257

257

AD　カン・タイクン
　　KAN TAI-KEUNG

DE　カン・タイクン
　　KAN TAI-KEUNG

　　ラム・ワイハン
　　LAM WAI HUNG

PH　C. K. ワン
　　C. K. WONG

CL　China National Academy
　　of Fine Art

Celebrating the NEW BORN
of the Museum of Design 祝賀設計博物館 誕生

258

258

AD　カン・タイクン
　　KAN TAI-KEUNG

DE　カン・タイクン
　　KAN TAI-KEUNG

PH　C. K. ワン
　　C. K. WONG

IL　カン・タイクン
　　KAN TAI-KEUNG

CL　The Museum
　　of Design Beijing

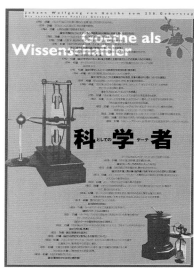

259

AD 工藤 強勝
TSUYOKATSU KUDO

DE 工藤 強勝
TSUYOKATSU KUDO

CW 粉川 哲夫
TETSUO KOGAWA

CL 東京ゲーテ記念館

259

260

260

AD 竹智 淳
JUN TAKECHI

DE 竹智 淳
JUN TAKECHI

CL 栗コーダー財団

261

261

AD フリーマン・ルー・シューホン
FREEMAN LAU SIU HONG

DE フリーマン・ルー・シューホン
FREEMAN LAU SIU HONG

CG レイ・ホー
RAY HO

CL Shanghai Graphic Designers
Association

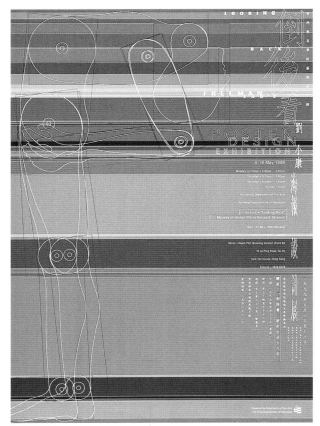

262

262

AD　フリーマン・ルー・シューホン
　　FREEMAN LAU SIU HONG

DE　フリーマン・ルー・シューホン
　　FREEMAN LAU SIU HONG

　　エリック・シャム
　　ERIC SHUM

CL　Kan & Lau Design Consultants

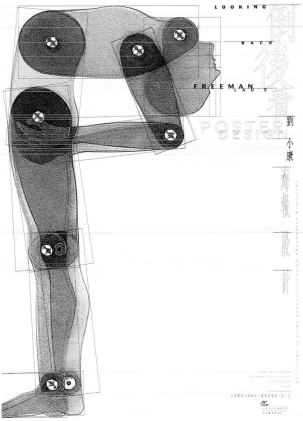

263

263

AD　フリーマン・ルー・シューホン
　　FREEMAN LAU SIU HONG

DE　フリーマン・ルー・シューホン
　　FREEMAN LAU SIU HONG

CL　Kan & Lau Design Consultants

264

AD シマダ タモツ
TAMOTSU SHIMADA

DE シマダ タモツ
TAMOTSU SHIMADA

CW 上村 慎也
SHINYA KAMIMURA

CL パラフィールド

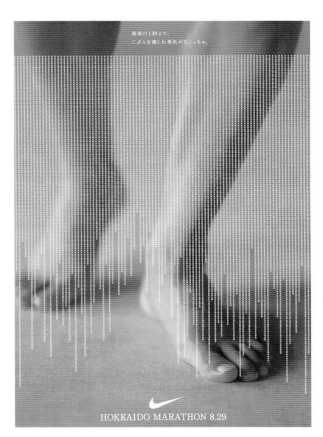

265

AD 西田 英一
EIICHI NISHIDA

DE 西田 英一
EIICHI NISHIDA

佐藤 卓哉
TAKUYA SATO

PH 村田 昇
NOBORU MURATA

CL NIKE JAPAN CORP.

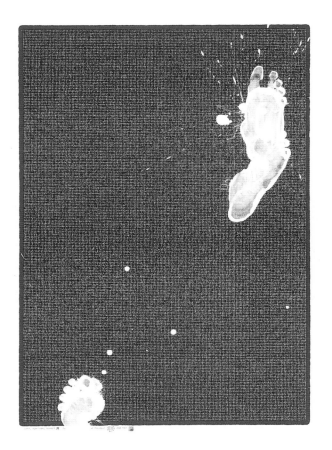

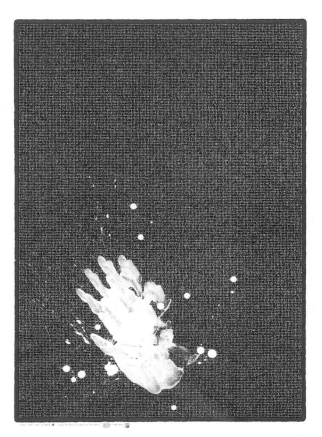

266

AD 大庭 三紀
MIKI OBA

DE 野村 美穂
MIHO NOMURA

CL GRAPHIC・π

266

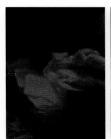

267

AD　佐藤賢治
　　KENJI　SATO

DE　佐藤賢治
　　KENJI　SATO

　　船見 奈未
　　NAMI　FUNAMI

CW　佐藤賢治
　　KENJI　SATO

PH　佐藤賢治
　　KENJI　SATO

CL　フレッシュネスバーガー、
　　ADプロジェクト

267

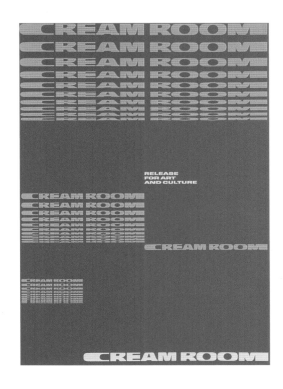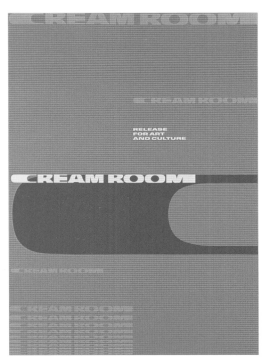

268

268

AD　杉崎 真之助
　　SHINNOSKE　SUGISAKI

DE　杉崎 真之助
　　SHINNOSKE　SUGISAKI

CL　クリームルーム

DON

DON   DON

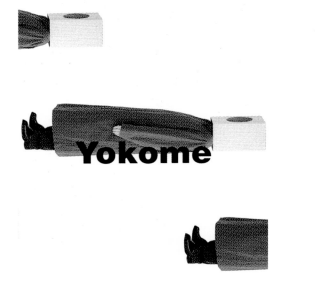

269

AD 三木 健
　　KEN MIKI

DE 三木 健
　　KEN MIKI

　　酒井田 成之
　　SHIGEYUKI SAKAIDA

PH 富浦 隆則
　　TAKANORI TOMIURA

CL 新富士製紙

270

270

AD　南部 俊安
　　TOSHIYASU NANBU

DE　南部 俊安
　　TOSHIYASU NANBU

CL　Taste Inc.

271

AD　野上 周一
　　SHUICHI NOGAMI

DE　野上 周一
　　SHUICHI NOGAMI

CL　野上デザイン事務所

271

272

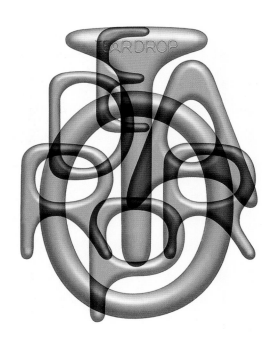

TEARDROP

273

272

AD　野上 周一
　　SHUICHI NOGAMI

DE　野上 周一
　　SHUICHI NOGAMI

CL　志木

273

AD　野上 周一
　　SHUICHI NOGAMI

DE　野上 周一
　　SHUICHI NOGAMI

CL　日本タイポグラフィ協会

274

275

276

AD 杉崎 真之助
SHINNOSKE SUGISAKI

DE 杉崎 真之助
SHINNOSKE SUGISAKI

CL 大阪府立現代美術センター

275

AD 杉崎 真之助
SHINNOSKE SUGISAKI

DE 杉崎 真之助
SHINNOSKE SUGISAKI

CL 日本グラフィックデザイナー協会

276

AD 佐藤 浩
HIROSHI SATO

DE 佐藤 浩
HIROSHI SATO

PH 目羅 勝
MASARU MERA

CA 黒澤 明
AKIRA KUROSAWA

CL アスミック・エース
エンタテインメント

GRAPHICS

二〇〇〇年

暦

御木幽石 書

日 月 火 水 木 金 土

一月

二月

三月

六月

八月

十月

十二月

十三月

日 月 火 水 木 金 土

277

DE 松石 博幸
HIROYUKI MATSUISHI

CL 一畫

277

162

Shimada Design Office
2-2-14 TY Bldg 7F Higashitenma kita-ku Osaka 530-0044 Japan tel 06 6352 1608 fax 06 6352 4009

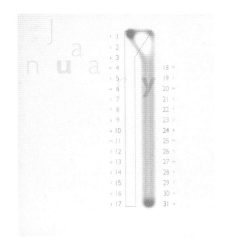

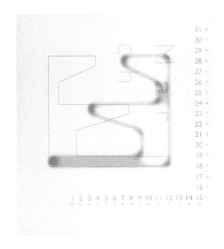

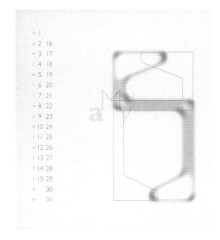

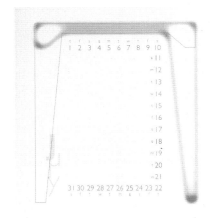

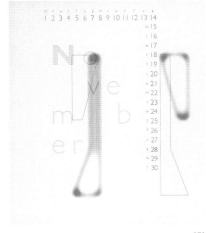

278

278

AD シマダ タモツ
TAMOTSU SHIMADA

DE シマダ タモツ
TAMOTSU SHIMADA

CL 嶋田デザイン事務所

数　字　動　物　誌　二　千

スクジー アニマル カレンダー 二〇〇〇

design and run

sun	mon	tue	wed	thu	fri	sat
		1	2	3	4	5
6	7	8	9	10	11	12
13	14	15	16	17	18	19
20	21	22	23	24	25	26
27	28	29				

february

20
00

sun	mon	tue	wed	thu	fri	sat
						1
2	3	4	5	6	7	8
9	10	11	12	13	14	15
16	17	18	19	20	21	22
23	24	25	26	27	28	29
30						

april

20
00

sun	mon	tue	wed	thu	fri	sat
			1	2	3	
4	5	6	7	8	9	10
11	12	13	14	15	16	17
18	19	20	21	22	23	24
25	26	27	28	29	30	

june

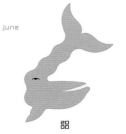

20
00

sun	mon	tue	wed	thu	fri	sat
		1	2	3	4	5
6	7	8	9	10	11	12
13	14	15	16	17	18	19
20	21	22	23	24	25	26
27	28	29	30	31		

august

20
00

sun	mon	tue	wed	thu	fri	sat
1	2	3	4	5	6	7
8	9	10	11	12	13	14
15	16	17	18	19	20	21
22	23	24	25	26	27	28
29	30	31				

october

20
00

sun	mon	tue	wed	thu	fri	sat
					1	2
3	4	5	6	7	8	9
10	11	12	13	14	15	16
17	18	19	20	21	22	23
24	25	26	27	28	29	30
31						

december

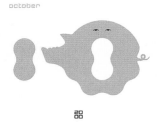

20
00

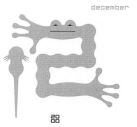

279

279

AD 大山 武
   TAKESHI OYAMA

DE 大山 武
   TAKESHI OYAMA

CL デザイン エンド ラン

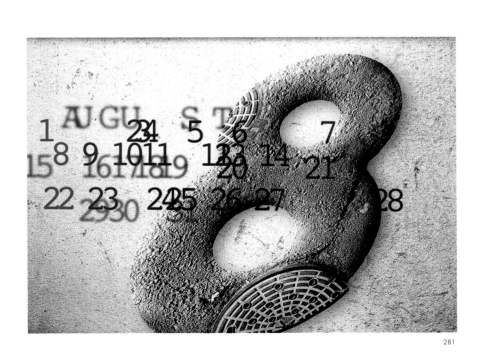

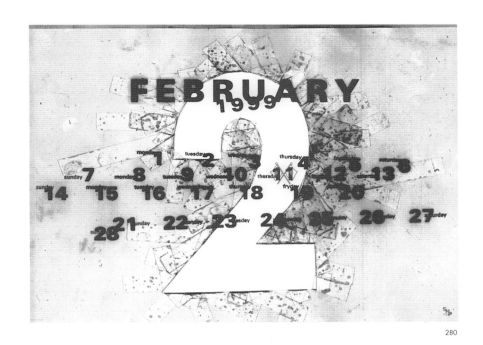

280

AD 高橋 善丸
    YOSHIMARU TAKAHASHI

DE 高橋 善丸
    YOSHIMARU TAKAHASHI

CL 新日本印刷

280

281

281

AD 高橋 善丸
    YOSHIMARU TAKAHASHI

DE 高橋 善丸
    YOSHIMARU TAKAHASHI

CL 新日本印刷

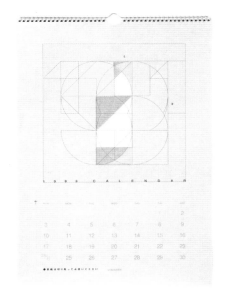

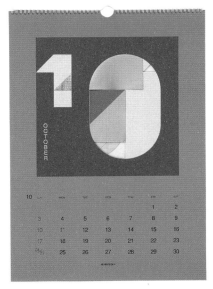

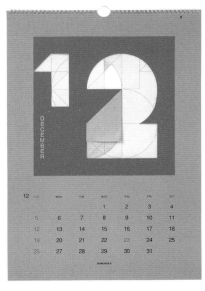

282

AD 奥村 昭夫
AKIO OKUMURA

DE 趙暉
HUI ZHAO

CL 平和紙業

282

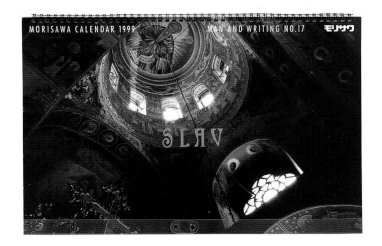

1
JANUARY

SUN	MON	TUE	WED	THU	FRI	SAT
					1	2
3	4	5	6	7	8	9
10	11	12	13	14	15	16
17	18	19	20	21	22	23
24	25	26	27	28	29	30
31						

モリサワ

6
JUNE

SUN	MON	TUE	WED	THU	FRI	SAT
		1	2	3	4	5
6	7	8	9	10	11	12
13	14	15	16	17	18	19
20	21	22	23	24	25	26
27	28	29	30			

モリサワ

8
AUGUST

SUN	MON	TUE	WED	THU	FRI	SAT
1	2	3	4	5	6	7
8	9	10	11	12	13	14
15	16	17	18	19	20	21
22	23	24	25	26	27	28
29	30	31				

モリサワ

283

AD 田中 一光
IKKO TANAKA

DE 田中 一光
IKKO TANAKA

大内 修
OSAMU OUCHI

PH 広川 泰士
TAISHI HIROKAWA

CL モリサワ

283

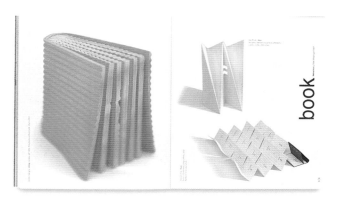

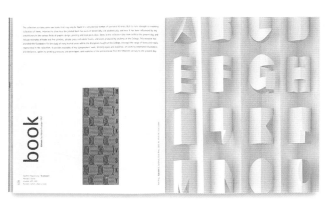

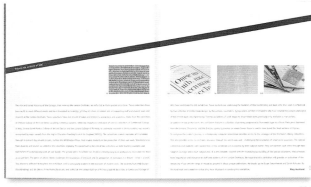

284

AD　リン・トリケット
　　LYNN TRICKETT

　　ブライアン・ウェブ
　　BRIAN WEBB

DE　カジャ・シーレン
　　KATJA THIELEN

CL　THE LONDON INSTITUTE

284

A pop-up 1999 calendar from the RSA Collection

285

285

AD リン・トリケット
LYNN TRICKETT

ブライアン・ウェブ
BRIAN WEBB

DE ハイジ・ライトフット
HEIDI LIGHTFOOT

コリナ・フレッシャー
CORINA FLETCHER

CL ROYAL SOCIETY OF ARTS

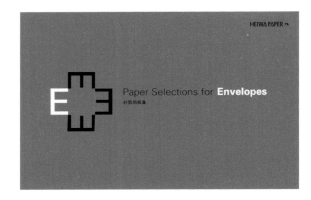

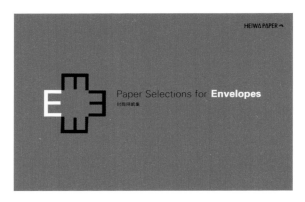

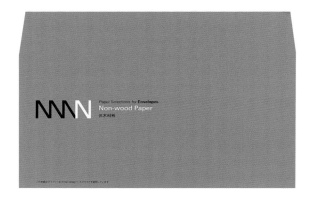

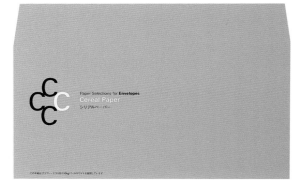

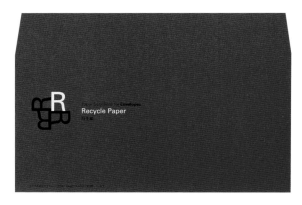

286

286

AD 三木 健
    KEN MIKI

DE 三木 健
    KEN MIKI

CL 平和紙業

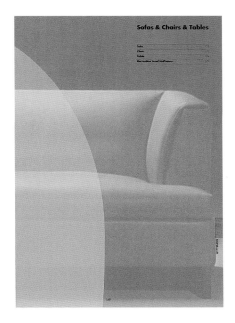

Sofas & Chairs & Tables

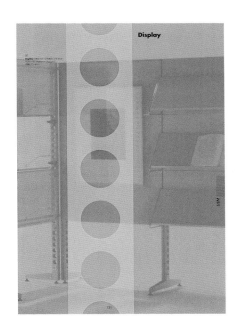

Display

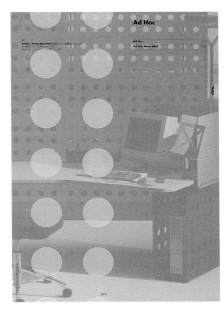

Ad Hoc

eleven22

Haller

287

AD 中川 憲造
KENZO NAKAGAWA

DE 森上 暁
SATOSHI MORIKAMI

中山 典科
NORIKA NAKAYAMA

CD 原田 孝行
TAKAYUKI HARADA

CL インター・オフィス

287

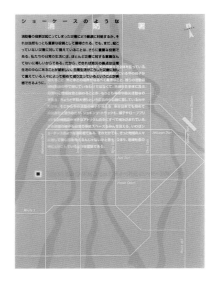

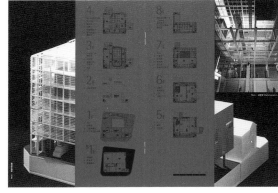

288

288

AD 中川 憲造
KENZO NAKAGAWA

DE 森上 暁
SATOSHI MORIKAMI

星 みゆき
MIYUKI HOSHI

CL 山本理顕設計工場

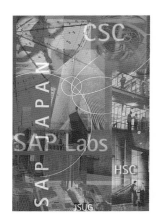

289

289

AD 新谷 秀実
HIDEMI SHINGAI

田中 俊明
TOSHIAKI TANAKA

DE 前島 理榮子
RIEKO MAEJIMA

CW 中崎 裕之
HIROYUKI NAKAZAKI

CL SAPジャパン

290

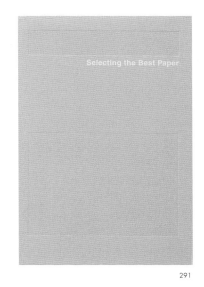

Selecting the Best Paper

291

PAPER VOICE   for nature and you vol.7

HEIWA PAPER

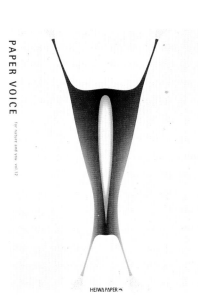

PAPER VOICE   for nature and you vol.12

HEIWA PAPER

PAPER VOICE   for nature and you vol.5

HEIWA PAPER

PAPER VOICE   for nature and you vol.9

HEIWA PAPER   292

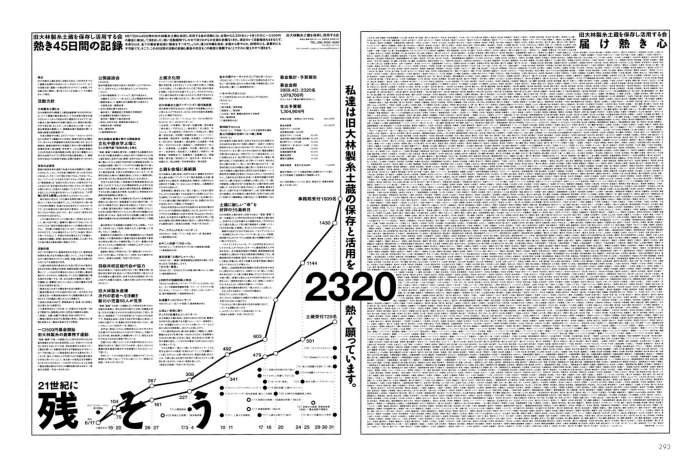

293

294

293

AD 味岡 伸太郎
    SHINTARO AJIOKA

DE 味岡 伸太郎
    SHINTARO AJIOKA

CL 旧大林製紙土蔵を保存し活用する会

294

AD 伊藤 勝一
    KATSUICHI ITO

DE 伊藤 勝一
    KATSUICHI ITO

    藤原 俊哉
    TOSHIYA FUJIWARA

CW 原 勝美
    KATSUMI HARA

IL 舟橋 全二
    ZENJI FUNABASHI

CL フジタ

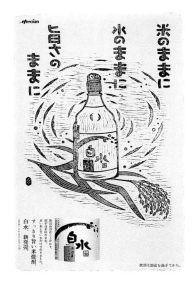

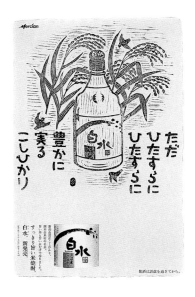

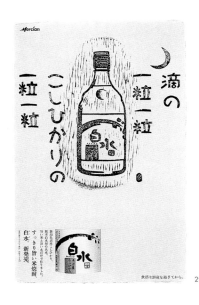

295

AD 明富士 治郎
JIRO AKEFUJI

井戸 尚美
NAOMI IDO

DE 鈴木 光太郎
KOTARO SUZUKI

CW 鈴木 聡一郎
SOICHIRO SUZUKI

IL 平松 尚樹
NAOKI HIRAMATSU

CL メルシャン

296

AD 工藤 強勝
TSUYOKATSU KUDO

DE 工藤 強勝
TSUYOKATSU KUDO

CW 竹尾
TAKEO

PH 加藤 力
TSUTOMU KATO

CL 竹尾

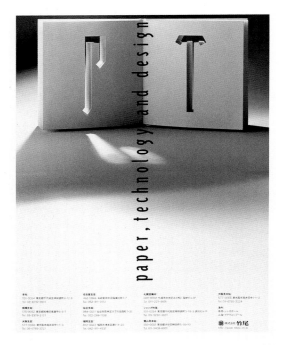

296

297

AD 味岡 伸太郎
SHINTARO AJIOKA

DE 味岡 伸太郎
SHINTARO AJIOKA

CL タイプバンク

297

298

AD 木下 勝弘
KATSUHIRO KINOSHITA

DE 木下 勝弘
KATSUHIRO KINOSHITA

CL モリサワ

299

AD 北川 正
TADASHI KITAGAWA

浦野 ひろみ
HIROMI URANO

DE 浦野 ひろみ
HIROMI URANO

CW 渋谷 政樹
MASAKI SHIBUYA

今井 雅子
MASAKO IMAI

PH 本道 はる美
HARUMI HONDO

IL 野村 美也子
MIYAKO NOMURA

CL なか卯

300

AD 平野 敬子
KEIKO HIRANO

DE 平野 敬子
KEIKO HIRANO

PH 佐治 康生
YASUO SAJI

CL 竹尾

301

AD 橋本 謙次郎
KENJIRO HASHIMOTO

DE 橋本 謙次郎
KENJIRO HASHIMOTO

CW 橋本 謙次郎
KENJIRO HASHIMOTO

CL STILL

302

AD アラン・チャン
ALAN CHAN

DE アラン・チャン
ALAN CHAN

CL Seiko Clock Inc.

THE MAGIC OF CHINESE CALLIGRAPHY

Designed by Alan Chan for Seiko Clock Inc. Japan

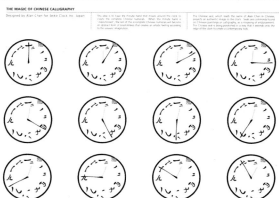

302

303

AD アラン・チャン
ALAN CHAN

DE アラン・チャン
ALAN CHAN

デビッド・ロー
DAVID LO

CL Numao Times Studio

303

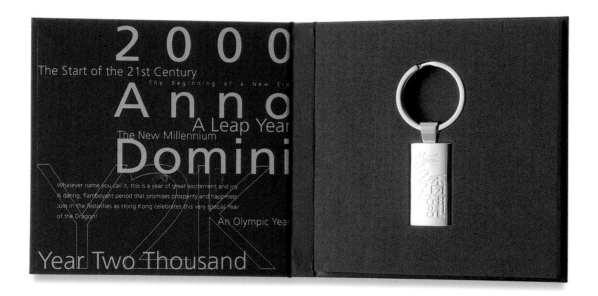

304

304

AD アラン・チャン
ALAN CHAN

DE アラン・チャン
ALAN CHAN

ミウ・チョイ
MIU CHOY

CW キャット・ティレル
CAT TYRELL

CL Alan Chan Creations Limited

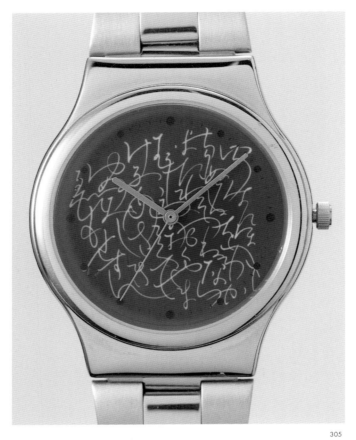

305

AD 篠原 榮太
EITA SHINOHARA

DE 篠原 榮太
EITA SHINOHARA

CL レターハウス

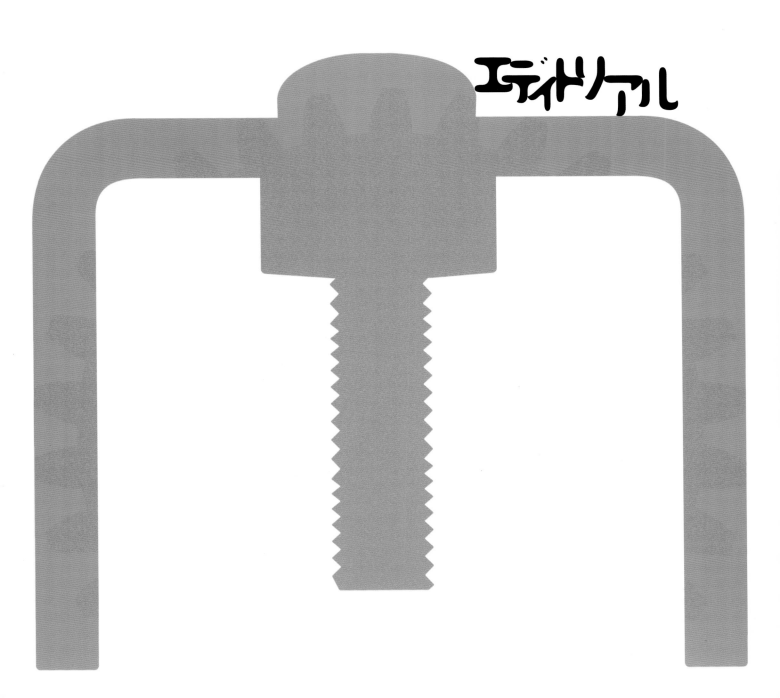

エディトリアル

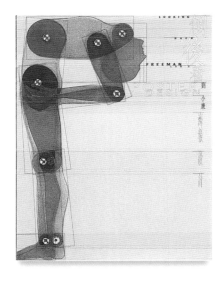

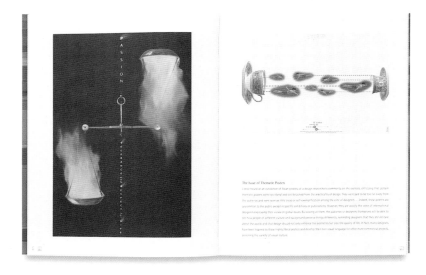

306

AD　フリーマン・ルー・シューホン
　　FREEMAN LAU SIU HONG

DE　フリーマン・ルー・シューホン
　　FREEMAN LAU SIU HONG

CL　Kan & Lau Design Consultants

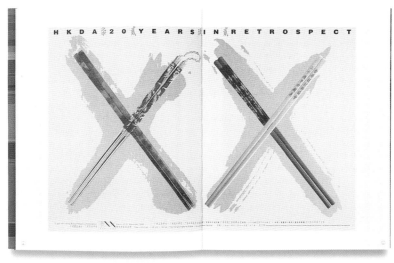

307

AD 篠原 榮太
EITA SHINOHARA

DE 篠原 榮太
EITA SHINOHARA

CL N舎

307

ITO Masao ITO Yumiko GOTO Shu TAMURA Shiro

The 6th Annual Iwate Contemporary Art Exhibition

伊藤昌夫 伊崎由美子 ゴトウシュウ 田村史郎

308

AD 工藤 強勝
TSUYOKATSU KUDO

DE 工藤 強勝
TSUYOKATSU KUDO

安田 真奈己
MANAMI YASUDA

CW 平澤 広
HIROSHI HIRASAWA

CL 萬鉄五郎記念美術館

308

309

AD 工藤 強勝
TSUYOKATSU KUDO

DE 工藤 強勝
TSUYOKATSU KUDO

安田 真奈己
MANAMI YASUDA

福本 裕子
YUKO FUKUMOTO

CW 黒川 公二
KOJI KUROKAWA

CL 佐倉市立美術館

309

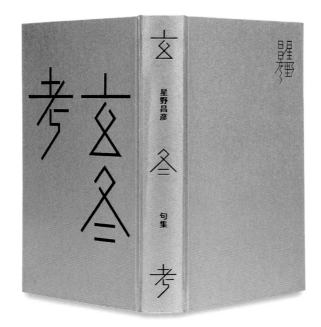

310
AD 味岡 伸太郎
SHINTARO AJIOKA

DE 味岡 伸太郎
SHINTARO AJIOKA

CL 星野昌彦

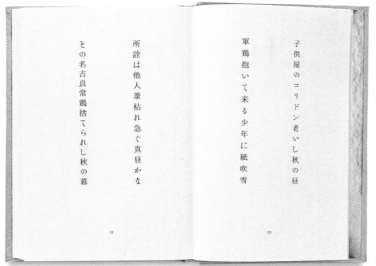

310

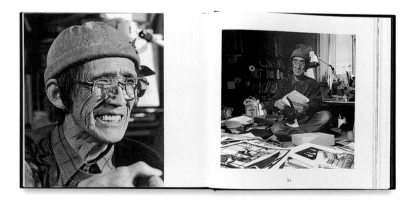

311

AD　味岡 伸太郎
　　SHINTARO AJIOKA

DE　味岡 伸太郎
　　SHINTARO AJIOKA

CL　水谷フォトスタジオ

311

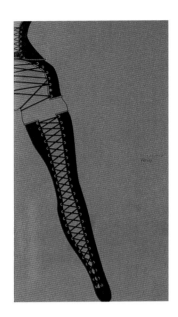

312

AD 奥村 昭夫
　　AKIO　OKUMURA

DE 桶本 尚子
　　TAKAKO　OKEMOTO

　　上田 満
　　MITSURU　UEDA

CW 前田 愛実
　　MANAMI　MAEDA

CL インターメディウム研究所

312

DCT

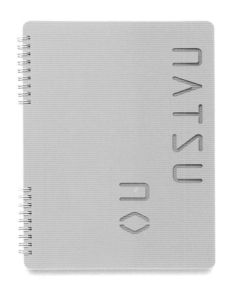

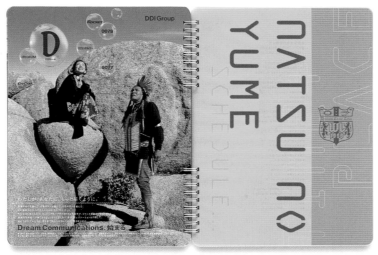

313

AD 海老名 淳
ATZSHI EVINA

DE 海老名 淳
ATZSHI EVINA

CL MSアーティスト・プロダクツ

313

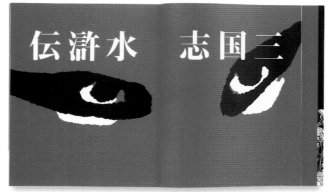

314

AD 太田 徹也
TETSUYA OHTA

DE 太田 徹也
TETSUYA OHTA

PH 富山 治夫
HARUO TOMIYAMA

CL TOW

314

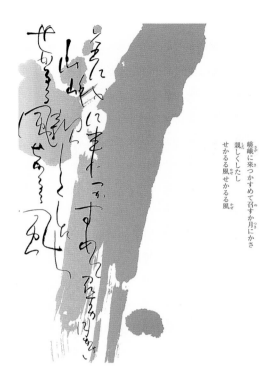

せかるる風せかるる風
親しくしたし
嵯峨に来つかすめて召すか月にかさ

折の至ればはれた祈りを
かく笛ふきむぎ笛吹くか
木か竹か見すかす霞影高き

315

AD　篠原 榮太
　　EITA SHINOHARA

DE　篠原 榮太
　　EITA SHINOHARA

CL　レターハウス

茎の香ぞ花にし似なば曽我の菊
今朝うたふ飲めかや瓶の葡萄酒
御意見がしみてして見し寒菊古

◉回文のたのしみ・おかしみ
うぐいすれた花は吸いくう
池の名はしらずめずらし花の影

316

AD 工藤 強勝
TSUYOKATSU KUDO

DE 工藤 強勝
TSUYOKATSU KUDO

CL 青土社

316

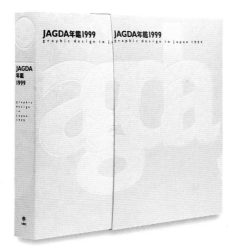

317

AD　工藤 強勝
　　　TSUYOKATSU KUDO

DE　工藤 強勝
　　　TSUYOKATSU KUDO

CD　松永 真
　　　SHIN MATSUNAGA

CL　日本グラフィックデザイナー協会

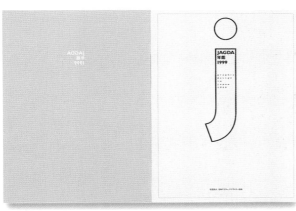

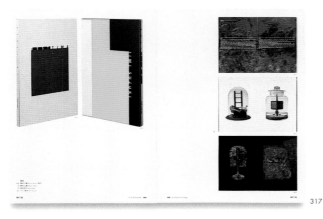

317

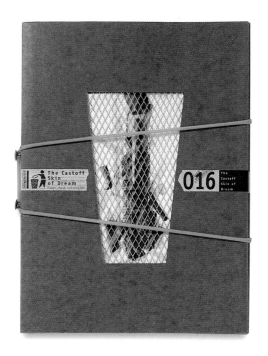

318

AD 高橋 善丸
YOSHIMARU TAKAHASHI

DE 高橋 善丸
YOSHIMARU TAKAHASHI

CL 竹尾

318

319

AD 高橋 善丸
　　YOSHIMARU　TAKAHASHI

DE 高橋 善丸
　　YOSHIMARU　TAKAHASHI

CL 詩遊社

319

320

AD 田中 一光
IKKO TANAKA

DE 太田 徹也
TETSUYA OHTA

CL トランスアート

320

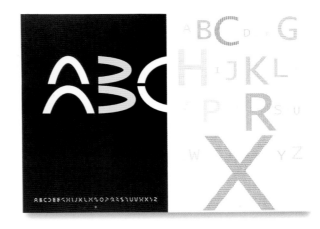

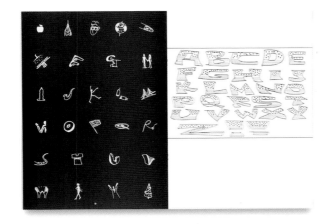

321

AD 奥村 昭夫
AKIO OKUMURA

DE 松原 博子
HIROKO MATSUBARA

CL インターメディウム研究所

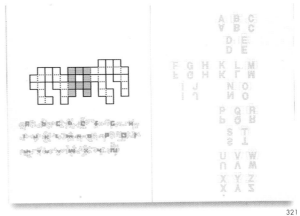

321

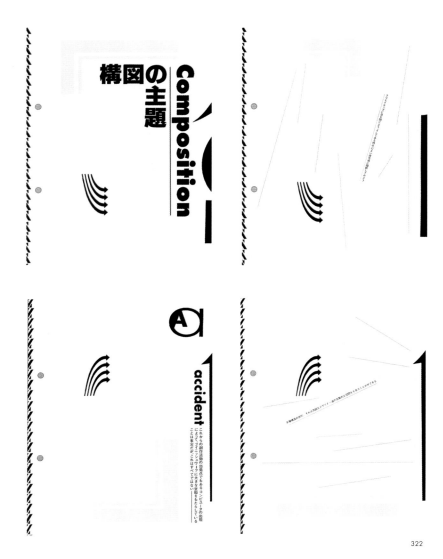

322

AD 篠原 榮太
EITA SHINOHARA

DE 篠原 榮太
EITA SHINOHARA

CL レターハウス

323

AD 工藤 強勝
TSUYOKATSU KUDO

DE 工藤 強勝
TSUYOKATSU KUDO

安田 真奈己
MANAMI YASUDA

CL 日経BP社

322

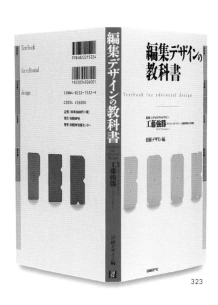

323

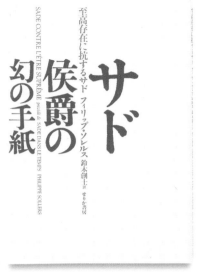

324

324

AD 工藤 強勝
TSUYOKATSU KUDO

DE 工藤 強勝
TSUYOKATSU KUDO

CL せりか書房

325

AD 工藤 強勝
TSUYOKATSU KUDO

DE 工藤 強勝
TSUYOKATSU KUDO

CL 彰国社

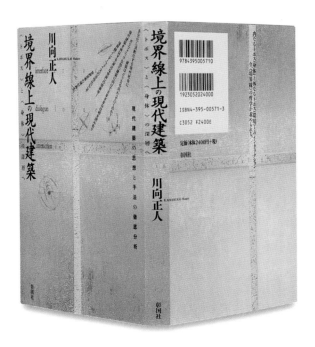

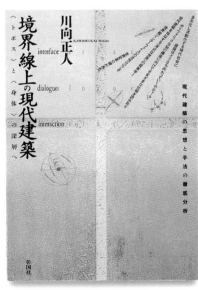

325

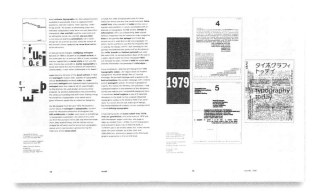

326

DE　ヘルムート・シュミット
　　HELMUT SCHMID

CL　mudra

327

AD　カン・タイクン
　　KAN TAI-KEUNG

DE　カン・タイクン
　　KAN TAI-KEUNG

CG　ニッキー・ラム・タットワイ
　　NICKEY LAM TAT WAI

IL　カン・タイクン
　　KAN TAI-KEUNG

CL　Shanghai Graphic Designers
　　Association

327

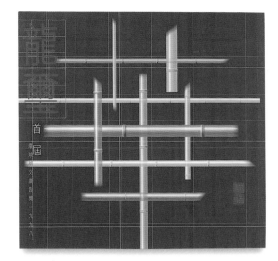

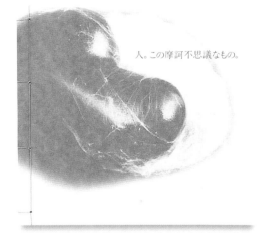

328

AD　アラン・チャン
　　ALAN CHAN

DE　アラン・チャン
　　ALAN CHAN

　　アルビン・チャン
　　ALVIN CHAN

　　ピーター・ロー
　　PETER LO

IL　ピーター・ロー
　　PETER LO

　　マーチン・ファン
　　MARTIN FUNG

　　ポリー・コー
　　POLLY KO

CL　Long Xi,Hong Kong

329

AD　小柳 文
　　AYA KOYANAGI

DE　小柳 文
　　AYA KOYANAGI

CW　小柳 文
　　AYA KOYANAGI

PH　小柳 文
　　AYA KOYANAGI

CL　小柳 文 クリエイト

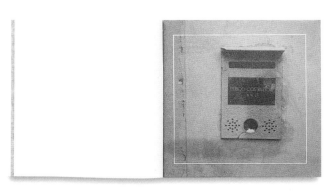

330

AD 海老名 淳
ATZSHI EVINA

DE 海老名 淳
ATZSHI EVINA

CL シティ出版

330

パッケージ

P A C K A G I ~ G

331
AD 味岡 伸太郎
   SHINTARO AJIOKA

DE 味岡 伸太郎
   SHINTARO AJIOKA

CL 入河屋

331

332

AD 中川 憲造
KENZO NAKAGAWA

DE 延山 博保
HIROYASU NOBUYAMA

小山 秀子
HIDEKO KOYAMA

CL タワーショップ

332

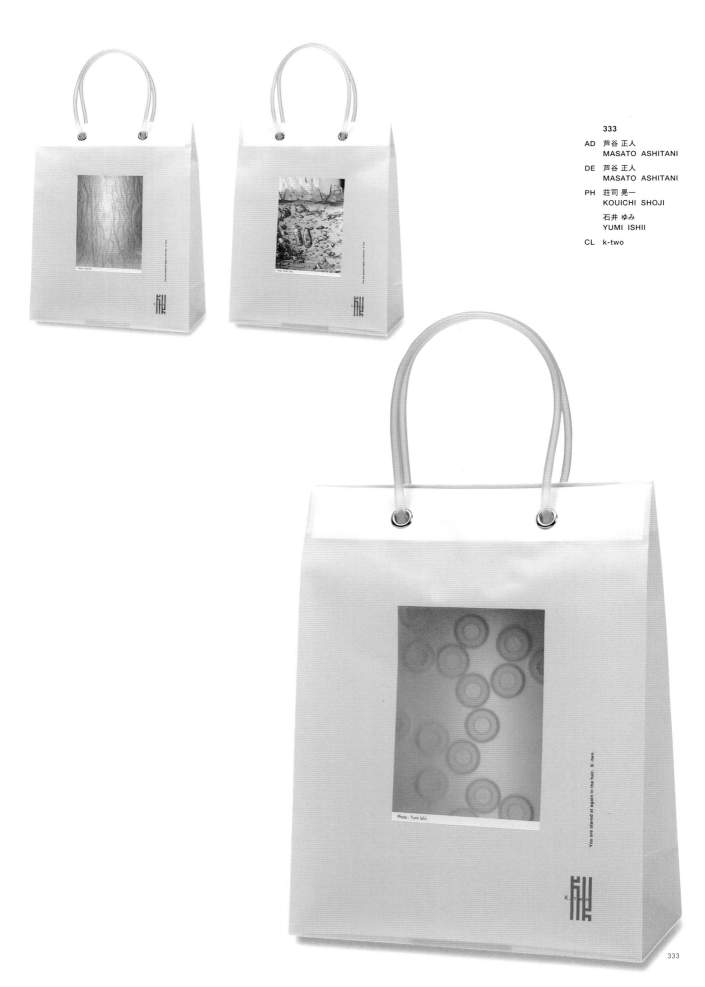

333

AD 芦谷 正人
MASATO ASHITANI

DE 芦谷 正人
MASATO ASHITANI

PH 荘司 晃一
KOUICHI SHOJI

石井 ゆみ
YUMI ISHII

CL k-two

334

AD 野上 周一
SHUICHI NOGAMI

DE 野上 周一
SHUICHI NOGAMI

CL 志木

334

335

AD メアリー・ルイス
MARY LEWIS

DE メアリー・ルイス
MARY LEWIS

PH チャーリー・ウエイト
CHARLIE WAITE

CL Vinhos Sogrape de Portugal SA

335

336
AD 八木 健夫
TATEO YAGI
DE 八木 健夫
TATEO YAGI
山口 美和子
MIWAKO YAMAGUCHI
CL 長野ステーションビル

337
AD 粟辻 美早
   MISA AWATSUJI
DE 粟辻 美早
   MISA AWATSUJI

   粟辻 麻喜
   MAKI AWATSUJI

   筒井 英子
   HIDEKO TSUTSUI
CL SAKE SHOP 福光屋

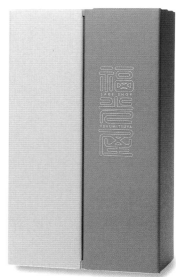

337

338

AD 峠田 充謙
MITSUNORI TAODA

DE 峠田 充謙
MITSUNORI TAODA

上田 知世子
CHIYOKO UEDA

CL セバスティアン インターナショナル

338

211

339

340

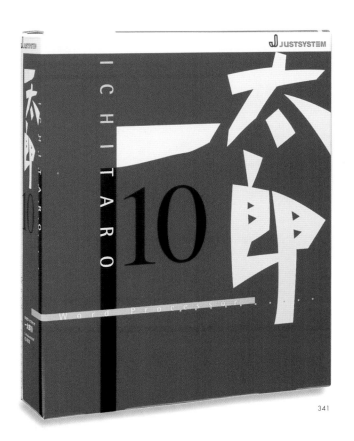

341

339
AD 田中 一光
IKKO TANAKA

DE 田中 一光
IKKO TANAKA

山本 寛
KAN YAMAMOTO

CL 西友

340
AD 中川 憲造
KENZO NAKAGAWA

DE 延山 博保
HIROYASU NOBUYAMA

清水 証
AKIRA SHIMIZU

CW 田中 あづさ
AZUSA TANAKA

CL 明治製菓

341
AD 飯尾 明彦
AKIHIKO IIO

DE 飯尾 明彦
AKIHIKO IIO

舟橋 全二
ZENJI FUNABASHI

IL 舟橋 全二
ZENJI FUNABASHI

CL ジャストシステム

DISPLAY
&
ENVIRONMENT

環境
二体

342

AD 水谷 孝次
KOJI MIZUTANI

DE 遠藤 一成
KAZUNARI ENDO

CL ボンイマージュ

342

215

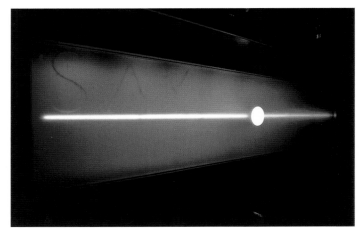

343

AD 工藤 青石
    AOSHI KUDO

DE 工藤 青石
    AOSHI KUDO

CL 資生堂

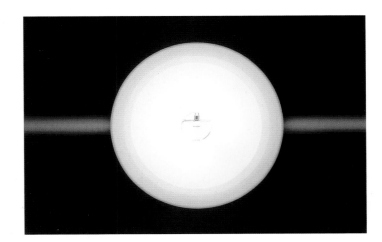

343

344

AD 坪内 祝義
TOKIYOSHI TSUBOUCHI

DE 坪内 祝義
TOKIYOSHI TSUBOUCHI

PH 藤塚 光政
MITSUMASA FUJITSUKA

CL エンゼルランドふくい

344

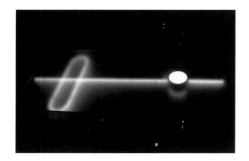

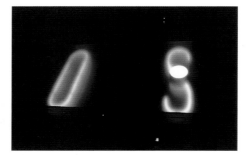

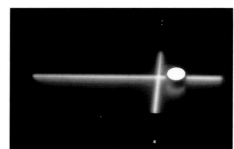

345

AD 工藤 青石
AOSHI KUDO

DE 工藤 青石
AOSHI KUDO

CL 資生堂

345

346

AD 中川 憲造
KENZO NAKAGAWA

瀬川 律子
RITSUKO SEGAWA

DE 森上 暁
SATOSHI MORIKAMI

印田 裕之
HIROYUKI INDA

CL 横浜みなとみらい21

346

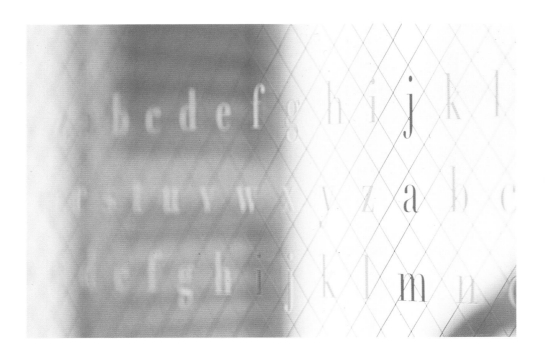

347

AD 藤本 孝明
　　TAKAAKI FUJIMOTO

DE 藤本 孝明
　　TAKAAKI FUJIMOTO

CL ヘア・ジャム

347

映像
デジタルメディア

VISUAL & DIGITAL MEDIA

Man and Writing

CD-ROM for
Macintosh and Windows

人間と文字

モリサワ

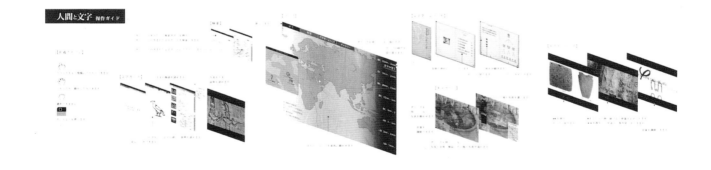

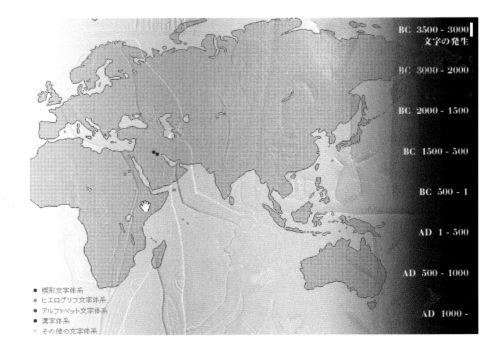

348

AD　田中 一光
　　　IKKO TANAKA

DE　田中 一光
　　　IKKO TANAKA

　　　大内 修
　　　OSAMU OUCHI

CL　モリサワ

文字を手にしてたった5,000年の人間

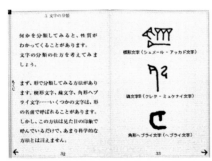

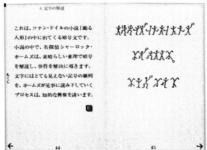

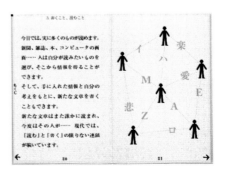

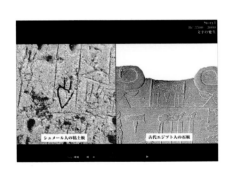

348

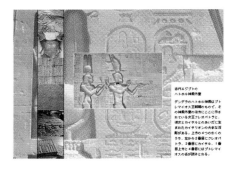

古代エジプトの
ハトホル神殿内壁

デンデラのハトホル神殿はプト
レマイオス王朝期のもので、そ
の神殿内壁の浮彫にここに示さ
れている女王クレオパトラと、
彼女とカイサリオンのあいだに生
まれたカイサリオンの大きな浮
彫がある。上方の4つのめくの
うち、左から2番目にクレオパ
トラ、3番目にカイサル、1番
目上方と4番目にはプトレマイ
オスの名が読めとれる。

エトルリアの石棺の奉納文

タルクィニアのモンテロッツィ
番地から出土した石棺の一つで、
その下方側面には、ここにも
「アマゾン女軍との戦い」が描か
れている。しかしこちらはテン
ペラ画法によっており、ギリシ
ア人の手が加わっているらしい。
エトルリア語刻文には「ラムザ・
フズクナリのために、息子ラルス・
アピアトルが奉納」などと記さ
れている。前4世紀。
フィレンツェ考古博物館蔵

348

AD　田中 一光
　　 IKKO TANAKA

DE　田中 一光
　　 IKKO TANAKA

　　 大内 修
　　 OSAMU OUCHI

CL　モリサワ

348

研究実験

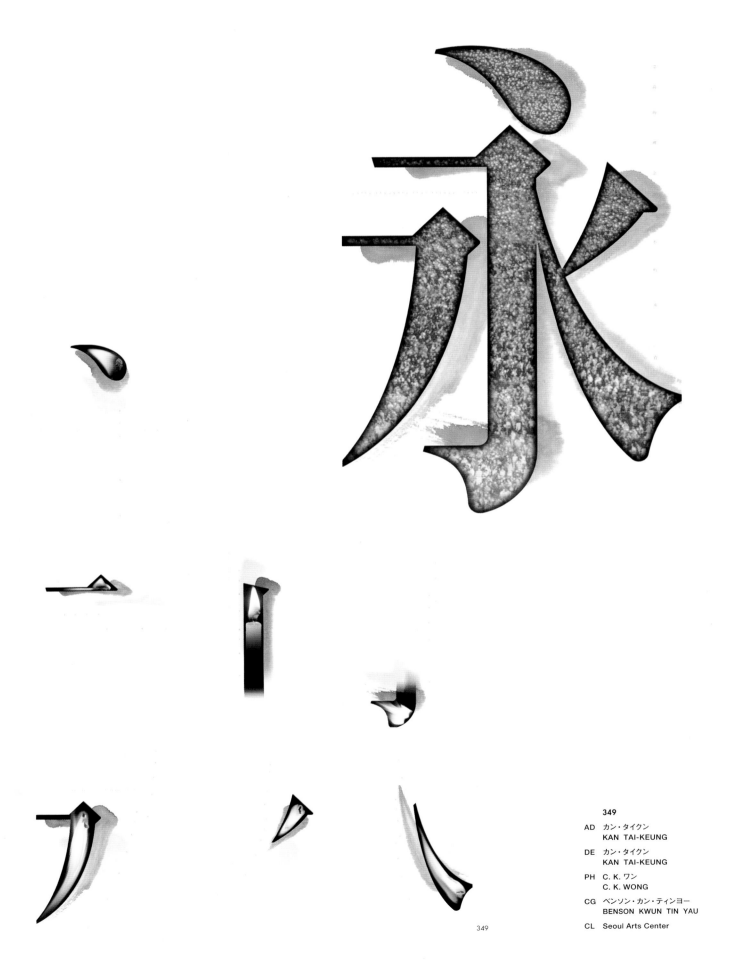

349

AD カン・タイクン
KAN TAI-KEUNG

DE カン・タイクン
KAN TAI-KEUNG

PH C. K. ワン
C. K. WONG

CG ベンソン・カン・ティンヨー
BENSON KWUN TIN YAU

CL Seoul Arts Center

349

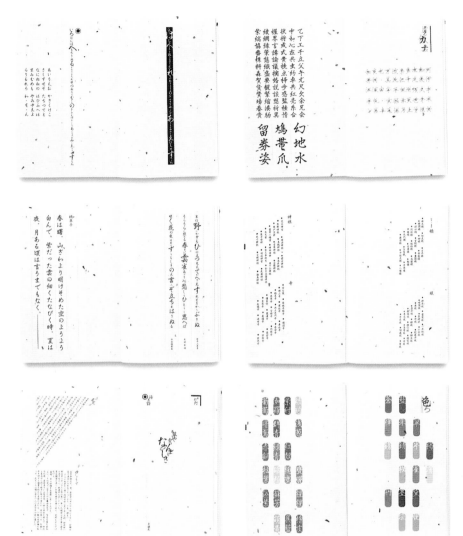

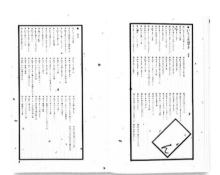

350

AD 篠原 榮太
　　EITA SHINOHARA

DE 篠原 榮太
　　EITA SHINOHARA

CL レターハウス

Design of visual dictionary for nameplate by Fil-typo

「Fil-typo図典」の制作と

Nameplateへの展開　抜粋 —

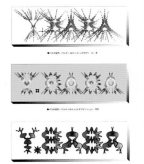

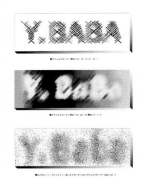

351

351

AD　馬場 雄二
　　 YUJI BABA

DE　馬場 雄二
　　 YUJI BABA

352

352
DE　トモ・ヒコ
TOMOHIKO

354

355

354

AD 奥村 昭夫
AKIO OKUMURA

DE 奥村 昭夫
AKIO OKUMURA

CL 日本グラフィックデザイナー協会

355

AD 大杉 学
MANABU OSUGI

DE 大杉 学
MANABU OSUGI

楠本 正敬
MASATAKA KUSUMOTO

CL 日本グラフィックデザイナー協会

356

356

AD　アラン・チャン
　　ALAN CHAN

DE　アラン・チャン
　　ALAN CHAN

　　ピーター・ロー
　　PETER LO

CL　Shanghai Graphic Designers
　　Association

357

AD　アラン・チャン
　　ALAN CHAN

DE　アラン・チャン
　　ALAN CHAN

　　デビッド・ロー
　　DAVID LO

CL　Shanghai Graphic Designers
　　Association

357

there
is
a
new
begin-
ning

new
beg
ning

for
every
end

there
is
a
new
begin-
ning

358

htypo
techno

359

358

DE　シュミット・ニコール
　　NICOLE SCHMID

CL　大阪芸術工科大学
　　視覚情報デザイン学科

359

DR　小泉 均
　　HITOSHI KOIZUMI

PR　真壁 友
　　TOMO MAKABE

ED　長谷川 直子
　　NAOKO HASEGAWA

CO　野上 タカヒロ
　　TAKAHIRO NOGAMI

CL　美術出版社

池上の道は果てるや青墨

kakyoku

夏曲

soshisha

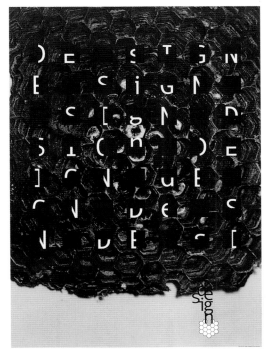

360

夏曲
soshisha

夏曲
soshisha

夏曲
soshisha

夏曲
soshisha

361

360

AD　滝川 正弘
　　MASAHIRO TAKIGAWA

DE　滝川 正弘
　　MASAHIRO TAKIGAWA

CD　高橋 修宏
　　NOBUHIRO TAKAHASHI

PH　滝川 正弘
　　MASAHIRO TAKIGAWA

CL　日本グラフィックデザイナー協会

361

AD　滝川 正弘
　　MASAHIRO TAKIGAWA

DE　滝川 正弘
　　MASAHIRO TAKIGAWA

CD　高橋 修宏
　　NOBUHIRO TAKAHASHI

CL　草子舎

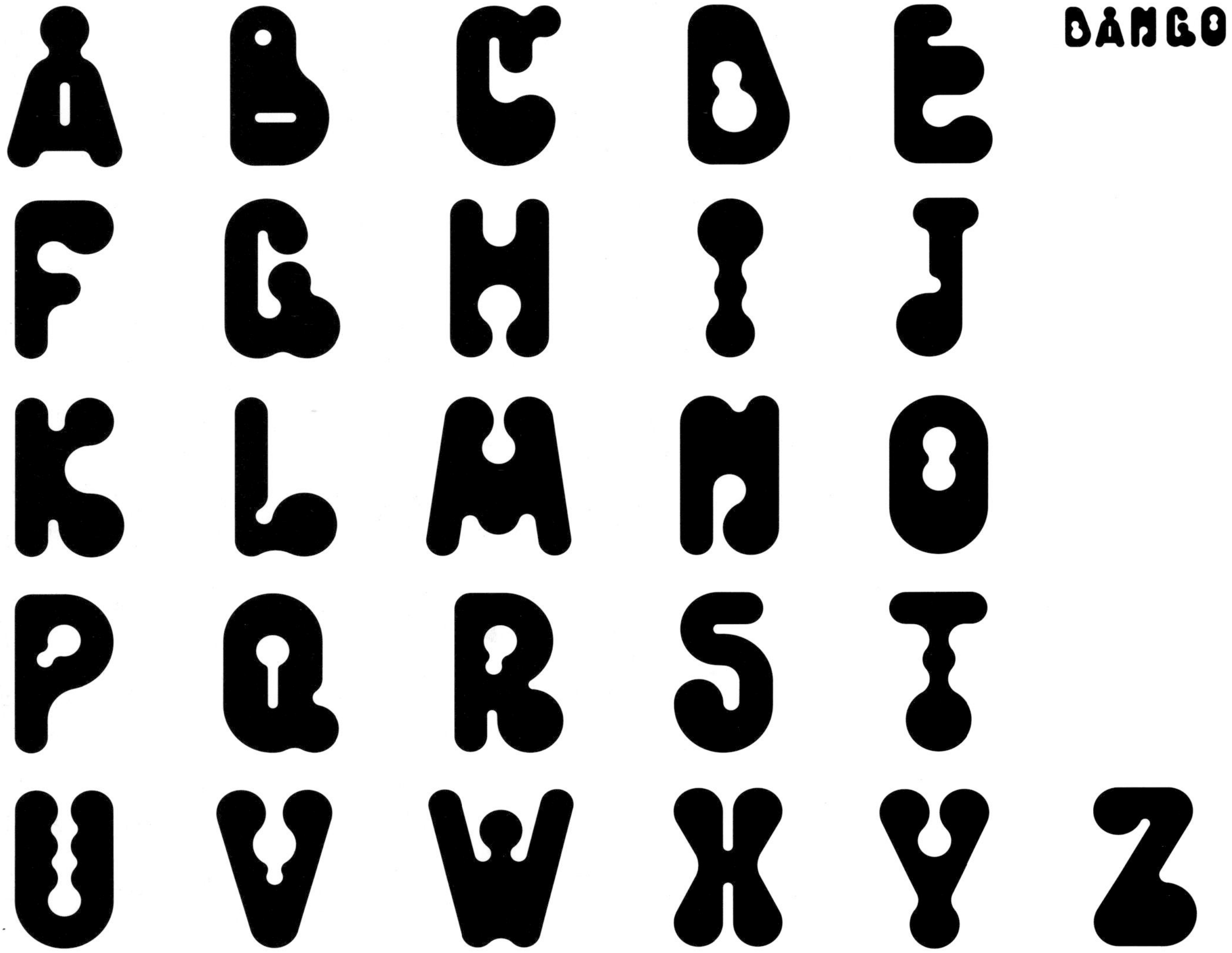

DANGO

A B C D E
F G H I J
K L M N O
P Q R S T
U V W X Y Z

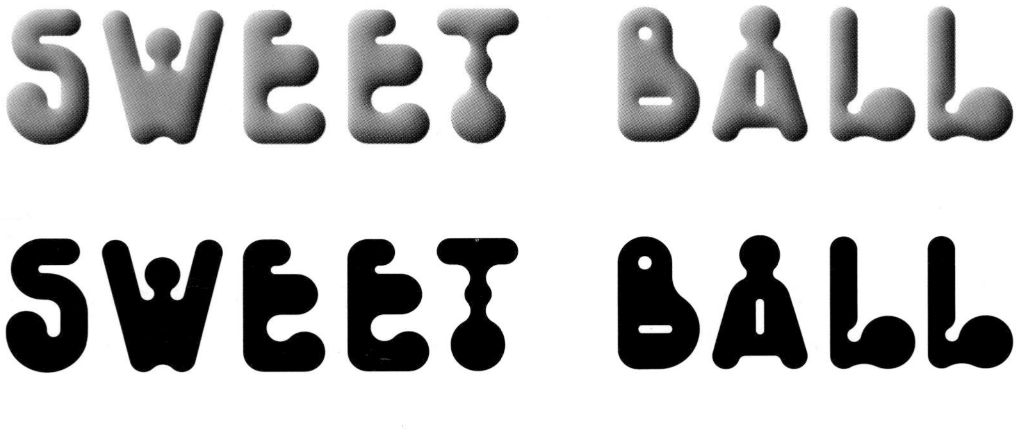

SWEET BALL

SWEET BALL

362
AD 高橋 善丸
YOSHIMARU TAKAHASHI

DE 高橋 善丸
YOSHIMARU TAKAHASHI

362

Penguin Time

ABCDEFGHIJKLM
NOPQRSTUVWXY
Zәe&ABCDEFGHIJKL
MNOPQRSTUVWXYZәe
1234567890!?,.-()
あいうえおがぎぐげご
なにぬねのまみむめも
やゆよわをんっ アイウ
エオカキクケコサシス
セソパピプペポッー、。

カオルです。… THIS IS Kәoru.
ヨのなかはせまいですね。………
…. SMALL WORLD, ISN'T IT?

363
AD 伊藤 勝一
KATSUICHI ITO
DE 伊藤 勝一
KATSUICHI ITO
藤原 俊哉
TOSHIYA FUJIWARA
CL 伊藤勝一デザイン室

またあえてうれしいです。……… GOOD TO SEE YOU AGAIN.
シャシンをとってもいい? ………… CAN I TAKE PICTURES?
どちらまでいくのですか? …… HOW FAR ARE YOU GOING?

363

364

364

AD 渡部 孝一
KOICHI WATANABE

DE 渡部 孝一
KOICHI WATANABE

CL 渡部孝一

365

AD 山口 馨
KAORU YAMAGUCHI

DE 山口 馨
KAORU YAMAGUCHI

CL パウ広告事務所

365

特集

新聞とタイポグラフィ

Special Report

Typography of the News Paper

文・構成 羽島 知之
Text & Construction
Tomoyuki Hajima

I. 明治の新聞
II. 新聞題字にみるタイポグラフィ
III. 新聞広告にみるタイポグラフィ

Newspapers in the Meiji Period
The Typography of Newspaper Mastheads
The Typography of Newspaper Advertising

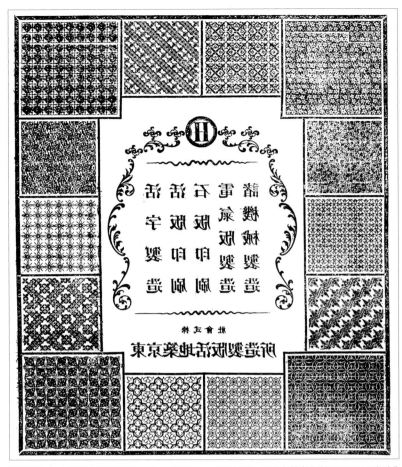

印刷に使うカットの模様と活字の母型をそのまま広告に使い、一見逆さと思わせる築地活版製造所ならではのアイデア広告（明治35年7月）　An innovative ad that could only be for Tsukiji Type Manufacturing: the characters are backwards. It was created directly from the company's print patterns and typeface (1902.7)

はじめに

今日、「新聞」といったら、人はどんなイメージを抱くのだろうか。毎朝夕に配達されてくるもの、朝日・毎日・読売のいわゆる三大新聞、駅売りのスポーツ紙などかもしれないが、この国の新聞が歩んできた道のりはあまり知られてないのではないか。もちろん新聞を何をもって新聞とするのかの定義はさまざまで、種類も一般紙、専門紙、機関紙、学校新聞、広報などいろいろである。しかしながら新聞は読んだら捨てるものだと思われている方は多いと考える。

ところが…。

私は中学時代に新聞に関心をもちはじめ、それから新聞や関係資料を収集するようになり、昭和31年に大学に入ってからは新聞歴史研究の草分け、小野秀雄先生に師事した。小野先生は新聞社自体にも保管されていない新聞について、各地の所蔵機関を回り、好事家を尋ね歩き、古書店などから古新聞を集め、当時すでに『日本新聞発達史』『新聞発生史論』『日本新聞史』など数々の主要著書を上梓されていたが、しかしまだなお日本の新聞歴史を知る上で未発見の資料、特定の困難なことがらがいくつもあるような、それがやっと学問的研究の対象になった新聞学のおかれた状況だった。小野先生は「歴史は全く資料次第である。確実な資料が出てくれば、根拠の薄弱な研究はたちまちだめになる」とおっしゃっていた。それにはやはり自分自身で収集しなければ新聞の歴史がわからない。もっといえば現物資料がどのような形で扱われていたのか、保存されてきたのか、印刷、紙のもつ風合い、付随する資料などを含めた新聞の向こう側にあるものまでも実際に見、手にしていかなければ時代の価値観や意識に迫ることはできないと私は思う。

時代のナマの資料である新聞は、ずっと人々の生き生きとした営みを伝えてきた。私はその記事内容もさることながら新聞がもつ、放つ世界に魅せられて収集を続けてきたが、ある時期からそのコレクションを通じて社会に開かれた歴史の構築の一助になればという思いも強くなっていった。

文久2年（1864）に誕生した日本の新聞は、古代から行われてきた板木に文字を刷って印刷する「木板整版」がスタートしている。慶応4年（1868）には、木活字を用いた組版刷りの新聞も木板整版にまざって登場、明治4年頃から本木昌造が

つくった鋳造活字が新聞紙面に登場する。以来、輪転印刷機が導入される明治20年代から、日本の新聞は鉛を高熱で溶かして活字を鋳造し組版をつくる、いわゆるホットタイプシステムによって製作されてきた。

近年、昭和40年代以降自動写植機を使いフィルムや印画紙に印字して版をつくるコールドタイプシステムやコンピュータにより整理大組みにまで技術革新は急速に進み、各新聞社は創業以来の「活字」に別れを告げている。

明治・大正・昭和・平成と移り変わる各時代の新聞の紙面には、タイポグラフィの歩みが凝縮されている。そんな意味から今回は「新聞とタイポグラフィ」と題して以下に示す3つの章の構成をとった。

I. 明治の新聞

わが国では江戸時代にいわゆる「かわら版」という庶民向けの読みもの情報紙が誕生したが、ここでは明治という時代に焦点をあて、「新聞」の発生から今日に繋がる企業化確立までの来歴をその時代のトピックとなった資料を紹介しながら概観していく。

II. 新聞題字にみるタイポグラフィ

新聞の顔ともいうべき新聞紙名、その題号は古くからフロント面の最上段または右上端に位置

している。その多くは毛筆書体によるもので、これをタイポグラフィ的関心をもって書体上に分類しながら考察を試みた。

III. 新聞広告にみるタイポグラフィ

タイポグラフィを文字をうまく表現しているもの、そのことによってコミュニケーションを快くはかることができることとしてみれば、広告ほどその要素を大きく備えるものはない。ここでは新聞広告の歴史を概観するとともに明治期の優れたレタリング、デザイン、レイアウトをもった広告作品を紹介してみたい。

主として日本に新聞が誕生し、現在の一般的な姿になる萌芽となった明治時代を中心に、資料を図版で掲載しながら歴史のあらましと、私なりにそこからうかがえるタイポグラフィについて提示してみた。

■フロント面の新聞錦絵

「東京日日新聞」第1号に掲載された記事をもとにつくられた"新聞錦絵"。夫の病気を治したい一心から旅の僧に読経を頼んだところ、刃物をもって迫られた。抵抗むなしく殺されたが、不貞の道を選ばなかった貞婦の話。

Introduction

What first comes to mind when you mention the word "newspaper" in Japan today? Most people will probably think of one of the so-called Big Three newspapers –the Asahi, Mainichi and Yomiuri – that are delivered to their doorstep every morning and afternoon, or perhaps the sports newspapers sold at station kiosks. Yet the history of newspapers in this country is not that well known. Of course, there is the initial problem of what exactly you define as a newspaper in the first place. After all, there are all kinds: regular papers, specialty papers, house organs, class newspapers, newsletters etc. etc. etc. The one thing almost everyone agrees on is that, once you read a newspaper, you throw it away. There are those, however, who would beg to differ.

When I was in junior high school, I conceived a fascination for newspapers. I began collecting newspapers and related materials, and after entering university in 1956 I studied under Professor Ono Hideo, the pioneering historian of newspapers. Professor Ono would go around libraries, visit collectors and rifle through used-book stores all over the country tracking down copies of old newspapers even the newspaper companies themselves no longer possessed. That was in spite of the fact that he

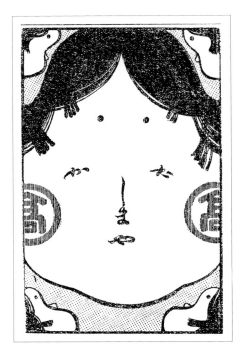

ほほを高島屋の商標で染めたおかめ。目、鼻、口が「たかしまやの5文字で表現されたユニークな作品（明治42年6月）
This unique specimen shows a homely face with the trademark of Takashimaya Drapers dyed on its cheeks. The eyes, nose and mouth consist of the five characters ta-ka-shi-ma-ya. (1909.6)

already had an impressive list of publications to his name, including his work Nihon Shimbun Hattatsu-shi ("History of the Development of Newspapers in Japan"), Shimbun Hasseisiron ("Historical Treatise on the Emergence of Newspapers"), and Nihon Shimbun-shi ("History of Newspapers in Japan"). Even so, the study of Japanese newspapers was barely out of the cradle as an academic discipline. Much archival material had yet to be discovered, and numerous obstacles still remained to the investigation of the history of the medium. Professor Ono was in the habit of saying that the study of history depends completely on the sources you have to work with: once you findreliable documentation, you can instantly debunk any research that lies on shaky foundations. Plus you cannot truly understand the history of newspapers without collecting them yourself. Only by observing in what manner the actual copies were handled, noting how they have been preserved, examining the printing on the page, feeling the paper, inspecting the materials they come with, I believe, can you hope to peer into the minds of the people of the day.

Newspapers mirror their particular age, and together they provide an unbroken record of the hustle and bustle of ordinary life. In collecting newspapers I have always been fascinated not just by the contents of the articles themselves but by the whole world each newspaper conjures up, and at a certain stage I found myself possessed by a growing desire to contribute to the study and popular understanding of history through my collections.

The first newspaper was published in Japan in 1862 using the ancient technique of woodblock printing, which involved engraving the text to be printed on a block of wood. In 1868 typeset newspapers using movable wooden type joined the woodblock-printed variety, and around 1871 the cast typeface developed by Motoki Shozo appeared on the pages of newspapers. After the introduction of the rotary press in the third decade of the Meiji era, Japanese newspapers were printed using the so-called hot-type system, which entailed melting lead at high temperatures for casting into type, then setting the text copy.

The years since the late 1960s have witnessed rapid advances in printing techniques like the introduction of the cold-type system, whereby plates are produced by printing on film or light-sensitive paper with a photocomposing machine, and the advent of computerized typesetting. With these innovations Japan's newspaper publishers finally bid farewell to movable type, on which they had depended since their earliest days.

The changing face of Japan's newspapers over

the course of the Meiji, Taisho, Showa and Heisei periods provides a compact overview of the evolution of typography in this country. It is with this in mind that I offer a feature entitled "Newspapers and Typography," which consists of three sections:

I. Newspapers in the Meiji Period

In Edo-period Japan there developed a type of broadsheet called a kawara-ban woodblock printing which catered to a popular readership. Here, however, we place the spotlight on the Meiji period as we survey the history of the newspaper in Japan from its origins through the evolution of journalism into the big business it is today. We shall interweave our overview with specific examples of newspapers from the day.

II.The Typography of Newspaper Mastheads

The masthead, which is as it were the "face" of the newspaper, is in Japan traditionally located at the top or upper right-hand corner of the front page. Most specimens are brush-written, and I have attempted to classify and analyze them typographically by calligraphic style.

III. The Typography of Newspaper Advertising

If typography is defined as the art of presenting text in such a manner as to communicate more effectively with one's audience, in no field does it have a greater role to play than advertising. Here we briefly trace the history of newspaper advertising in Japan. We also present actual specimens of advertising from the Meiji period that are outstanding for their lettering, design and layout.

I offer an illustrated outline of the history of newspapers in Japan interwoven with my own personal perspective on the evolution of typography in this country. My chief focus is on the Meiji period, when the medium first emerged and developed into its present form.

Color front-page print

A color print based on an article in the first issue of the Tokyo Nichinichi Shimbun. A woman asked an itinerant Buddhist monk to recite a sutra on behalf of her husband in the pious hope this might help him recover from his illness. The monk however turned on her with a dagger. Resistance proved futile and she was killed, but she refused to compromise her virtue to the end.

Ⅰ. 明治の新聞

わが国最初の日刊紙「横浜毎日新聞」が生まれたのは明治3年(1870)、また現存する最古の「東京日日新聞」(毎日新聞東京本社版の前身)が創刊されたのが明治5年、近代新聞発祥の"明治"の文化的意義は極めて大きい。

現在、社団法人・日本新聞協会に加盟している日刊新聞は111社あるが、改題や統合などにより題号が変わっているものも含めて、この"明治"を創刊日としている社は40を超え、そのうち30余紙が輝かしい100周年を通過している。

1. 新聞の先駆

この明治から数えて6年前にあたる文久2年(1862)に、日本邦字新聞の始祖「官板バタヒヤ新聞」が誕生している。

これ以前、鎖国令をしいた徳川幕府は、外国事情を知るために、オランダに貿易を許可する条件として世界情勢を報告させた。この報告書は「和蘭風説書」とよばれ老中格に限り回覧させていた。幕府が鎖国政策をすてて開国にふみ切って以来、オランダはこの風説書に替えて「ヤバッシュ・クーラント」という政府の機関新聞を献上するようになった。幕府は洋学所である蕃書調所(文久2年洋書調所と改称)を設置、これを翻訳して江戸の書肆「老皂館」萬屋兵四郎に販売させたのが「官板バタヒヤ新聞」である。現在の新聞とはほど遠く、木活字で印刷した和半紙二つ折り数葉をとじ合わせた小冊子で、この年の1月から2月にかけて23巻が発行されている。

その後は「官板海外新聞」と改題され、8月から9月までに9巻、また「海外新聞別集」として上中下3冊が発行されている。上下2巻はアメリカの新聞から南北戦争の模様をイラスト入りで、中巻はオランダの新聞から幕府遣欧使節一行の消息記事といった特集版になっている。

これが動機となり洋書調所は、中国各地で英米の宣教師が発行していた中国新聞にも目をつけ、句読点をつけた「官板中外新報」「官板香港新聞」「官板六合叢談」などの翻刻新聞を文久年間に発行した。

一方、来日した外国人による外字新聞の発行はこれより早く、文久元年5月に長崎で英人ハンサードが週2回刊で、「The Nagasaki Shipping Rist and Advertiser」を創刊している。この新聞はハンサードが横浜に移転したため10月の第28号で廃刊となり、11月から横浜で「The Japan Herald」と改称されて発刊、大正3年まで続刊された。以

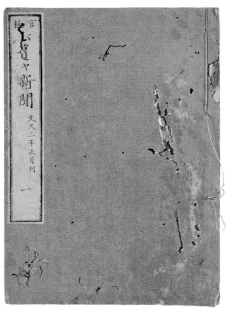

官板バタヒヤ新聞 Kanpan Batahiya Simbun

後、横浜・神戸・長崎などの外国人居留地で、居留民を対象に海外事情と日本の国内情勢を伝える外字新聞の発行は相次いだ。幕府はこの国内発行の外字新聞にも情報源を求め、会訳社という翻訳筆記の団体をつくり、文久3年5月、横浜でポルトガル人ローザの発行した「Japan Commercial News」の邦訳「日本貿易新聞」をはじめ、「横浜新聞」「日本交易新聞」「別段新聞」「日本新聞」など数多くのタイトルの筆写新聞をつくらせ有料で回覧させた。

元治元年(1864)、アメリカに帰化した日本人、ジョセフ・ヒコ(日本名・浜田彦蔵)は、手書きの「新聞誌」を発刊、翌年5月に「海外新聞」と改題、岸田吟香らの協力を得て、最新の海外ニュースや商況、広告などを木版印刷で慶応2年第26号まで発行した。この海外新聞はニュースの速報性、刊行の定期性、読者対象を一般人に向けている点においても、従来の官板新聞とはまったく異なった特徴をもち、わが国最初の民間新聞として特筆に値する。慶応3年(1867)には、英国

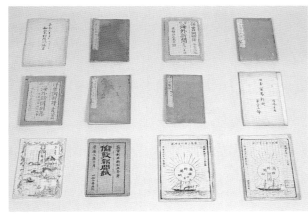

幕末・明治初期の冊子型新聞
Pamphlet-style newspapers of the late Tokugawa and early Meiji periods

I.Newspapers in the Meiji Period

The Meiji period is of tremendous cultural significance in the birth of the mod Shimbun, was established in the third year of the era, 1870, and the oldest newspaper still in print today, the Tokyo Nichinichi Shimbun (precursor of the Tokyo edition of the Mainichi Shimbun), appeared two years later in 1872.

The Japan Newspaper Association currently counts a membership of 110 daily newspapers. Of these, if we include papers that have changed their titles due to renaming or mergers, more than forty were established in the Meiji period, and thirty-odd have the distinction of being over a hundred years old.

1. Precursors of the Newspaper

Six years before the beginning of the Meiji period, in 1862, the first ever Japanese-language newspaper appeared: the Kampan Batahia Shimbun or "Official Batavia News". Earlier, during the country's long years of self-imposed isolation, the Tokugawa shogunate kept abreast of developments abroad by requiring the Dutch to report to it on the world situation in return for permission to trade. This report, known as the Oranda Fusetsu-gaki, was circulated confidentially among the Shogun's senior councilors. After the shogunate decided to abandon its policy of national seclusion and open the country to the outside world, the Dutch began submitting a government newspaper called the Javasche Courant instead. The shogunate forwarded the copies of this newspaper for translation to a special agency it had established to study Western learning, the Office for the Investigation of Barbarian Writings (renamed the Office for the Investigation of Western Writings in 1862). The translated version was the Kampan Batavia Shimbun, which was sold through the Edo bookseller Yorozuya Heishiro, proprietor of the Rosokan. It bore precious little resemblance to a modern newspaper, consisting of several folio sheets of Japanese paper printed on with wooden type and bound into a pamphlet. A total of 23 issues appeared in January and February of that year.The paper was subsequently renamed the Kampan Kaigai Shimbun ("Official Overseas News"), of which nine issues were published in August and September. A special three-volume supplement, the Kaigai Shimbun Besshu, also appeared. The first and last volume provided an illustrated account of the US Civi War incorpora ting material from American

人ベーリーが「萬国新聞紙」を創刊、その第3集には横浜元町でパン・ビスケット・バターを販売した日本人最初の広告主、中川屋嘉兵衛の広告も登場する。

2. 維新前後の新聞

徳川幕府が崩壊し大政奉還によって新政府が出現した翌年にあたる慶応4年（1868）、維新戦争の動乱とともに国内ニュース報道に力を入れた民間の手による新聞や官報など50紙近くが創刊された。まず新政府は2月に「太政官日誌」（京都）を発刊、官軍の佐幕派に対する戦況を報道、ついで4月に「各国新聞紙」と「内外新聞」が大阪で、5月に「都鄙新聞」（京都）と7月「新聞論破・湊川濯余」（神戸）などが新政府を支持し佐幕派新聞を攻撃した。

一方、旧幕府の本拠地の江戸・横浜では、佐幕派新聞が相次いで創刊、2月の柳河春三の「中外

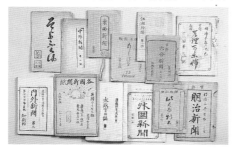

慶応4年から明治2年に創刊された新聞
Newspapers established from 1868 to 1869

新聞」をはじめ、福地源一郎の「江湖新聞」、米人ヴァン・リードの「横浜新報もしほ草」や「そよふく風」「遠近新聞」「内外新報」「東西新聞」「公私雑報」「日々新聞」などが一斉に新政府の横暴ぶりを非難した。「中外新聞」は5月15日に上野の山で勃発した戦争のニュースを翌日に号数なしの「別段中外新聞」として発行、これがわが国最初の号外といわれている。

官軍は江戸を占拠して間もない6月、新聞の取締りを強化し一旦、全新聞の発行を禁止して許可を得て発行すべきことを命じた。新政府は明治2年（1869）2月に「新聞紙印行条例」を制定、積極的に新聞の発行を許可することにしたため前年、禁止になった「中外新聞」や「遠近新聞」が復刊、「明治新聞」や「六合新聞」なども新たに創刊されたが、いずれも短命で廃刊した。

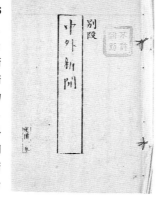

Betsudan Chugai Simbun

newspapers, while the second volume reported on an official Japanese mission to Europe based on Dutch newspapers.

The Chinese-language newspapers published by British and American missionaries in various parts of China also caught the eye of the Office for the Investigation of Western Writings, which in the early 1860s reprinted a number of these with punctuation added for ease of reading. These include the Kampan Chugai Shimbun, the Kampan Hong Kong Shimbun and the Kampan Rikugo Shimbun. The first newspaper published by a foreigner in Japan appeared even earlier. In May 1861, in Nagasaki, the Englishman ??Hansard founded The Nagasaki Shipping List and Advertiser, which came out twice a week.

This paper was discontinued after 28 issues the same October, when Hansard moved to Yokohama. There it resumed publication in November with a new title, The Japan Herald, under which masthead it appeared continuously until 1914. Subsequently a whole flurry of European-language newspapers sprung up in the foreign settlements in Yokohama, Kobe, Nagasaki and elsewhere to keep resident Westerners informed of developments in Japan and abroad. The shogunate tapped these locally-published foreign papers for information as well. Setting up a team of translators and writers called the Kaiyakusha, in May 1863 it issued a Japanese version of the Japan Commercial News, which was published in Yokohama by a Portuguese by the name of ??Rosa, under the title the Nihon Boeki Shimbun. It went on issue a veritable spate of similarly transcribed newspapers with names like the Yokohama Shimbun, the Nihon Koeki Shimbun, the Betsudan Shimbun and the Nihon Shimbun, which it circulated for a fee.

In 1864 Joseph Heco (Hamada Hikozo in his native Japanese), a Japanese who was a naturalized American citizen, founded a handwritten newspaper called the Shimbun-shi. The next May he renamed it the Kaigai Shimbun ("Overseas News"), a woodblock-printed publication produced with the assistance of Kishida Ginko which carried the latest news from abroad, commercial reports and advertising. This went through 26 issues until 1866. The Kaigai Shimbun, which differed completely from the official publications that preceded it in several key respects -- its up-to-date reporting, the regularity with which it appeared, the fact it catered to a general readership -- occupies a special

place in history as Japan's first privately-published newspaper. In 1867 the Englishman Bailey founded the Bankoku Shimbun-shi ("International News"), the third issue of which carried an advertisement for Japan's first commercial sponsor: one Nakagawaya Kahei, a vendor of bread, biscuits and butter in the Motomachi district of Yokohama.

2. Newspapers around the Time of the Meiji Restoration

In 1868, amidst the confusion of the civil wars ushered in by the collapse of the Tokugawa regime the previous year, when the last Shogun surrendered his powers and a new government was installed, almost fifty private newspapers and official gazettes sprung up that offered extensive coverage of domestic news.

In February the new government began publishing the Dajokan Nisshi ("Journal of the Council of State") in Kyoto, which reported on the campaigns waged by imperial forces against Tokugawa loyalists. This was followed by the establishment of the Kakkoku Shimbun-shi and Naigai Shimbun in Osaka in April, the Tohi Shimbun in Kyoto in May, and the Shimbun Rompa: Minatogawa takuyo Senzen in Kobe in July, all of which supported the new government and attacked pro-shogunate rivals. Meanwhile Edo and Yokohama, the stronghold of the ancien regime, became a fertile breeding ground for pro-shogunate newspapers beginning with Yanagawa Shunsan's Chugai Shimbun in February. Others include Fukuchi Genichiro's Koko Shimbun, the American Van Reed's Yokohama Shimbun Moshihogusa, Soyofuku Kaze, Ochikochi Shimbun, Naigai Shimbun, Tozai Shimbun, Koshi Zappo and Nichinichi Shimbun. These were unanimous in condemning the new government for its high-handed policies.

The day after fighting broke out on the heights of Ueno on May 15, the Chugai Shimbun published an unnumbered edition carrying news of the clash entitled the Betsudan Chugai Shimbun ("Chugai Shimbun Special"). This is believed to be Japan's first newspaper extra. In June, soon after occupying Edo, the imperial forces launched a crackdown on the press. Newspapers were banned across the board, and in future publishers were required to obtain a permit. With the adoption of the Newspaper Publication Ordinance in February 1869, the Meiji government switched to a policy of licensing newspapers more readily. As a result the Chugai Shimbun and Ochikochi Shimbun, which had been banned the previous year, were able to resume publication and several new papers came out, including the Meiji Shimbun and Rikugo Shimbun. All these newspapers, however, proved short-lived.

3. 最初の日刊新聞登場

明治3年12月8日には、わが国最初の日刊紙「横浜毎日新聞」が創刊された。外国新聞をまねてスタイルを一新、従来の和紙 二つ折冊子型木版刷りを、輸入西洋紙に鉛活字（創刊当初は木活字）を用いての両面刷りに変え、わが国の近代新聞の祖といわれる画期的な新聞の出現となった。

翌4年には「新聞雑誌」をはじめ、廃藩置県を契機として各地に新聞が発生、7年くらいまでに「名古屋新聞」「若松新聞誌」（福島）、「信飛新聞」（長野）、「毎週新聞」（横浜）、「北湊新聞」（新潟）、「大阪新聞」「神戸港新聞」、「京都新報」、「日注雑記」（広島）、「鳥取県新報」、「抜萃新聞」（香川）、「木更津新聞」（千葉）ほか続々と発刊され、この傾向は年々増加し全国に及んだ。

明治5年には東京初の日刊紙「東京日日新聞」や英国人ブラックの「日新真事誌」、郵便の父・前島密の「郵便報知新聞」や成島柳北の「朝野新聞」の前身「公文通誌」なども発刊された。

冊子型から一枚刷りになった最初の日刊新聞
The first daily newspaper to go from pamphlet style to a broadsheet

4. 官権派と民権派の新聞

明治6年、征韓論にやぶれた板垣退助らは翌7年「民撰議員設立の建白書」を提出して、国会の開設と代議政治確立を提唱、「日新真事誌」に発表した。これを契機に自由民権運動が急速に全国に広まり、新聞紙上で激しい言論戦が展開された。政府の立場を擁護する新聞は官権派新聞と呼ばれ、その代表的なものは福地源一郎（桜痴）の「東京日日新聞」だった。福地は東京日日を官報代用紙とし、官報掲載の特権を得、役人や知識階級に多く読まれるようになったため、政府に対して強い立場をもつ新聞になった。

一方、民権運動の立場を支持する民権派新聞は「東京曙新聞」（新聞雑誌改題）、「日新真事誌」などで、民権論者の論調や投書を掲載して激しく対立した。このため政府は8年7月讒謗律を公布し、新聞紙条例を改正したため、この傾向は一層激しくなり全国的に政論新聞の全盛時代を迎えた。

西南戦争を取材する福地源一郎　Fukuchi Genichiro covering the Satsuma Rebellion

3. The First Daily Newspaper

On December 8, 1870, Japan's first daily newspaper was born, the Yokohama Mainichi Shimbun ("Yokohama Daily News"). This was a truly historic event, for it marked the emergence of the ancestor of the modern Japanese newspaper. Modeled after Western newspapers, this publication was unlike anything ever seen before. Instead of a sheaf of woodblock-printed folio sheets of Japanese paper bound into a pamphlet as heretofore, it consisted of imported paper printed on both sides with lead type (wooden type at first).

The next year, 1871, saw the final abolition of the feudal domains, and the Shimbun Zasshi became the first of a wave of newspapers that began popping up all over the country. By 1874 these included the Nagoya Shimbun, Wakamatsu Shimbun-shi (Fukushima), Shimpi Shimbun (Nagano), Maishu Shimbun (Yokohama), Hokuso Shimbun (Niigata), Osaka Shimbun, Kobe-ko Shimbun, Kyoto Shimpo, Nitchu Zakki (Hiroshima), Tottori-ken Shimpo, Bassui Shimbun (Kagawa) and Kisarazu Shimbun (Chiba). Within the next several years newspapers spread to every corner of Japan. In 1872 Tokyo got its first daily newspaper, the Tokyo Nichinichi Shimbun ("Tokyo Daily News"). A number of other newspapers came out the same year, including the Englishman Black's Nisshin Shinji-shi, the Yubin Hochi Shimbun, founded by the father of Japan's postal system, Maejima Hisoka, and the Kobun Tsushi, precursor of Narushima Ryuhoku's Choya Shimbun.

4. Government Prerogative versus Popular Rights

In 1874 Itagaki Taisuke, who had resigned from the government the previous year after being thwarted in his plans for a war against Korea, submitted a memorial calling for the formation of an assembly chosen by the people and the establishment of a system of representative government. This document, which was carried in the pages of the Nisshin Shinji-shi, unleashed a movement for "freedom and popular rights" that spread like wildfire throughout the country, and a furious debate ensued in the press. Pro-government newspapers defended the official line, as typified by the Tokyo Nichinichi Shimbun of Fukuchi Genichiro (also known by his sobriquet Ochi). Fukuchi obtained the right to publish official notices and in effect turned the Tokyo Nichinichi into a government mouthpiece. The paper thus became favorite reading among officialdom and the intelligentsia, for which reason it came to exercise considerable influence in government circles. Advocates of the popular rights movement, on the other hand, like the Tokyo

5. 小新聞と新聞錦絵の流行

こんな中で政治に無関心とされる庶民や婦女子向けに政治問題をさけ、総ルビつき平仮名まじりの口語体で、雑報（いまの社会面記事）や続きもの（連載小説）など娯楽本位の新聞が出現した。政論新聞が大判の体裁だったので大新聞と呼ばれたのに対し、この種の新聞は型も小さかったので小新聞と呼ばれて区別された。小新聞の代表的なものには、明治7年に子安峻らが創刊した「読売新聞」をはじめ、「東京絵入新聞」「仮名読新聞」「東京平仮名絵入新聞」「有喜世新聞」や、関西で発行された「朝日新聞」や「浪花新聞」「西京新聞」などがあり、大新聞を圧倒する勢いのものも見られ、明治中期までは大新聞と小新聞が共存、読売や朝日は政論を含む一般新聞に発展していった。

また明治7、8年頃の新聞には、絵も写真も入っていなかったため、新聞に載った興味本位の記事をえらび戯作者の文章と浮世絵師の絵を錦絵に仕立てて、絵草紙屋から出版することが流行した。これが新聞錦絵といわれ、代表的なものは「東京日日新聞」と「郵便報知新聞」で、大きさは週刊誌2ページ大、内容は殺人事件や色ごと、孝行美談、珍談奇聞などの題材が中心だった。中でも東京日日を担当した画家・落合芳幾（歌川国芳の弟子）の絵は、写実的で殺伐な光景が生々しく描かれているものが多く人気を博した。

東京と大阪で発行された小新聞
Tabloid newspapers published in Tokyo and Osaka

囲みの記事から作られた新聞錦絵、旅籠の近代化に尽くした遠州の本多留平　Newspaper color news prints using boxed articles. Shown is Tomehei Honda of Totomi Province, who worked hard at modernizing inns.

乗馬中の芸者が老人を転倒させる「郵便報知」の新聞錦絵
A geisha on a horse pushes over an old man. Color news print from the Yubin Hochi Shimbun.

which their readers had little enthusiasm, in favor of "human-interest" stories (as we might call them) and serialized novels. They were written in the spoken language of the day, with all Chinese characters spelt out phonetically and inflectional endings added in the hiragana syllabary for ease of reading. Such papers were known as "koshimbun," "little papers" or "tabloids" as we might say, to distinguish them from the politically-oriented broadsheets ("oshimbun"). Examples are the Yomiuri Shimbun, founded by Koyasu Takashi in 1874, the Tokyo Eiri Shimbun, the Kana-yomi Shimbun, the Tokyo Hiragana Eiri Shimbun and the Ukiyo Shimbun, as well as the Asahi Shimbun, Naniwa Shimbun and Saikyo Shimbun in the Kansai. Some of these "tabloids" came to far outsell the broadsheets. The two types of newspaper coexisted until the mid Meiji period, and the Yomiuri and Asahi eventually evolved into general-interest papers that carried political news as well. Back in

those days newspapers did not carry pictures or photos, and around 1874 or 1875 it became the vogue to bring out color prints illustrating sensational stories from the paper through sellers of woodblock prints. A writer of popular stories would compose the text, while an ukiyo-e artist would produce the illustration itself. Such prints, known as "shimbun nishiki-e" or "color news prints," came out weekly in a two-page format, typical examples being those issued by the Tokyo Nichinichi Shimbun and Yubin Hochi Shimbun. Their subject matter ranged from murder and romantic intrigue to virtuous tales of filial piety and anything out of the ordinary.

The work of Ochiai Yoshiku (a pupil of Utagawa Kuniyoshi), who did illustrations for the Tokyo Nichinichi Shimbun, was especially popular for its lurid realism and bloodthirsty depictions.

Akebono Shimbun (as the Shimbun Zasshi had been renamed) and the Nisshin Shinji-shi, carried articles and letters by proponents of constitutional government that were scathing in tone. In July 1875, therefore, the government promulgated the Libel Statute and revised the Newspaper Ordinance. But debate only grew more intense, and political journalism entered a golden age throughout Japan.

5. "Tabloids" and Color News Prints Come into Vogue

Meanwhile another type of newspaper emerged designed primarily for entertainment. These papers catered to the tastes of women and the lower classes by avoiding political news, for

6. 政党新聞の出現

西南戦争が契機となり自由民権運動が急速に盛り上がり、有力新聞が相次いで政党の機関紙になっていった。

明治14年（1881）の国会開設の詔勅により、まず板垣退助を総理とする自由党が結成され、翌15年には大隈重信総理の立憲改進党、福地源一郎総裁の立憲帝政党などが乱立、新聞も全国的にこれらの政党の系列紙になり、名実ともに政党新聞時代が到来した。その代表ともいわれる15年創刊の「自由新聞」は、発行規則の冒頭で「政党ニ新聞ナキハ軍隊ニ武器ナキト一般ナリ」

6. The Rise of Party Newspapers

The campaign for freedom and popular rights reached a crescendo after the Satsuma Rebellion, and the leading papers became mouthpieces for different political parties.

In 1881, in the wake of an imperial edict promising the establishment of a Diet, the Liberal Party was established under the chairmanship of Itagaki Taisuke, joined the next year by Okuma Shigenobu's Progressive Party and Fukuchi Genichiro's Imperial Government Party. Newspapers throughout the country became affiliated with one or another of these rival organizations, and Japanese journalism came to be dominated by party politics. A typical example is the Jiyu Shimbun ("Liberal News") founded in 1882, whose "Rules of Publication" opened with this bold assertion: "A political party without a newspaper is like an army without weapons."

The main affiliations of the newspapers of the day are given below.

- Papers affiliated with the Liberal Party:
Over thirty papers, including the Jiyu Shimbun, Jiyuto, Eiri Jiyu Shimbun, Asahi Shimbun, Nihon Rikken Seito Shimbun, Shin Aichi, Tohoku Jiyu Shimbun and Kainan Shimbun.
- Papers affiliated with the Progressive Party:
Over thirty papers, including the Yubin Hochi Shimbun, Tokyo Yokohama Mainichi Shimbun,

主な政党新聞　The main political party newspapers

と記し、新聞の重要性を説いている。
おもな新聞の系列は下記の通り

●自由党系
「自由新聞」「自由燈」「絵入自由新聞」「朝日新聞」「日本立憲政党新聞」「新愛知」「東北自由新聞」「海南新聞」など30余紙

●立憲改進党系
「郵便報知新聞」「東京横浜毎日新聞」「改進新聞」「大阪新報」「神戸新聞」「山陽新聞」「名古屋新聞」「福岡日日新聞」「熊本新聞」など30余紙

●立憲帝政党系
「東京日日新聞」「明治日報」「東洋新報」「福島新聞」「信濃毎日新聞」「静岡新聞」
「山梨日日新聞」「大東日報」など20余紙

14年7月、北海道開拓使官有物払い下げ問題が起こると、新聞を中心とする言論界が一丸となり、政府攻撃を展開した。苦慮した政府は政党新聞の言論活動に対して、発行停止または禁止

明治10年の新聞番付　1877 ranked list of newspapers

Kaishin Shimbun, Osaka Shimpo, Kobe Shimbun, Sanyo Shimbun, Nagoya Shimbun, Fukuoka Nichinichi Shimbun and Kumamoto Shimbun.

-Papers affiliated with the Imperial Government Party:
Over twenty papers, including the Tokyo Nichinichi Shimbun, Meiji Nippo, Toyo Shimpo, Fukushima Shimbun, Shinano Mainichi Shimbun, Shizuoka Shimbun, Yamanashi Nichinichi Shimbun and Daito Nippo.

When a scandal broken out over the sale of state-owned property in Hokkaido in July 1881, the press unleashed a concerted attack on the government. The harried authorities struck back with a crackdown, suspending or banning publication of party newspapers. In April 1883 further restrictions were imposed on freedom of speech in the form of the Revised Newspaper Ordinance, nicknamed the Newspaper Eradication Act. Party newspapers went into decline as a result, and some were forced to suspend or cease publication altogether. Circulation plummeted, and in 1885 even the Jiyu Shimbun went out of print.

などの弾圧を加え、16年4月には新聞撲滅法との
異名をとった改正新聞紙条例で、言論活動の取
締りを一段と強化したために政党新聞は没落、休
廃刊に追い込まれるものまであった。各紙の部数
も急減し「自由新聞」も18年に廃刊となった。

7. 不偏不営の大衆新聞

政治記事や論説を主体とした硬い紙面の政党新
聞にかわって、不偏不党を標榜した大衆新聞が
登場する。明治15年3月、慶応義塾の創立者、福
沢諭吉は自力で「時事新報」を創刊した。政治
第一主義を廃し、経済および社会記事を中心と
した大衆的中立新聞をモットーにしたために読者
は急増、短期間で一躍、大新聞の座を確保した。
一方、政党新聞の没落により、正論を主として
きた大新聞も編集、経営方針を改め、大衆新聞
に転換しなくてはならなくなった。「郵便報知新
聞」は定価を引き下げ、紙面は雑報を第一とし、
連載小説をのせるなど紙面の刷新をはかった。
また、22年元旦からは朝版4ページと夕版2ペー
ジの朝夕刊二回配達制を試みるが永続きせず、
一年余りで中止された。
朝日新聞社は、政府のたび重なる弾圧によって
経営不振に陥っていた「めさまし新聞」を買収、
明治21年7月には「東京朝日新聞」の題号でス
タート、大阪系新聞社の東京進出第一号になっ
た。同年、「今日新聞」が「都新聞」と改題、「や
まと新聞」「国民新聞」「中央新聞」「萬朝報」な
ど、東京の新聞界は編集方針や紙面に異彩を放

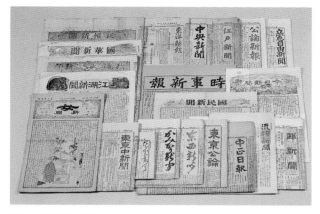

明治20年代の東京の諸新聞　Tokyo newspapers of the decade from 1887 to 1896

明治末期の新聞紙型と下は輪転印刷機
The matrix for a late-Meiji period newspaper.
Below is a rotary press.

7. Non-partisan Newspapers for the Masses

Party newspapers, whose austere-looking pages were dominated by political news and commentary, were replaced by non-partisan publications that catered to a more general audience. In March 1882 Fukuzawa Yukichi, founder of Keio University, independently started up the Jiji Shimpo ("Current Events") with the express goal of creating an unbiased newspaper with a mass appeal – one that gave pride of place to economic and social news rather than the intricacies of politics. The idea worked. Readership soared, and the Jiji Shimpo rapidly carved out a niche for itself as one of the country's leading journalistic organs.

With the decline of the party mouthpieces, meanwhile, the major papers, which had hitherto been content to pontificate from on high, were forced to overhaul their editorial and management policies in order to appeal to the broader public. The Yubin Hochi Shimbun cut its price and gave itself a brand new look: its pages were now devoted primarily to stories of general interest supplemented by serialized novels. Starting on New Year's Day 1889, it also experimented with two deliveries a day, a four-page morning edition and a two-page evening edition. The attempt fizzled out, however, in little more than a year.

The Asahi Shimbun for its part bought up the Mesamashi Shimbun, which had fallen on hard times in the face of constant government harassment, and in July 1888 relaunched it as the Tokyo Asahi Shimbun. This was the first example of an Osaka-based newspaper expanding into Tokyo. The same year the Konnichi Shimbun was retitled the Miyako Shimbun, and soon readers in Tokyo had an impressive selection of popular newspapers from which to choose, like the Yamato Shimbun, Kokumin Shimbun, Chuo Shimbun or Yorozu Choho, each of which had its own distinctive look and editorial bent. This, the third decade of the Meiji period, also witnessed major innovations in newspaper production. The telegraph and telephone became indispensable tools of the journalist's trade, while the flatbed press was replaced by the rotary press, which was capable of performing large print jobs in a short time.

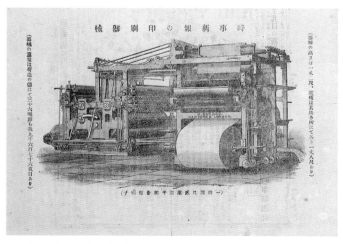

つ大衆新聞でにぎわった。この明治20年代には、
新聞の製作面にも大きな改革があらわれた。ニュ
ースの取材に電報・電話が威力を発揮し、印刷
面では平盤印刷機に変わり、短時間で大部数が
刷れる輪転印刷機がお目見えした。

8. 新聞の企業化確立

明治27年8月に日清戦争が勃発、国民の血を湧かせ戦意を高揚させる戦況号外が連日各社から競って発行され、号外売りという新しい職業も誕生した。37〜8年の日露戦争では戦時報道や号外合戦はさらにエスカレートし社運をかけて各社は競争した。各新聞社は従軍記者からの報告と当局の発表によって紙面を作成したが大阪の朝日、毎日両社の号外合戦は異常で、開戦中朝日が389、毎日が498回という驚異的な数の号外を発行、多額の経費をついやす結果になった。戦況を刻々と知ろうという購読者の飛躍的激増で、新聞の発行部数も大幅に伸びた。新聞社間の販売競争も一層激しくなり、夕刊紙の発行、地方版の新設、ページ数の増大、色刷り付録のサービス、各種の人気投票や博覧会などの事業や新企画が実施され、新聞社は企業化確立の時代に入った。

戦争による部数の伸びは新聞広告の媒体価値を高め、大型広告や連合広告なども増え、広告収入が新聞社の大きな財源にもなった。色刷輪転機も導入され、肖像や風景に写真版も登場読者を驚かせた。

一方、明治30年代には社会問題や労働問題に関する論議や記事が新聞紙面に頻繁に掲載されるようになり、「平民新聞」をはじめ「東京社会新聞」「直言」など社会主義者による機関紙が横行する。しかし明治43年の大逆事件を境に、社会主義に対する取締りが一段と強化され、後をたたなかった社会主義新聞も姿を消して行った。明治45年7月20日、宮内省は天皇陛下のご病気を発表し新聞各社は連日、病状を報道するが、7月30日午前零時43分に天皇は崩御、黒枠つきの崩御号外は深夜の街を走った。大阪では朝日が寝静まっている家々に号外を配達、配る者も配達人に起こされる人も、涙の感慨をもって号外を手にしたといわれ、朝日は評判を高めた。つづく新元号は「大正」となり、それを知らせる号外をもって輝かしい明治は45年で幕を閉じた。

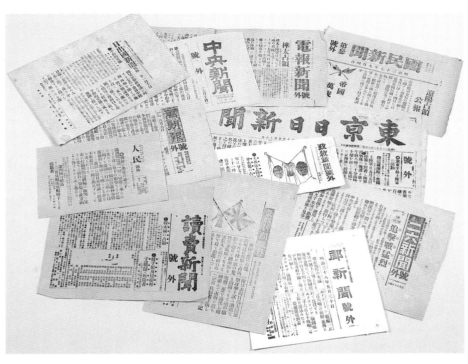

市中をにぎわした東京各紙の日露戦争を伝える号外　Extras by Tokyo newspapers that electrified the city with news of the Russo-Japanese war

写真が入った色刷り紙面
Newspapers with color
photographs

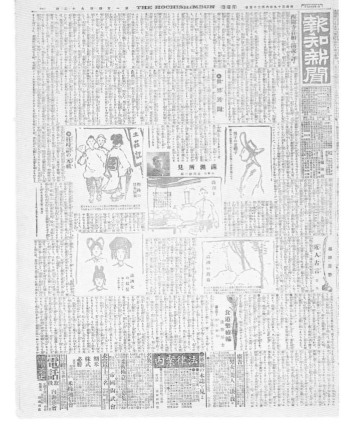

中央は見事なグラデーションをかけたカラー印刷　Color printing with excellent gradation in the center

明治中期にはじまった美人画の色刷り付録　Color supplements depicting beautiful women that began in the mid-Meiji period

8. The Emergence of Journalism as a Big Business

In August 1894 the Sino-Japanese War broke out, and newspapers vied to publish extras on an almost daily basis that stoked popular enthusiasm and boosted morale with updates on the conflict. Indeed, a whole new profession was born, selling extras. The Russo-Japanese War of 1904-05 saw a further escalation of this competition as newspapers staked their very future on their ability to report on the hostilities and churn out extras. Each paper's reportage consisted of a combination of accounts by war correspondents and official announcements. The Osaka editions of the Asahi and Mainichi in particular went overboard in their rivalry. Over the course of the conflict the Asahi brought out 389 extras and the Mainichi an amazing 498. Both companies spent a small fortune in the process. Meanwhile newspaper subscriptions increased dramatically as people sought up-to-the-minute accounts of the war, and circulation skyrocketed. Competition to sell more copies intensified as papers brought out evening editions, launched local versions, added extra pages, produced color supplements, and started new ventures like organizing popularity contests and sponsoring exhibitions. Journalism was becoming big business.

The growth in circulation sparked by the war increased newspapers' value as an advertising medium. Advertising income became a major source of revenue as papers began to carry a growing number of large-size and serial ads. Color rotary presses appeared, and photographic plates of people and scenery dazzled readers.

During the fourth decade of the Meiji era a good deal of ink also came to be spilt over social and labor issues, and mouthpieces of the socialist cause like the Heimin Shimbun, Tokyo Shakai Shimbun and Chokugen became rampant. However, a severe crackdown on socialism followed a plot to assassinate the Emperor in 1910 that led to mass arrests, and socialist newspapers, for all their resilience, finally disappeared. On July 20, 1912, the Ministry of the Imperial Household announced that the Emperor was ailing, and the newspapers provided daily updates on his illness. At 12:43 a.m. on July 30 he passed away, and extras bordered in black conveyed the sad news through the streets of the night. In Osaka the Asahi distributed its extra directly to the sleeping households of the city.

Both delivery boy and awakened occupant, it is said, stood newspaper in hand, choked with tears, and the Asahi enjoyed a surge in popularity. The new Emperor's reign was called Taisho, and the extra that reported the new name brought the 45 glorious years of the Meiji era to a close.

明治末期のの社会主義新聞　Socialist newspapers of the late Meiji period

Ⅱ. 新聞題字にみるタイポグラフィ

1.新聞題字に関する覚え書き

私が新聞というものについて収集、研究するようになったきっかけも、実はこの新聞題字にある。戦後間もない昭和24年、目黒八中2年生のとき、国語の授業のグループ研究で新聞の種類について調べ、全国各地で発行されている一般紙・専門紙・機関紙・学級新聞・広報など、200種近い新聞の題字を集め、大きな日本地図の上に張りつけて展示した。それから新聞題字の収集がはじまる。新聞社の名札でもある新聞題字には百社百様それぞれの個性豊かな顔があった。さまざまな毛筆体やデザイン文字、またバックの地紋にはその地域や、新聞の特徴を表現する興味深い絵や模様が生々しく描かれていた。そんな題字ほしさに、雑誌の連絡欄で全国各地にペンフレンドを求め、相手が希望する郵便切手や絵はがきなどとその地方で発行されている新聞を交換してもらったり、外出時には駅の新聞スタンドに目を輝かせたりしたものだった。

高校時代に文通していた香川県のコレクターから送られてきた日露戦争当時の古い新聞に魅了され、題字から新聞本紙の収集に変わって行く。以来、神田の古書店街や、古書即売展の常連となり、10数年前からは早朝からの骨董市も欠かすことなく半世紀近くをかけて江戸時代のかわら版から、幕末明治・大正・昭和・平成の今日に至る新聞・号外を中心に関連の錦絵や新聞人の肉筆の書簡や色紙、新聞売りの箱や看板・ハッピ、ジャーナリズム全般にわたる書籍文献など、およそ10万点以上を所蔵、「新聞資料ライブラリー・羽島コレクション」と称して関係各方面の利用に供してきた。

やまと新聞の創刊号の見開き広告（明治19年10月）題号を立体的な文字にして各層の人々がかつぎあげている。
Double-page advertisement in the inaugural issue of the Yamato Shimbun (August 1886).
The three-dimensional title characters are carried by people representing various segments of society.

II. The Typography of Newspaper Mastheads

1. Personal Notes on Newspaper Mastheads

Newspaper mastheads are in fact what got me started collecting and studying newspapers.

In 1949, when I was in Second Year at Meguro No. 8 Junior High, we did a group project on types of newspapers in my Japanese class. We collected almost 200 mastheads from various papers published nationwide-regular papers, specialty papers, house organs, class newspapers, newsletters etc. which we then pasted for display on a large map of Japan. That is how I started collecting newspaper mastheads. Mastheads are like the nameplate of a newspaper, and to my youthful eyes every one looked excitingly distinctive. They featured a myriad different kinds of calligraphy and stylized font, and the fascinating motifs and patterns that formed their backgrounds were richly evocative of the character of each individual newspaper and the locale where it was published. In my eagerness to collect these mastheads, I looked for pen-friends all over the country through the correspondence columns of magazines. I would send them any stamps or pictures they wanted in return for newspapers published where they lived. And whenever I went anywhere, my eyes would sparkle at the sight of a newspaper stand on the station platform.

One day, when I was in high school, a collector in Kagawa Prefecture with whom I was in correspondence sent me an old paper dating back to the Russo-Japanese War. I was mesmerized. From then on my interest shifted from merely cutting out mastheads to acquiring whole papers. Ever since I have been a denizen of the used-book-store district of Kanda and haunted used-book sales, and for more than a decade now I have attended the early-morning antique market without fail. Over the course of close to half century I have brought together some 100,000 pieces: kawara-ban tile-block prints from the Edo period, newspapers and newspaper extras ranging in date from the last years of the Tokugawa shogunate through the Meiji, Taisho, Showa and present Heisei eras, color news prints, autograph letters and calligraphies by newspapermen, newspaper vendors' boxes, placards and happi coats, and a wide range of books on all aspects of journalism. This collection, christened the Hajima Library of Newspaper Archives, I have made available for the use of interested parties.

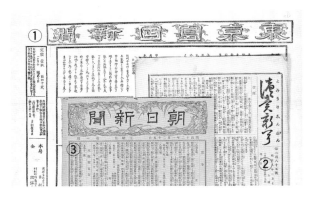

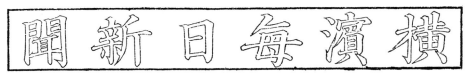

わが国最初の日刊紙はりんかく線による楷書体　The title of Japan's first daily newspaper was the regular script style in outline form.

2.個性が生かされた新聞題字

幕末から明治の冊子型新聞は表紙に、大判一枚刷りになってからの新聞は第一面の最上段または右肩に、新聞名が記されている。百数十年を経た現代の新聞にもこの伝統は守られているが、この新聞の顔ともいう文字「新聞題字」は、新聞紙面に登場するタイポグラフィの代表格である。この題字を書体上から分類してみると、活字体、毛筆、デザイン文字に分けられるが、明治期の新聞の大半は毛筆文字で、書体は隷書と楷書が圧倒的に多く使われている。隷書体の新聞題字には、「大阪毎日新聞」「絵入自由新聞」「都新聞」「上毛新聞」「朝日新聞」、楷書体のものにはわが国最初の日刊紙「横浜毎日新聞」をはじめ「東京曙新聞」「江戸新聞」「政論」「東海日報」などが該当する。隷書体のもつ装飾性や楷書体の読みやすさ、わかりやすさなどの理由で、この二つの書体が多くの新聞に使われたものと思われる。

ほかに明治期の新聞には、現代人に読みにくくなじめない行書体と草書体の題字がある。行書体は「山陰新聞」「東京横浜毎日新聞」「信濃日報」、草書体は「ひらかな新聞」「めさまし新聞」「かみなり新聞」「日曜新聞」などだが、筆記用具が毛筆中心であった当時の人々の草書に対する感覚や理解力の高さをうかがい知ることができる。新聞題字で興味深いのは、明治5年（1873）に創刊された「東京日日新聞」①の第1号である。タブロイド判で和紙片面に木板整版で刷られたものだが、題字は最上段に「東京圓圖新聞」となっている。この題字は篆書の名人と呼ばれた謙堂によって書かれているが、圓・圖はともに「日」という字で、お日さまのことを金鳥ともいい縁起をかついで使われたといわれている。ところが読者には読みにくかったようで、第12号から「東京日日新聞」に変更、7年12月以降は福地桜痴の書いた行書体の題字に変更している。また特筆されるのは、記事の本文に使用していた明朝活字を、明治14年8月から木版の冊子型新聞や明治最初の新聞にみられる書体に似た清朝体に切り替えたことである。23年2月までつづき再び明朝体に戻っているが、新聞社で定着していた字体を一時期にせよ、なぜ変えたのかは文字表現と伝達性、視覚的効果の面からも興味深い。

清朝体時代の東京日日新聞
The Tokyo Nichinichi Shimbun when it used the Shincho typeface

2.Newspaper Mastheads: Every One Unique

The news pamphlets of the late Edo and Meiji periods carried their title on the front cover, while the broadsheets that supplanted them featured their name on the top or upper right of the front page. Today's newspapers, well over a century later, still preserve that tradition. The masthead of the newspaper, the "face" it presents to the world, is a veritable showcase of newspaper typography.

The typography of mastheads can be classified stylistically into printed characters, brush-written characters and stylized characters. Most Meiji-era mastheads are brush-written, the vast majority being in one of two styles of Chinese calligraphy, the angular reisho ("clerical script") or the more supple kaisho ("regular script"). Newspapers featuring reisho script include the Osaka Mainichi Shimbun, Eiri Jiyu Shimbun, Miyako Shimbun, Jomo Shimbun and Asahi Shimbun. Newspapers featuring kaisho script include Japan's first daily, the Yokohama Mainichi Shimbun, as well as the Tokyo Akebono Shimbun, Edo Shimbun, Seiron and Tokai Nippo. The popularity of the two styles can be attributed to the decorativeness of the former and the readability of the latter.

Other Meiji-period mastheads are written in two highly cursive styles most Japanese today would have difficulty deciphering, gyosho ("running script") and the even more fluid sosho ("grass script"). Samples of gyosho may be seen in the Sanin Shimbun, Tokyo Yokohama Mainichi Shimbun and Shinano Nippo, of sosho in the Hiragana Shimbun, Mezamashi Shimbun, Kaminari Shimbun and Nichiyo Shimbun. In those days the most common writing implement was the brush, and these mastheads offer a glimpse of how at home people were back then with cursive script.

A fascinating example of a masthead is that of the first issue of the Tokyo Nichinichi Shimbun, which was launched in 1873. This was a tabloid-size publication consisting of Japanese paper woodblock-printed on one side only.

The name of the newspaper appeared in the characters Tokyo X(nichi) Y(nichi)Simbun in the hand of a celebrated master of the seal script, Kendo. The characters X and Y are both forms of 日 nichi, "sun" or "day." The sun is also known as the Golden Bird, and these forms of the character were used, it is said, for their auspicious associations. Readers, however, evidently found them almost illegible, for from the second issue the masthead promptly changed to the more common Tokyo nichinichi Shimbun. On July a new title appeared brushed in running script by Fukuchi Ochi. Also noteworthy is the fact that, in August 1881, the mincho typeface previously used for the text of the articles was replaced by shincho, which resembles the style of font found in woodblock-printed news pamphlets and the earliest Meiji newspapers. In February 1890 the paper reverted to mincho. Nonetheless, the question of why it chose to abandon its accustomed typeface, albeit temporary, is an intriguing one in terms of the visual impact of the printed word and its ability to communicate information.

The Yomiuri Shimbun, founded soon after in 1874, started out as a compact-sized paper published on alternate days, and its masthead was originally printed in mincho typeface. In January 1876 the calligrapher Sase Tokusho

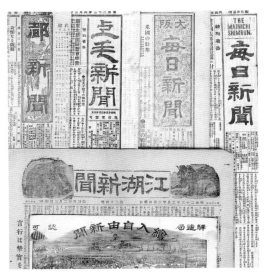

隷書体　reishotai

行書体　gyoshotai

篆書体　tenshotai

「毛筆字体見本」右から篆書、隷書、楷書、行書、草書『現代商業美術全集』第15巻「実用図案文字集」より　Samples of brush-drawn characters. From right to left: tensho (seal script), reisho (clerical script), kaisho (regular script), gyosho (running script) and sosho (grass script). From the catalog of applied design characters in Gendai Shogyo Bijutsu Zenshu ("Complete Anthology of Modern Commercial Art") 15

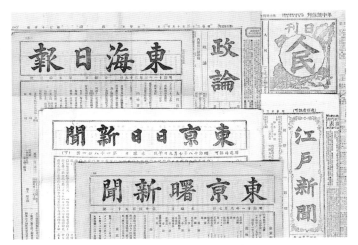

楷書体　kaishotai

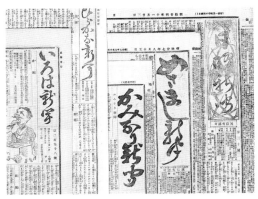

草書体　soshotai

手書の明朝体とゴシック体　Brush-written Mincho typeface and gothic style

「朝日新聞」の"新"の字が作られた「宗聖観記」の字体
The two characters from the Zongsheng Guanji that were used to create the character shin ("new") for the title of the Asahi Shimbun

追って7年に創刊された「読売新聞」②は創刊当初、隔日刊の小型新聞で題字は明朝活字を使っていた。9年1月に書家の佐瀬得所に依頼し草書体の題字に改めた。「よみうり志んぶん」と仮名つきだったが、あまりに草体すぎ「読」が「涜」とも見え評判が悪く、10日間でこの題字の使用を中止、従来からの活字体を拡大したものに変更、さらに14年1月から永坂石埭の行書体の題字に変わっていく。

一方、12年に大阪で創刊された「朝日新聞」③は、初代主幹だった津田貞が「昇る旭日─それは希望と光明の表徴であり、毎朝早く配達される新聞もまた無知のトビラを開く朝日だ」というところから発案された題号といわれている。題字の文字は中国唐代の名筆として知られる欧陽詢の「宗聖観記」からとられた。同書の原字には「新」の字がなく、親のヘンと栐のツクリから作字して意匠化を狙って手が入れられた文字で周囲は浪速の蘆の模様を配して新聞の顔をつくっている。

いま私たちが手にする「毎日新聞」は、平成3年11月の新生スタートを機に紙面を一新し、題字もポピュラーな明朝体に改めた。現代の造形性を配慮して、線の太さや全体の構成が工夫され、すっきりとシャープな印象が目立つ。題字の上にはコーポレート・シンボルの「毎日の目」が配され、個性が強調された題字になっている。

明治期新聞題字の筆者には、書の世界で能書と認められた多彩な顔ぶれが見られる。長三洲、勝海舟、山岡鉄舟、池原日南、佐瀬得所、三条実美らだが、池原は福沢諭吉の「時事新報」をはじめ「明治日報」「郵便報知新聞」「大阪新報」ほか10年間に20数社の新聞題字を手がけている。

一度にたくさんの題字を集めてみると、あらためて毛筆文字の表現力の豊かさや幅広さ、そして筆者ひいては新聞各社の個性やこだわりが伝わってくる。

was commissioned to produce a new masthead in grass script, which however met with a poor reception. Though accompanied by hiragana spelling out the words Yomiuri Shimbun phonetically, the ideographs were so highly stylized that for example the strokes representing the character 読 yomi("read") could well be mistaken for X("break") and ten days later the new masthead was abandoned in favor of an enlarged version of the printed title used previously. This was supplanted in January 1881 by a masthead brushed in running script by Nagasaka sekitai. The Asahi Shimbun was launched in Osaka in 1879. The name, literally "Morning Sun Newspaper," is said to be the brainchild of the first editor, Tsuda Tei. It alludes to the fact that, just as the rising sun is the symbol of hope and light, a newspaper delivered early each morning opens the door to illumination. The characters used in the masthead were culled from the Zongsheng Guanji, a work by the celebrated Chinese Tang-Dynasty calligrapher Ouyang Xun. That composition does not, however, contain the third ideograph of the paper's name, 新 shin ("news"), which was therefore created by combining the left side of the character 親 and the right side of the character 栐. The words were then bordered with a pattern of the reeds of Naniwa. The result is a design that is both elaborate and distinctive.

The Mainichi Shimbun we read today acquired its present look in a facelift in November 1991, when the masthead was redone in the popular mincho typeface. The thickness of the lines and overall layout have been carefully tailored to contemporary notions of plastic design, and the sleek, sharp appearance immediately catches the eye. The masthead is crowned with the paper's corporate symbol, the "eyes of the Mainichi,"which make it instantly recognizable. The mastheads of the Meiji period were written by a veritable who's-who of accomplished calligraphers of the day – personages like Cho Sanshu, Katsu Kaishu, Yamaoka Tesshu, Ikehara Nichinan, Sase Tokusho and Sanjo Sanemi. Ikehara produced mastheads for over

twenty newspapers over the course of a decade, including Fukuzawa Yukichi's Jiji Shimpo, the Meiji Nippo, Yubin Hochi Shimbun and Osaka Shimpo. Collecting large numbers of mastheads reminds one of the expressiveness and diversity of brush-written calligraphy, and offers a glimpse into the character and quirks of the individuals who composed them and of the papers they graced.

Ⅲ. 新聞広告にみるタイポグラフィ

1.新聞広告に関する覚え書き

日本の活字製造の祖である本木昌造が開発した鋳造活字が明朝体であったためか明治以降、今日に至るまで新聞活字も明朝体が紙面の大半をしめている。

この傾向は見出し文字に至るまで、明治期全般にわたる特徴のようだが、文明開化期の新聞広告にはイラストやマーク、手書き文字などを組みあわせたタイポグラフィの息吹きを感じさせる広告が見受けられる。

そもそも私が新聞広告に特別な興味を抱いたのは、30年以前のことである。広告会社に勤務していた昭和42年、明治100年を記念して、「近代日本の礎を築いた偉大な明治」と題した新聞一頁広告を企画した。明治時代の新聞広告を再現し、その余白に簡単な説明文と現在の企業イメージを表現したキャッチフレーズを入れた。現存する企業の過去をふり返り明治のころ、すでにこのような広告によって日本の企業はたくましく歩みはじめていたことを見直すもので、関係各方面の話題をよんだ。このとき長年集めてきた古い新聞の中から興味深いイラストやコピーの入った広告を探し出し、一千点を超える作品に接した。

ついで昭和57年、東京コピーライターズクラブが設立20周年を記念して「一行の力・コピーライター展」を東京池袋の西武デパートで開催した。ポスター、新聞・雑誌の広告作品を時代別に分類展示するコーナーに、私のコレクションから新聞と新聞広告のオリジナルを提供、新聞広告に対する興味が一段と高まった。各時代の新聞から、これと思う広告を見つけては大小を問わず複写したりスクラップしていった。その数はまたたく間に数千点を越え、いつか一冊の本にし、忘れ去られた広告作品を後世に伝えて行きたいという思いを抱いた。

平成4年には珍広告・傑作広告を集め、天野祐吉氏の痛烈な広告批評で人気を博した文春ビジュアル文庫の『嘘八百シリーズ』明治編・大正編・昭和戦前編三部作にも大半の資料を提供、あらためて広告表現の面白さを痛感した。追って平成6年には読売新聞社広告局が同社の創刊120周年を記念して『新聞広告カタログ　広告はニュースだ』を製作した。これは新聞広告の歴史を時代およびテーマ別に図版を中心にまとめ、その流れを概観したもので、

このときも明治から昭和までの新聞広告はほとんど私の所蔵資料が使われた。

そんな折、以前にも『号外』シリーズ全12巻を刊行した大空社から、ぜひ『新聞広告美術大系』として出版したいという話を受け、1万点を越す大量の新聞広告の資料が日の目を見ることになり、昨年1月末に明治編・全5巻が誕生した。

この企画では、明治・大正・昭和戦前期までを通して新聞に掲載されたイラスト広告を中心に、業種別にその変遷を顧みることを主眼とした。初期の拙劣な作品から、アールヌーボー、アールデコの影響を感じさせるモダンなものまで、広告表現はバラエティーに富んでいる。

今回は、明治の新聞広告の中からタイポグラフィ的関心をもって図版を選んでみたが、紙幅の都合でほんの一部しか紹介できなかった。従って以下の明治期新聞広告の歩みの記述に登場する広告作品の図版はほとんど載せられていない。さらに詳しくご覧になりたい方は図書館で『新聞広告美術大系』（全5巻）を手にしていただきたい。

さて、「広告」という文字が初めて新聞に登場するのは明治5年（1873）の「横浜毎日新聞」だが、一般的に使われるようになるのは7〜8年になってからである。また幕末の新聞から広告の意味で使用されたことばは多彩で、告白・引札・禀告・告條・報告・布告・汎告・口上などがある。

Shimbun Kokoku Bijutsu Taikei

III. The Typography of Newspaper Advertising

1. Personal Notes on Newspaper Advertising

The mincho typeface has dominated the pages of Japanese newspapers ever since the Meiji period, perhaps because it was the font developed by the father of typeface production in Japan, Motoki Shozo.

This tendency continued throughout the Meiji period, and even headlines were composed in mincho. Nonetheless, newspaper advertising from the years of rapid westernization under the banner of "civilization and enlightenment" displays hints of considerable typographical flair in the way it integrates illustrations, symbols and handwritten text.

I first developed a special fascination for newspaper advertising thirty years ago. Back then I was working at an advertising agency, and in 1967 I was involved in planning a series of one-page newspaper ads commemorating the centennial of the Meiji Restoration entitled "The Glorious Meiji Era: Laying the Foundations of Modern Japan." This featured reprints of newspaper ads from the Meiji period, in the blank space around which was placed a simple explanatory caption along with a catchphrase summing up the company's current image. The series, looking back as it did over the history of some of the firms of the day, stirred up a good deal of interest. It was a reminder of how, already back in the Meiji period, Japanese corporations had taken their first confident strides forward with the help of advertising. For the project I rummaged through the old newspapers I had collected over the years searching for ads with interesting illustrations and copy. I must have looked at over a thousand different ads.

A number of years later, in 1982, the Tokyo Copywriters Club organized an exhibition to mark its twentieth anniversary called "Copywriting: The Power of a Phrase," which was held at the Seibu Department Store in the Ikebukuro district of Tokyo. One corner featured a display of posters and newspaper and magazine ads classified chronologically, for which I lent originals of newspapers and newspaper ads from my collection. This further stimulated my curiosity for the subject, and from then on, whenever I came across an ad in an old newspaper that caught my eye, regardless of how big or small, I would make a copy of it and add it to my scrapbook. Virtually overnight I found myself with several thousand ads on my hands, and it began to occur to me that one day I should bring out a book in order to preserve these long-forgotten works for posterity.

In 1992 I was brought once again to the realization of just how fascinating advertising is as a form of expression when I contributed most of the materials for the Uso Happyaku Series published by the Bunshun Visual Library. This set of three volumes, one each devoted to the Meiji period, the Taisho period, and the pre-war phase of the Showa period, brought together curiosities and masterpieces of advertising from the past, supplemented with scathing commentary by Amano Yukichi that left readers delighted. Then, in 1994, the Advertising Department of the Yomiuri Shimbun produced the Catalog of Newspaper Advertising: Advertising Are News to commemorate the paper's 120th anniversary. This tome offered a profusely illustrated overview of the history of newspaper advertising by period and subject. The vast majority of ads from the Meiji through Showa periods that appeared were from my collection. This extensive collection of over 10,000 newspaper ads, meanwhile, drew a step closer to seeing the light of day when Ozora-sha, the publisher that had earlier brought out my twelve-volume anthology of newspaper extras, offered to publish it under the title Shimbun Kokoku Bijutsu Taikei ("Newspaper Advertising Art Series"). The first five volumes, on the Meiji period, appeared at the end of January last year.

The primary objective of this publication is to trace, by industry, the evolution of illustrated newspapers advertisements over the course of the Meiji and Taisho periods and the pre-war phase of the Showa period. The advertising from these decades displays tremendous variety. It ranges from the crude attempts of early years to modernistic designs that betray the influence of art nouveau and art deco.

For this article I have selected illustrations of Meiji-period newspaper ads that are of typographical interest. Constraints of space, however, have imposed severe limitations on my choice of materials to include, and I have been unable to illustrate most of the pieces discussed in the following survey. Readers who wish to delve further into the subject are requested to consult the five-volume Shimbun Kokoku Bijutsu Taikei at their library.

The first appearance in a newspaper of the modern Japanese word for "advertisement," kokoku, was in the Yokohama Mainichi Shimbun in 1872, although the term did not come into general usage until 1874 or 1875. Newspapers from the last years of the Tokugawa period feature a wide array of terms for advertisements, such as kokuhaku, hikifuda, rinkoku, kokujo, hokoku, fukoku, hankoku and kojo.

2. 明治初期の広告

明治初年の新聞広告は活字の羅列でスタート
したが、4年には太平洋蒸気船のイラスト入り
広告も登場する。8〜9年にはイラストや手書
きコピーを自ら書いたアド・マン「精錡水」
の岸田吟香や、「宝丹」の守田治兵衛など偉才
の薬品広告が注目を集めた。広告出稿量で群
を抜いていたのは書籍広告で、明治9年国文社
が出した「官許・假名附布告全報」の広告は、
外国から取り寄せた銅版画を用い、読者のみ
ならず他の広告主を驚かせた。10年代の前半
には三越の前身「ゑちご屋」、のちにはたばこ
の広告主として有名になった「岩谷松平」、宝
丹・精錡水に次ぐ神薬の「資生堂」、歯痛止め
の「千金丹」、小町水・水おしろいの「平尾賛
平」や、西洋入歯、時計、武器力劍、地図な
どと広範な業種の広告が登場する。平尾賛平
は11年に売薬業岳陽堂を開店、おしろい下
「小町水」の発売をはじめ、「小町あらひ粉」
など洋風化粧品の開祖で、24年には「ダイヤ
モンド歯磨」も発売している。

また、16年には媒体社側の「時事新報」が福
沢諭吉の「商人に告ぐる文」と題した社説を
掲載、新聞広告が他の広告手段と比較してい
かに廉価であるかを力説し、効果的な新聞広
告の勧誘をして話題を呼んだ。

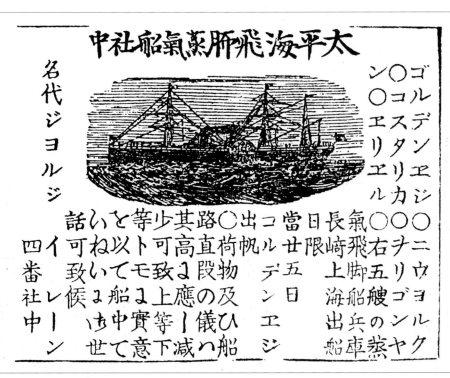

清朝体木活字の出船広告（明治4年1月）　Ad for a departing ship in wooden shincho typeface.(1871.1)

鉛活字に銅版カットを入れた蒸気船の出帆広告（明治8年7月）　Ad for a departing steamship in lead typeface with copperplate illustration.(1875.7)

廣告

くちぐ

又ならのチずくちぐハ
の印相対ひ候若此印なきもの
度店の品を熟之候間御改の
可被下候
アメリカニウヨーク府ベェア
イル通百二十七番井ニ八十番ビ

私店のランプ油ハ道々盛に賣れ
出し候處外々て私店の印ろ似せ
紛敷油を賣出し候者有之此
度真偽見分けのため箱井ニ
"Devoe's Brilliant"
"Devoe's"

「広告」の文字や、英字が配された舶来品の広告（明治8年）
Ad for imported goods featuring the word kokoku
("advertisement") and snatches of English text. (1875)

2. Advertising in the Early Meiji Period

For the first few years of the Meiji period newspaper ads consisted of nothing but columns of text, but in the fourth year of the era, 1871, an illustrated ad for Pacific Steamship appeared. In 1875-76 the eyes of readers were greeted by the sight of ads for medicaments designed by brilliant minds like Morita Jihei (Hotan) and "ad man" Kishida Ginko, who himself produced the illustration and handwritten copy for his plug for Seikisui. Far and away the most common type of advertisement was for books, and in 1876 an ad for a collection of official edicts (complete with phonetic readings) published under government license by Kokubunsha amazed not

文明開化の象徴。蒸気機関車の銅版カットが引き立っている（明治9年2月）
Symbol of "civilization and enlightenment." The copperplate illustration of the steam locomotive immediately catches the eye.
(1876.2)

just readers but other advertisers as well: it was printed with a copperplate ordered from abroad. As the Meiji era entered its second decade, ads appeared for all kinds of proprietors and products: Echigoya, the predecessor of Mitsukoshi Drapers, Iwaya Shohei, later famous for cigarette ads, Shiseido, a cure-all like Hotan and Seikisui, Senkintan for relief of toothache, Hirao Sampei's Komachisui foundation and liquid face powder, western-style false teeth, timepieces, swords and weapons, maps etc. Hirao Sampei, who began selling the foundation Komachisui at his newly-opened Gakuyodo pharmacy in 1878, was pioneer of western-style cosmetics like Komachi washing powder. In 1891 he added Diamond Tooth Powder to his lineup.

In 1883 the Jiji Shimpo carried an editorial by Fukuzawa Yukichi entitled "Declaration to Merchants," which created something of a stir. This succeeded in attracting new advertising business by emphasizing how much cheaper newspapers were than other advertising media.

簡単なタイトルの出版広告だがまわり
の飾りケイが生きている（明治12年2月）
These publishers' ads give simply the title of the publication, but the decorative borders are appealing.
(1879.2)

見出し活字に変化をつけながらカット図の周囲にきめ細かく組版している新聞発売広告（明治14年6月）
The text is closely spaced around the illustration, while the typeface of the headline adds a touch of variety. (1881.6)

II.新聞題字編でとり上げた清朝体の「東京日日新聞」の広告。
社名や見出しは明朝体の大型活字が用いられている（明治18年7月）
An ad from the Tokyo Nichinichi Shimbun in shincho font, discussed in Section II on newspaper mastheads. The company name and headline are in large-size mincho.(1885.7)

ビールのラベルと活字で引き立つ組版（明治18年12月）　A striking layout combining beer label and typeset copy.(1885.12)

3. 明治中期の広告

明治20年代に入ると、器械ランプ、空気ランプの広告が、22年には、金庫製造の元祖とうたった竹内善次郎、荻原弥吉や東京金庫、大倉金庫などが火事や盗難から財産を守るために金庫の必要性をイラスト入り広告で訴え競い合う。興業ものの広告では、不可思議奇術、大曲馬、浅草花屋敷などがあり、三井・三菱・安田などの銀行の広告、猟銃や護身用のピストル販売の川口銃砲店や金丸謙次郎の広告も目立っている。石けんや歯磨の広告も盛んで、長瀬富郎の「花王石鹸」も23年10月に発売された。

この時期には新聞の発行部数も伸び新聞広告の媒体価値も高まった。1ページ全面を含む大型広告や連合広告、案内広告なども増加、フロントページを全部広告に使う社も出現し、広告収入が新聞社の盛衰を決めるとまでいわれるようになった。

紙面に見る興味深い特徴は、広告のレイアウトに一段と進歩がみられ、多くの広告主が商品名や会社名などに特注の手書き文字を使い、イラストや写真の入った広告原稿を作成するようになったことだ。東京芸術大学の前身、東京美術学校に図按科が創設されるのは明治29年（1896）で、この頃の広告主にはまだ広告課や宣伝課は皆無に等しかった。めずらしかった職業の図案書きも、版下屋とか石版工と呼ばれる職人扱いで、原稿の製作や版下などは新聞社の広告部に

商品にマッチしたイラスト、文字の大きさの変化、周囲の模様などに一段の進歩がみられる洋服店の広告（明治20年1月）
This ad shows signs of considerable progress: an illustration to match the product, variation in font size, the pattern around the border etc.(1887.1)

直接、作らせていた広告主も多かった。新聞社側の広告スペースも自由で、広告主の要望に応じて丸・三角・菱形、化粧品に至ってはビンの形や、わざと目立たせるために横向きや逆さまに広告を入れたりすることも可能だった。

イラストの中に文字を配した広告代理店らしい斬新な広告（明治23年10月）
An unconventional ad for an advertising agency, with text incorporated right into the illustration.(1890.10)

3. Advertising in the Mid Meiji Period

The third decade of the Meiji period witnessed the appearance of ads for mechanical lamps and air lamps. In 1889 Japan's first manufacturers of safes-- individuals like Takeuchi Zenjiro and Ogiwara Yakichi and companies like Tokyo Safe and Okura Safe – vied to sell their wares with illustrated ads emphasizing the importance of protecting one's property from fire and theft with a strongbox. There were also ads for magic shows, circuses and places of entertainment like the Asakusa Flower Mansion.(amusement park) Banks such as Mitsui, Mitsubishi and Yasuda similarly promoted their services, while the Kawaguchi Gun Shop and Kanemaru Kenjiro flogged hunting rifles and pistols for self-defense. Ads for soap and tooth powder also became common. Nagase Tomio's Kao Soap debuted in October 1890.

Newspapers' value as an advertising medium grew as circulation climbed. Large-size and even full-page ads, serialized ads and classified ads became increasingly common. Some papers began devoting their whole front page to advertising. Advertising revenue could now make or break a newspaper.

One interesting development was greater sophistication in ad layout. Many advertisers started using customized hand-drawn lettering for product and company names and incorporating illustrations and photos in their ads. Tokyo Art School, precursor of Tokyo National University of Fine Arts and Music, first offered a course in design in 1896. Corporate advertising and PR departments were virtually non-existent back in those days, and designers still a rare breed – were treated as artisans and referred to as copy artists or lithographers. Many companies got the newspaper advertising departments to produce and lay out their ads for them. Newspapers for their part were extremely flexible with the space they provided to advertisers. Ads could be round, triangular or lozenge-shaped as the client required, or even bottle-shaped in the case of cosmetics. It was even possible to place your ad sideways or upside down as a way to catch the eye.

The fourth decade of the Meiji era was marked by an increase in advertising for mainstream products and services. The year 1901 was something of a vintage year for large-size ads, many splashed across the whole page. The Sobu, Narita and Sanyo lines and Japan Railways published notices of new train service and offered information on tourist excursions and the quickest routes to temples and shrines at New Year's. Teikoku Briquette and Shibaura Manufacturing flogged generators. Tokyo Machinery Manufacturing plugged rotary

胃と腸で周囲をデザインしたグロテスクな薬の広告（明治21年1月）
A striking ad with border of stomach and guts. (1888.1)

ポンチ絵風のイラスト。手書き白ヌキ文字も登場する本の広告（明治23年3月）
A Punch-style illustration with hand-drawn characters in white on black. (1890.3)

「欧米製の活字に代わり、当所の活字を」という築地活版製造所の広告（明治24年12月）
Ad for Tsukiji Type Manufacturing plugging that company's typeface as an alternative to western-made fonts. (1891.12)

文字だけが多かった書籍広告にもイラストが入る（明治24年1月）
Illustrations finally begin to grace ads for books, which previously consisted wholly of text. (1891.1)

横浜居留地の外国人商人の懐中時計広告。角ゴシック体を使いイラストを毎回変えている（明治27年10月）
Ad for pocket watches sold by a western merchant in the foreign quarter of Yokohama. Note the angular Gothic font. A different illustration was featured each time. (1894.10)

30年代になると硬派ものの広告も増えてくる。34年には、総武・成田・山陽・日本鉄道などの路線開通や初詣・観光案内の広告、帝国練炭、芝浦製作所の発電機、新聞輪転印刷機の東京機械製作所や、日本鉄工、日本郵船、内国通運の小荷物取集広告など、全頁を含む大型広告が目立っている。また、文明の進歩で広告が日常生活面への大ニュースになった。ほかに興味深いものにガスや電気の広告がある。

東京電燈は「電燈の効用」と題して
▽電燈は静かに光を放ち、其之線はすこしも動揺せざるを以て、人の眼を害することなし…
と、ローソクやランプのように炎がゆらゆらすることがなく目にやさしい光であることをPRしている。井上電気製造はアセチリンガスによる新発明の置洋燈を発表、東京瓦斯は、ガスを使うと煮物が簡単で便利なこと、西洋風呂や水道用湯沸器、瓦斯七輪、瓦斯用置暖爐など、まだ一般の人々には目新しい情報を、大きなスペースに絵入りで広告している。このほかにも米国製のモノプレックス電話機「丸菱商会」、自動涼風機「峰川商会」、内外人力車製造「伊藤竹三郎」などの生活必需品がずらりと並ぶ。食品では銀座木村屋総本店のパン・ビスケット、味の素、万上味醂に、ヤマサ、キッコーマン、ヒゲタなどの醬油や牛肉、宇治茶、小麦粉、牛乳。ビールはサッポロ・キリン・エビス・アサヒ・東京・カブト・浅田・丸三・大里・東陽と銘柄が豊富な上、デザイン的にもすぐれた広告が多かった。酒類の広告で出荷量が抜群に多かったのは蜂印葡萄酒で、赤玉ポートワイン、大黒天印葡萄酒、ヘルメスウヰスキーなどを圧倒していた。

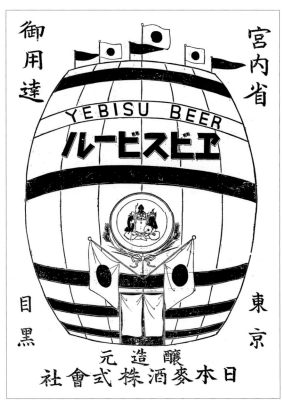

エビスビールの全ページ広告。文字はすべて手書きだが、立体のゴシックのロゴが新しい（明治36年5月）
Full-page ad for Yebisu Beer. The characters are all hand-drawn. The 3D-style Gothic logo is new. (1903.5)

出稿量が多かった蜂印ブドウ酒の広告。はたして現在こんなキャラクターのソムリエはいるだろうか？（明治38年8月）
Ad for Bee's Brand Wine, one of the more heavily advertised products of the time. You have to wonder whether there are still sommeliers like this character today. (1905.8)

presses for newspapers, and Japan Ironworks was equally assiduous in promoting its wares. NYK Line and Naikoku Express trumpeted parcel delivery service. Advertising was becoming a vital source of news on how the latest advances in civilization were improving daily life. Also of great interest are ads for gas and electricity. Tokyo Electric Lamp placed an ad entitled "Virtues of the Electric Light Bulb," which explained:The electric light bulb is harmless to the eye because it emits light softly and its rays do not waver in the least......

The point is that electric lights are gentle on the eyes since they do not flicker like the flame of a candle or gas lamp. Inoue Electrical Manufacturing unveiled a new invention, a portable lamp that burned acetylene gas. Tokyo Gas lavished considerable space on illustrated ads that explained how simple and handy gas was for stewing foods, and told of wonders like western-style baths, water heaters, gas stoves and portable gas heaters. Papers were full of ads for daily necessities: Marubishi Trading's Monoplex phones from the US, Minegawa Trading's automatic fans, Ito Takezaburo's Naigai Rickshaw Manufacturing. Kimuraya's main store in Ginza plugged bread and biscuits, while other ads promoted foodstuffs like Ajinomoto, Manjo mirin (sweet wine), Yamasa, Kikkoman and Higeta soy sauce, beef, tea from Uji, flour and milk. Beer came in a host of brands --Sapporo, Kirin, Yebisu, Asahi, Tokyo, Kabuto, Asada, Marusan, Osato, Toyo-- whose ads were often brilliantly designed. As for liquor, Bee's Brand Wine pulled far ahead of the pack in sheer volume of advertising, leaving the likes of Akadama Port Wine, Daikokuten Brand Wine and Hermes Whisky in the dust.

Advertising proliferated further as 8-14 page newspapers became the norm. Ads for books, magazines, medicinal cosmetics and cigarettes abounded. Plugs for medicines were especially common, though quite a few had fishy-sounding names and promised remarkable benefits. "Cure your gonorrhea quickly with Kairingan pills." "Jokyusan, guaranteed to help you get pregnant." "Biseisan for projecting the voice." "Rikkogan for sexual disorders." There were remedies for everything: leprosy, tuberculosis, bed-wetting, ringworm, chilblains, athlete's foot, hemorrhoids. Among the more unusual blurbs: "Practice birth control, avoid sexual contamination, prevent syphilis and enjoy the pleasure with Roedzak, No. 1 in the land."

新聞の頁数も8〜14が普通になると広告掲載量も一段と増え、書籍・雑誌・医薬化粧品・煙草などの広告が氾濫した。中でも目立ったのは薬品の広告で、眉唾な薬名や効能のものがかなりあった。「りん患者早く直し玉へ・快麻丸」、「子のできる保障薬・女宮散」、「こえのでる薬・美声散」、「生殖器病・立効丸」ほか、らい病、肺病、寝小便、いんきんたむし、霜やけ、水虫、痔などの特効薬に多かった。効能やキャッチフレーズの変り種は、「避妊・男女不潔・梅毒予防・快楽欲望に天下一品のルーデルサック」、「酒不可飲・酒者百難の基、さけきらいになる薬、礼状は8千余通」、「良薬は口に甘し・浅田飴」、津村順天堂は子宮病欠の道の薬として中湯を発売、「見よ見よ10年の血の道3週間にて全治す」と、目立つイラスト入りでオーバーな表現の広告を出している。一方、三共のタカヂアスターゼ、大木五蔵圓、太田胃散、大学目薬、今治水、宝丹、毒掃丸など今日でもおなじみの薬も出稿されていた。

化粧品は31年に桃谷順天堂のにきびとり「美顔水」、32年に平尾賛平の「おしどり香油」「パール練香油」、そして35年頃からは洋風化粧品が流行し、大崎組はフランス・パリの「鶴香水」、元祖衛生歯磨石鹸を販売していた福原資生堂も化粧品部門を開設、化粧水「オイデルミレ」や練おしろいを発売した。歯みがきには大きなもの、強いもの、高価なものを象徴する、象印・ライオン・ダイヤモンドなどの商品名のついた広告が目立っている。

ご婦人向けで、漢字にルビ付き薬品広告（明治30年1月）
All the Chinese characters are accompanied by phonetic readings in hiragana to assist the ladies.(1897.1)

細かいコピーは不要というのか、目立つイラストで視覚的効果をねらっているタバコの広告（明治35年5月）
The eye-catching illustration of tabako ad ,makes an immediate visual impact. No need for detailed copy here. (1902.5)

"Drink not, for alcohol is the source of all evils! Medicine for coming off the bottle. Over 8,000 testimonials received." "Good medicine tastes sweet. Asada drops." Tsumura Juntendo came out with a medicine called Chujoto for dizziness and other symptoms associated with uterine disorders, for which it placed an eye-catching illustrated ad that was extravagant in its claims: "Look! Look! Ten years of uterine troubles, completely cured in just three weeks!" A number of medicines still familiar in Japan today also graced the ads of the time: Sankyo's Takaji Astaze, Oki Gozoen, Ohta Stomach Powder, Daigaku Eye Drops, Konjisui, Hotan, Dokusogan.

Cosmetics were big as well. In 1898 Momotani Juntendo's pimple remover Bigansui appeared, followed in 1899 by Hirao Sampei's Oshidori Hair Oil and Pearl Pomade. Western-style cosmetics came into vogue around 1902. Osaki-gumi offered "Crane Perfume" from Paris. Fukuhara Shiseido, which had pioneered the sale of sanitary tooth powder and soap in Japan, established a cosmetics division and brought out Eauderumine toilet water and facial paste. Tooth powder was advertised under brand names like Elephant Brand, Lion and Diamond – terms suggestive of size, strength and exclusive price.

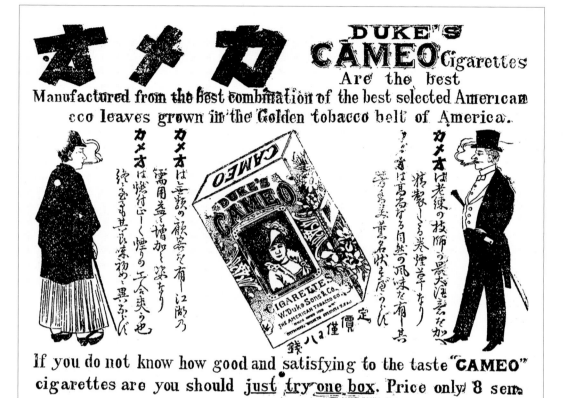

商品のパッケージ。和洋スモーカーのイラスト。英文に手書き文字が入れられインパクトの強い興味深い広告（明治33年12月）
A product package flanked by illustrations of a Japanese and westerner smoking.
This interesting specimen, which combines English text with handwritten Japanese, exerts quite an impact.(1900.12)

眼帯をかけた婦人のイラストも興味深いが、大学目薬の手書き文字が独特な上、文字にアミがかかっている（明治38年11月）
The illustration of the woman with the eye-patch is certainly interesting, but also note the hand-drawn characters Daigaku Megusuri ("Daigaku Eye Drops") with their hatching and distinctive design.(1905.11)

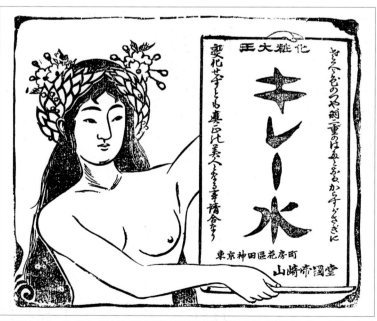

商品名にふさわしいキレイな人。その上ヌードとは、斬新な化粧品の広告に当時の読者の驚く顔が目に浮かぶ（明治39年5月）
The lovely young lady perfectly complements the name of the product: Beauty Water. The nude is daring, and one can easily imagine the shocked look on the faces of contemporary readers.(1906.5)

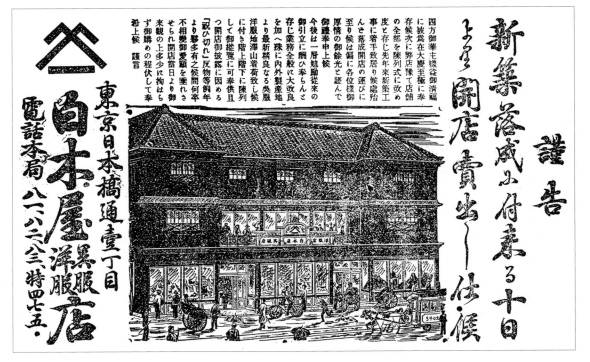

今はなき老舗の百貨店・白木屋は店先のイラストに毛筆と活字を上手に配している（明治36年9月）
This ad for the now-defunct Drapers Shirokiya skillfully combines brush-written calligraphy and typeset text with an illustration of the storefront. (1903.9)

各種製品と商店名だけを配した帽子店の印象広告（明治38年6月）
An impressionistic ad featuring simply the name of the store with an illustration of its hats. (1905.6)

懐中時計をイメージしたデザインに、オールゴシック体の手書き文字が生かされている作品例（明治38年8月）
Hand-drawn characters, all in Gothic style, on a pattern of pocket watches. (1905.8)

元和2年創業と歴史を感じるが、明朝に長体活字やゴシック、英文を配したフレッシュなレイアウトが注目される醤油店の広告（明治38年7月）
The words "founded in 1616" are redolent of history, but the layout itself, with its combination of mincho, elongated type, Gothic characters and English text, creates a fresh impression. (1905.7)

4. 明治後期の広告

明治末期には、わが国新聞史上最初にして最後といわれる224頁の超大型の記念号が「時事新報」の創刊25周年で発行された。掲載された広告件数も583件と驚異的な量で、当時の主要広告主を網羅している。たとえば三越呉服店の最初の2ページ見開き広告は、マルに越の商標を中央に置き、四隅に美女を配して曲線と植物模様のアールヌーボーのワクで囲んだシンプルなデザインだが、強烈な印象を与える秀作である。三越はこの時代からポスターなどにも岡田三郎助や橋口五葉など著名画家に作らせており、宣伝活動は群を抜いていた。

こうした新聞広告の比重増大と大型広告の流行は、ロゴや商品名の文字、デザインやコピーにも一段の進歩をもたらすようになる。スペースいっぱいに文字のみを配した原稿は影をひそめ、商標や製品のパッケージ、カットや広告をやわらげる女性のイラスト、アールヌーボーやアールデコの影響を感じさせるモダンなものまで、表現はバラエティーに富んでくる。

こうしたさまざまな広告表現の発展の中で注目したいのは、木活字は別として明治期の新聞広告のコピーにはほとんど明朝体しか使われていないことである。ゴシック体も明治10年代の後半には作られたといわれているが、新聞の紙面を見る限り記事の見出しや本文に至るまで皆無に等しい。広告の中には商品名や社名などにいくらかのゴシック体を見かけるが、いずれも活字でなく手書文字である。一般の印刷所ではゴジック活字を所持しているところもあったが、新聞社は明朝体以外の活字を揃えていなかったため記事や見出しはおろか、たとえ広告主から依頼があってもゴシックの組版には対応できなかったのではないかと推察できる。一方、逆に広告を目立たせるための手書き文字やイラストによるレイアウトは、このような影響で急速に発達したと見るのが妥当のようだ。

アールヌーボー調のイラストに手書きのゴシック体、活字を配した三井呉服店の変形広告（明治37年4月）
An unusually shaped ad of Mitsui with handwritten Gothic text, typeset copy and an art-nouveau illustration.（1904.4）

三越初の見開き広告（明治40年3月）
The first spread ad of Mitsukoshi Drapers.（1907.3）

分厚い224頁の記念号
A 224-Page whopper making the 25th anniversary of the Jiji Shimpo.

4.Advertising in the Late Meiji Period

At the end of the Meiji period the biggest commemorative number in the history of Japanese journalism either before or after appeared -- a 224-page whopper marking the 25th anniversary of the Jiji Shimpo. This contains an amazing 583 ads representing virtually all the major sponsors of the day. It opens, for example, with a two-page spread for Mitsukoshi Drapers. The design is simple -- the character for koshi surrounded by a circle in the center, beautiful women in each of the four corners, an art-nouveau border of curved lines and plants -- but it is masterful in the force of the impression it makes. Mitsukoshi was far ahead of its contemporaries on the publicity front, and around this time it began commissioning well-known painters such as Okada Saburosuke and Hashiguchi Goyo to produce posters for it.

The growing prominence of newspaper advertising and increasing popularity of large ads spurred further innovations in logos, the lettering used for product names, design and copywriting. Blocks of text filling every available inch gave way to a far richer variety of expression: trademarks, depictions of product packaging, pictures, illustrations of young ladies to soften up the page. Some ads, clearly influenced by art nouveau and art deco, were highly modern-looking.

In spite of this tremendous diversity, it is noteworthy that the copy of Meiji-period newspaper ads was almost invariably printed in the mincho typeface, except when wooden type was used. The Japanese Gothic font is said to have been developed in the mid 1880s, yet it is totally absent from either the text or headlines of newspaper articles. The occasional ad is found with a product or company name in Gothic-style characters, but these are written by hand, not typeset. While regular print shops may sometimes have stocked Gothic type, it can be conjectured that newspaper publishers possessed nothing but mincho. That is why articles and headlines are all in that font, and newspapers would have been incapable of setting ads in Gothic even if their clients had wanted them to. This state of affairs, it is reasonable to assume, sparked the rapid evolution of hand-drawn lettering and illustrated layouts as ways to jazz up ads.

斬新な図案文字を商品名にした久保田紙店。説明文はひらかなのみの力作（明治40年11月）
The product name is given in boldly stylized characters. The copy is all in hiragana. A veritable tour de force. (1907.11)

丸善初の全面広告。手書き文字や明朝体活字の中にゴシック体が要所にみられる（明治40年3月）
Book Store Maruzen's first full-page ad. Gothic appears in key places amidst the handwritten characters and mincho type. (1907.3)

ビンの形のイラストに写真版を配し影つきの「クラブ阿らい粉」の手書き文字も秀作な化粧品広告（明治40年3月）
Another masterpiece, with photographic plates on a bottle-shaped background and the hand-drawn characters for "Club Araiko" bordered with shadows. (1907.3)

「クリスマス」の文字に丸ゴシックが登場。サンタクロースのイラストを入れた和菓子屋の広告（明治40年12月）
A confectioner's ad with an illustration of Santa Claus. The word "Christmas" is written in rounded Gothic. (1907.12)

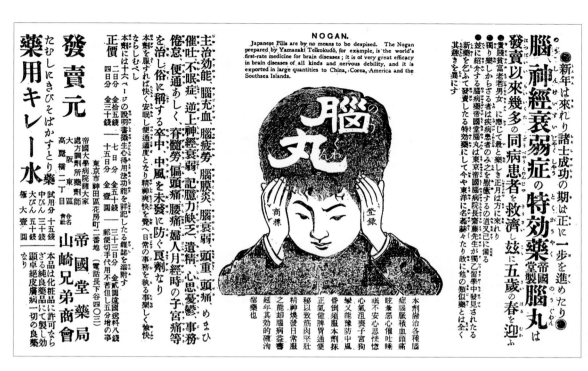

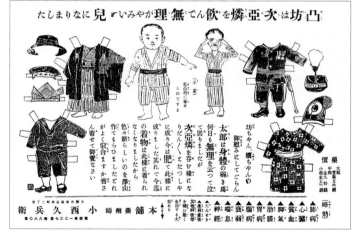

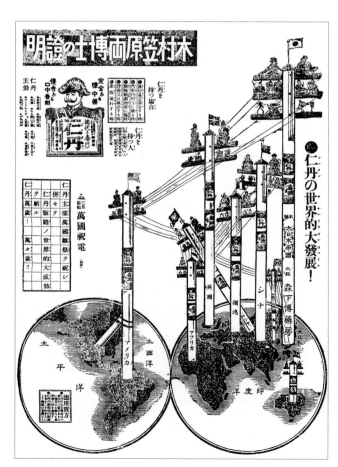

製品とともにヨーロッパから輸入したデザインに明朝体活字を組み合わせた洋酒の広告（明治43年12月）
Like the liquor it advertises, this design is imported straight from Europe. The text is added in mincho font.（1910.12）

商標とラーヂ自転車の丸ゴシックの白抜きが、際だって目立つ（明治43年8月）
The trademark and words "Rudge Bicycles" in white on black leap off the page.（1910.8）

毛筆で「プリミヤは自転車の王なり」と書く洋装の女性。輸入自転車の広告に和洋折衷を感じる（明治44年4月）
A woman in western attire writes the words "Premier is the King of Bicycles" with a brush. Ads for imported bicycles show a blend of Japanese and western motifs.（1911.4）

おわりに
新聞博物館開館に向けて

前述したように中学時代に、国語の先生との交流がきっかけで始めた新聞に関する資料集め。以後も、さまざまな人々とのドラマチックな出会いを経て、約半世紀の歳月を重ねながら、その数も優に10万点を超える膨大なものになった。

古いものには限りがあるものの、江戸時代から幕末・明治・大正・昭和そして平成にわたる私が集めた資料は、年々増え続け敷地内にある書庫も満杯となった。こうした資料は収集家が少ないせいか、私の収蔵品も「新聞資料ライブラリー・羽島コレクション」としてテレビ・ラジオや新聞、雑誌などで機会あるごとに紹介された。加えて私設文庫が国立国会図書館が編集した「全国特殊コレクション要覧」など各種のディレクトリー集に掲載されるに至って、マスコミ各社や研究者・団体などからの問い合わせや資料の請求が増え、近年では年間100件を軽く超える有様となった。増え続ける資料、そして問い合せ。小さな文庫の限界をつくづく感じながら、収集・整理・運営の一切を私一人でまかなっている毎日が10数年前から続いてきた。阪神淡路大震災以来、火災や地震などの心配も重なり、資料維持について不安は高まるばかり。

そんな折、(社)日本新聞協会から『2000年秋、横浜にオープンする日本新聞博物館「ニュースパーク」構想に協力してほしい』との要請を受けた。つまり私のコレクションを必要としているのである。

「世に博物館の類は、多種多様にある。されど、激動の時代を彩ってきたもっとも知的な文化遺産『新聞』の博物館は、なぜかいまだに存在しない。文化国家を標榜する手前、これはまことに遺憾の極みといえるだろう」

1985年10月の新聞週間に朝日新聞に掲載された因藤泉石氏のコメントだが、これを読んで以来、新聞博物館の実現を待ち望んでいた私には、嬉しい申し出だった。

新聞一枚は、一葉一片断簡零墨といえども実に貴重な「ナマ資料」である。わが国の新聞歴史は、やっと一世紀を超えた程度だというのに、全国各地で発行された新聞の多くは天災あるいは人災によって消滅、雲散してしまっている。主だった新聞は近年マイクロフィルムやCD-ROM、復刻版などにより図書館や研究機関に収められているが、近代日本の文化的なこのナマ資料を保存し後世に残すことは、歴史を検証する上で

も次の世代に対するわれわれの責務であると考えている。

しかし、手塩にかけて収集してきたコレクションは、どれ一つとっても大切な子供のようなもの、いざとなると博物館で大きく育てたいと思う一方で、いつまでも手元に置きたいとの思いが交差する。でも、こんな出会いもまたとないだろう。新聞協会は輪転機などハードな資料は揃えているが、新聞や号外などソフトな資料は皆無に等しいという。新聞原紙はまさにソフト。ソフトを揃えられるのは私だけと思い悩んだ挙句、コレクションの一切を新聞博物館に譲渡し、事業に協力することにした。

現在、横浜市では今年10月の完成を目指し、横浜市中区の県庁前に12階建てのメディア・情報関連産業の総合施設「横浜市情報文化センター」の建設を進めている。多目的ホールやパブリックスペースなどを配置したセンターの目玉の一つが「日本新聞博物館」である。近代新聞の発祥地・横浜にふさわしい新名所ができることになる。横浜市では中・高校生の修学旅行の見学コースにPRしていくというが、若い世代に私のコレクションがどう映るか、いまから夢が膨らむ。

私は37年間勤めてきた広告会社を退職、98年4月から博物館担当の特別専門委員として博物館の分室でスタッフとともに資料の分類や整理にあたっているが、集めた資料の中には購入したまま放置してあったものもあり、再会の喜びといおうか、意外な発見に興奮を覚えるときもある。

個人コレクションは、収集者が不要になり処分または亡くなるなどの理由で散逸したり、あまり利用度のない機関に移され死蔵されるケースも多い。その点、私がライフワークとして生涯をかけて集めてきたコレクションは、もうすぐ日の目を見ることができ幸である。

日本新聞博物館が入る「横浜情報文化センター」ビル

コレクションが展示されるのは、新聞博物館の中の「歴史展示ゾーン」と「企画展示ゾーン」。このコーナーは日本と世界の新聞歴史街道となる。新聞の歴史を実物、模型、映像、レプリカによって見せる仕組みだ。そして、江戸末期からの事件・世相を次々に紹介しながら、新聞の歩みをたどる"道しるべ"として役立つのが私の資料というわけだ。

新聞の発生期、近代新聞の成立期、戦時統制期、日本の民主化と新聞の復興期、新聞の高度成長期、多メディア時代の6ジャンルに分けて、それぞれの時代の息吹きと背景を伝えようというのが狙いである。

私の一つ一つの資料が多くの人と出会える、そんな新聞博物館の開館の前に、『日本タイポグラフィ年鑑2000』の特集ページを与えられたことは大変に光栄なことだと感じている。とはいえ浅学非才の身、専門家の方々には不備な内容ではなはだ恐縮だが、これを機会にタイポグラフィに関していっそう理解を深めて行きたいと思っている。お気づきの点など、ご教示たまわれれば望外の喜びである。

なお本稿作成にあたり、企画の段階からお手伝いいただいた福間敏彦氏をはじめ、写真や資料・情報提供などさまざまな面でご協力いただいた(株)東京機械製作所、(財)日本新聞教育文化財団、(株)日本図書センター、(株)大空社ほか、これまで私の収集や研究に対してご支援いただいたみなさまに、深く感謝を申し上げる。

参考文献
▽ 小野秀雄著「日本新聞発達史」大11
▽ 北原義雄編「現代商業美術全集」昭4
▽ 日本電報通信社編「日本新聞広告史」昭15
▽ 伊藤正徳著「新聞五十年史」昭18
▽ 小野秀雄著「日本新聞史」昭24
▽ 日本電報通信社編「広告五十年史」昭26
▽ 博報堂編「広告六十年」 昭30
▽ 内川芳美編「日本広告発達史」(上巻) 昭51
▽ 落合茂著「花王広告史」(上巻) 昭52
▽ 中井幸一著「日本広告表現技術史」 平3
▽ 羽島知之編著「新聞の歴史」1 平9
▽ 羽島知之編著「新聞広告美術大系」平11

●執筆者紹介
羽島知之(はじまともゆき)
昭和10年(1935)東京生れ。東洋大学経済学部卒。
(株)三栄広告社取締役を経て、(財)日本新聞教育文化財団博物館担当特別専門委員。東洋文化新聞研究会代表。
●主な編著書
『新聞雑誌特秘調査』昭和54年(大正出版)、『号外』シリーズ全12巻 平成7〜9年、『カストリ新聞』平成7年、『新聞広告美術大系』明治編 平成11年(以上大空社)、『写真絵画集成・新聞の歴史』平成9年(日本図書センター)

Afterword:

The New Museum of Journalism As I have already described, it was my Japanese teacher who first set me on the path to collecting newspapers. In the intervening half century I have amassed a huge collection well in excess of 100,000 items.

In the process I have enjoyed all kinds of dramatic encounters. Although the number of older items is limited, the materials that I have brought together range in date from Edo times and the last years of the Tokugawa regime through the Meiji, Taisho, Showa and Heisei periods. My holdings are growing by the year, and the storage facilities on site have reached bursting point. Evidently there are few collectors of this type of thing, for the Hajima Library of Newspaper Archives, as it is known, is not infrequently featured on television and radio and in newspapers and magazines. My personal library is also listed in various directories, including the Catalog of Special Collections Nationwide compiled by the National Diet Library. Thus I receive a growing number of inquiries and requests for materials from the media, researchers and various organizations –in recent years, well over a hundred annually. Yet for over a decade now the whole thing has been a one-man operation – collecting, sorting, administration-- and I am acutely aware of the limitations of a small private library like this. How do you handle the ever expanding collection and constant stream of inquiries? The massive Hanshin-Awaji temblor, which added fire and earthquake to my list of concerns, made me more worried than ever about how to maintain the collection.

It was around that time that the Japan Newspaper Association approached me for my help with the News Park project, a plan to open a museum of Japanese journalism in Yokohama in the fall of 2000. In a nutshell, they wanted me to donate my collection.

"There are all kinds of museums. But for some reason no museum yet exists dedicated to the newspaper, that most intellectual facet of our cultural heritage that has been the counterpoint to an age of constant upheaval. As we dedicate ourselves to the goal of building a nation of culture, this is most regrettable."

That comment of Indo Senseki appeared in the Asahi Shimbun during Newspaper Week in October 1985. Ever since reading those words, I have looked forward to the day when someone would establish a museum of journalism. The Association's overtures, therefore, were most welcome.

Every page, every last scrap of a newspaper is a valuable document of the past. The newspaper in Japan is barely over a century old, yet the majority of papers published through the length and breadth of this country have vanished without a trace, the victim of various natural or man-made disasters. In recent years libraries and research institutions have brought together major newspapers on microfilm or CD-ROM or in reprinted editions.

Nonetheless, it is our duty to posterity and to the investigation of history, I believe, to pass on these cultural records of modern Japan to future generations. But every single item in this collection I have lovingly nurtured over the years is like a precious child to me. My hopes of seeing it grow into something bigger in the context of a museum were mingled with a desire to keep it forever by my side. Yet this was a once-in-a-lifetime opportunity. The Newspaper Association said it had plenty of "hardware" like rotary presses, but its holdings of "software" –newspapers and newspaper extras -- were virtually nil. The original papers themselves are the software, I told myself, and I am the only one who can supply them. And so, after much heart-searching, I finally decided to cooperate and hand over my whole collection.

A twelve-story media and information complex called the Yokohama City Information Culture Center is currently under construction across from the prefectural government building in Yokohama's Naka Ward, with a scheduled completion date of next October. Along with a multipurpose hall and public space, one of the facility's biggest attractions will be the Museum of Japanese Journalism –a fitting addition to the sights of Yokohama, birthplace of the modern Japanese newspaper. The City of Yokohama says it will recommend the museum as a stop on junior and senior high school tours. Seeing what impression my collection makes on the younger generation will be like a dream come true.

In April 1998, after retiring from the advertising agency I had been with for 37 years, I became special advisor to the museum. Ever since, I have been working alongside staff at the museum's office sifting through and classifying materials. Certain items I have never looked at virtually since the day I bought them, and sometimes I experience the joy of meeting an old friend mingled with the thrill of unexpected discovery.

Many private collections become dispersed when their owners lose interest or pass away. Others end up gathering dust in some seldom-visited institution. Thus I count myself lucky, for the collection I have devoted my whole life to amassing is about to see the light of day. The collection will grace the museum's History Exhibition Zone and Special Exhibition Zone. This corner is designed to be a highway through the history of newspapers in Japan and around the world. It will show how journalism has evolved using actual newspapers, models, film and replicas. The items from my collection will serve as signposts of major developments along the way while offering a kaleidoscopic survey of incidents and social conditions since the late Edo period. The display is to be divided into six phases: the origin of newspapers, the emergence of the modern paper, wartime controls, the democratization of Japan and the revival of the press, newspapers during the years of rapid economic expansion, and the multimedia age. The idea is to convey the background and ambience of each era.

The Museum of Japanese Journalism, where a large audience will be able to see the individual items in my collection firsthand, is soon to open, and it is a tremendous honor to be able to contribute this feature to Applied Typography 10 at such a time. Yet I can make no claim to learning, and I am afraid experts in the field will find much to criticize.

Nonetheless, I intend to take advantage of this opportunity to enhance my understanding of typography. I would be delighted if readers would enlighten me on any points they might notice.

Finally, I would like to express my deep appreciation to Mr. Fukuma Toshihiko, who assisted in preparing this manuscript from the planning stage ; Tokyo Kikai Seisakusho, Ltd., the Japan Newspaper Education Cultural Foundation, Nihon Tosho Center Co., Ltd., Ozora-sha, Ltd., and everyone else who assisted by providing photos, documentation and information; and all the many individuals who have helped me over the years with collecting and research.

Bibliography

Ono Hideo, Nihon Shimbun Hattatsu-shi ("History of the Development of Newspapers in Japan"), 1922.

Kitahara Yoshio (ed.), Gendai Shogyo Bijutsu Zenshu ("Complete Anthology of Modern Commercial Art"), 1929.

Japan Telegraphic Communication Co., Ltd. (ed.), Nihon Shimbun Kokoku-shi ("History of Japanese Newspaper Advertising"), 1940.

Ito Masanori, Shimbun Gojunen-shi ("Fifty Years of Newspapers"), 1943.

Ono Hideo, Nihon Shimbun-shi ("History of Newspapers in Japan"), 1949.

Japan Telegraphic Communication Co., Ltd. (ed.), Kokoku Gojunen-shi ("Fifty Years of Advertising"), 1951.

Hakuhodo (ed.), Kokoku Rokujunen-shi ("Sixty Years of Advertising"), 1955.

Uchikawa Yoshimi (ed), Nihon Kokoku Hattatsu-shi ("History of the Development of Japanese Advertising"), Vol. I, 1976.

Ochiai Shigeru, Kao Kokoku-shi ("History of Kao Advertising"), Vol. I, 1977.

Nakai Koichi, Nihon Kokoku Hyogen Gijutsu-shi ("History of Japanese Techniques of Advertising Expression"), 1991.

Hajima Tomoyuki (ed.), Shimbun no Rekishi I ("History of Newspapers I"), 1997.

Hajima Tomoyuki (ed.), Shimbun Kokoku Bijutsu Taikei ("Newspaper Advertising Art Series"), 1999.

About the Author

Hajima Tomoyuki was born in Tokyo in 1935. A graduate of the Department of Economics of Toyo University, he has served on the board of directors of Sanei Advertising Co., Ltd., and is currently special museum advisor to the Japan Newspaper Education Cultural Foundation. He also chairs the Oriental Cultural Newspapers Research Association.

Mr. Hajima's chief publications are Shimbun Zasshi Tokuhi Chosa ("Confidential Survey of Newspapers and Magazines") (Taisho Publishing, 1979); the 12-volume Gogai ("Newspaper Extras") series (1995-97), Kasutori Shimbun ("Lowbrow Newspapers") (1995), and Shimbun Kokoku Bijutsu Taikei ("Newspaper Advertising Art Series"), Meiji Period (1999) (all published by Ozora-sha); and Shashin Kaiga Shusei: Shimbun no Rekishi ("Anthology of Photographs and Pictures: The History of Newspapers") (Nihon Tosho Center, 1997).

INDEX

掲載作家一覧
Art Directors & Designers Index

会 員 名 簿
Member's list

個人会員
Individual member

50音順
Member's Directory is not in
English alphabetical order.

相澤 竹夫
(有) アルファルファ
〒106-0032 東京都港区六本木6-11-17-5A
Takeo Aizawa
Alfalfa Inc.
6-11-17-5A Ropponngi, Minato-ku,
Tokyo 106-0032
Tel. 03-5770-6470　Fax. 03-5770-6471

相羽 高徳
(株) グラフィクス アンド デザイニング
〒108-0071 東京都港区白金台3-3-1
G&Dアルケミックハウス
Takanori Aiba
Graphics & Designing Inc.
G & D Aichemic House 3-3-1 Shirokanedai,
Minato-ku, Tokyo 108-0071
Tel. 03-3449-1541　Fax. 03-3449-1542

赤松 陽構造
(株) 日映美術
〒151-0051 東京都渋谷区千駄ヶ谷4-5-15
ストークメイジュ 206
Hicozo Akamatsu
NICHIEI ART CO., LTD
Stork Meijyu 206 4-5-15 Sendagaya,
Shibuya-ku, Tokyo 151-0051
Tel. 03-3403-2409　Fax. 03-3403-2491
E-mail: nichiart@ce.mbn.or.jp

秋元 克士
アド・エンジニアーズ・オブ・トーキョー
〒102-0084 東京都千代田区二番町2-12
平田ビル内
Yoshio Akimoto
Advertising Engineers of Tokyo Inc.
Hirata Bldg. 2-12 Niban-cho, Chiyoda-ku,
Tokyo 102-0084
Tel. 03-3264-3841(代)　Fax. 03-3264-6206

浅石 征浩
浅石デザイン研究所
〒155-0031 東京都世田谷区北沢2-37-2-302
Yukihiro Asaishi
Asaishi Design Office
2-37-2-302 Kitazawa, Setagaya-ku,
Tokyo 155-0031
Tel. 03-5790-5498　Fax. 03-5790-5499
E-mail: asaishi@mars.dtinet.or.jp

淺埜 勝
(株)・アーサー・ハンドレッド・カンパニー
〒150-0034 東京都渋谷区代官山町4-1
代官山マンション#705
Katsu Asano
ASA 100 COMPANY
Daikanyama Mansion 705 4-1 Daikanyamacho,
Shibuya-ku, Tokyo 150-0034
Tel. 03-3462-1988　Fax. 03-3462-1050
E-mail: asa100@sepia.ocn.ne.jp

浅野 豊久
(有) インター・ウェイブ
〒104-0061 東京都中央区銀座4-11-2
栄ビル5F
Toyohisa Asano
INTER-WAVE INCORPORATED
Sakae Bldg.5F 4-11-2 Ginza,
Cyuo-ku,Tokyo 104-0061
Tel. 03-3248-2382　Fax. 03-3248-2384
E-mail: wj4t-asn@asahi-net.or.jp

浅見 博
浅見デザイン室
〒192-0045 東京都八王子市大和田町7-4-1-3F
Hiroshi Asami
Asami Design Studio
7-4-1-3F Owadacho, Hachioji-shi,
Tokyo 192-0045
Tel. 0426-60-0635　Fax. 0426-60-0636
E-mail: hasami@ja2.so-net.ne.jp

味岡 伸太郎
(有) スタッフ
〒441-8011 愛知県豊橋市菰口町1-43
Shintaro Ajioka
Design Studio Staff
1-43 Komoguchi-cho, Toyohashi-shi,
Aichi 441-8011
Tel. 0532-32-4871　Fax. 0532-32-7134
E-mail: ajioka-s@jf6.so-net.ne.jp
http://www05.u-page.so-net.ne.jp/jf6/ajioka-s/

芦部 圀昭
〒158-0096 東京都世田谷区玉川台1-14-5
Kuniaki Ashibe
1-14-5 Tamagawadai,
Setagaya-ku, Tokyo 158-0096
Tel. Fax. 03-3700-1912

有澤 逸男 (号・祥南)
デザイン ラボ AW
〒257-0002 神奈川県秦野市鶴巻南4-7-1
鶴巻ガーデンシティプラザ 306号
Itsuo Arisawa
Design Lab. AW
Tsurumaki Garden City Plaza 306
4-7-1 Tsurumaki-minami, Hadano-shi,
Kanagawa 257-0002
Tel. Fax. 0463-76-5427
E-mail: arisawa@fsinet.or.jp

井口 やすひさ
IGUCHI
〒112-0011 東京都文京区千石1-19-2-401
Yasuhisa Iguchi
IGUCHI
1-19-2-401 Sengoku,
Bunkyo-ku, Tokyo 112-0011
Tel. Fax. 03-5977-1550
E-mail: iguchi7@sepia.ocn.ne.jp

池上 貴文
池上貴文デザイン室
〒468-0033 愛知県名古屋市天白区一つ山1-65
一つ山荘東 T-B-305
Takafumi Ikegami
Hitotsuyama-so T-B-305 1-65 Hitotsuyama,
Tenpaku-ku, Nagoya 468-0033
Docomo. 090-156-45187　Fax. 052-807-6915
Email: blues@love.email.ne.jp

石山 俊郎
(株) イクス
〒153-0043 東京都目黒区東山3-16-2
Toshiro Ishiyama
ICS Corporation
3-16-2 Higashiyama,
Meguro-ku, Tokyo 153-0043
Tel. 03-3719-5178　Fax. 03-3719-7611
E-mail: ics@i.bekkoame.ne.jp

今井 毅
日本プリンテクス(株)
〒162-0065 東京都新宿区住吉町1-16
Tsuyoshi Imai
NIPPON PRINT AND GRAPHICS INC.
1-16 Sumiyoshi-cho, Shinjuku-ku,
Tokyo 162-0065
Tel. 03-3358-8100 (代)　Fax.03-3358-8148

池田 毅
(株) アイ工房
〒530-0003 大阪府大阪市北区堂島2-1-5
サントリーアネックス1101
Takeshi Ikeda
Ai Kobo
Suntory Annex 1101 2-1-5 Dojima,
Kita-ku, Osaka 530-0003
Tel. 06-6341-8541　Fax. 06-6341-8543

伊勢谷 浩
伊勢谷浩デザイン室
〒010-0343 秋田県男鹿市脇本田谷沢字豆沢54
Hiroshi Iseya
Iseya Hiroshi Design Room
54 Mamesawa Aza Tayazawa,
Wakimoto, Oga-shi, Akita 010-0343
Tel. 0185-22-2016　Fax. 0185-22-2017
E-mail: iseya@wc4.so-net.ne.jp

IMAKITA DESIGN RESEARCH
今北 紘一
(有) 今北デザイン研究所
〒530-0047 大阪府大阪市北区西天満4-5-5
京阪マーキス梅田312
Koichi Imakita
Imakita Design Research Inc.
Keihan Marquis Umeda 312
4-5-5 Nishitenma, Kita-ku, Osaka 530-0047
Tel. 06-6364-6640　Fax. 06-6364-6140

jacket inc.
I think this is the beginning of
a beautiful design.
池田 秀夫
(株) ジャケット
〒160-0022 東京都新宿区新宿1-12-12-801
Hideo Ikeda
Jacket Inc.
1-12-12-801 Shinjuku, Shinjuku-ku,
Tokyo 160-0022
Tel. 03-3352-5733　Fax. 03-3352-6559
E-mail: jacket@fa2.so-net.ne.jp
http://www01.u-page.so-net.ne.jp/fa2/jacket/

板倉 忠則
(株) 板倉デザイン研究所
〒550-0014 大阪府大阪市西区北堀江1-12-9-1001
Tadanori Itakura
Itakura Design Institute Inc.
1-12-9-1001 Kitahorie, Nishi-ku,
Osaka 550-0014
Tel. 06-6534-5630　Fax. 06-6534-4025
E-mail: itakurad@osk3.web.ne.jp
http://www.itakurad.com/

今田 欣一
(有) 今田欣一デザイン室
〒170-0013 東京都豊島区東池袋5-7-6
スカイコート池袋第2 902
Kinichi Imada
Imada Kinichi Design Room
5-7-6-902 Higashiikebukuro,
Toshima-ku, Tokyo 170-0013
Tel. 03-5979-7378　Fax. 03-5979-7379
E-mail: kinkido@m08.alpha-net.ne.jp
http://www.alpha-net.ne.jp/users2/kinkido/

池田 縁
〒424-0212 静岡県清水市八木間町1954
Yukari Ikeda
1954 Yagima-cho, Shimizu-shi,
Shizuoka 424-0212
Tel. Fax. 0543-69-6416

KI
伊藤 勝一
(株) 伊藤勝一デザイン室
〒106-0031 東京都港区西麻布3-20-9
ハイネス麻布 606号
Katsuichi Ito
Katsuichi Ito Design Office
Highness-azabu 606 3-20-9 Nishiazabu,
Minato-ku, Tokyo 106-0031
Tel. 03-3408-5560　Fax. 03-3408-5855
E-mail: k-ito-dr@zc4.so-net.ne.jp

KI
入江 健介
(株) 麹谷・入江デザイン室
〒107-0062 東京都港区南青山2-29-13
鈴青ビル2F
Kensuke Irie
Kojitani, Irie & Inc.
2-29-13 Minamiaoyama,
Minato-ku, Tokyo 107-0062
Tel. 03-3478-0011　Fax. 03-3478-0012
E-mail: CXS02261@nifty.ne.jp

DOCCO
DESIGN
INC.
石川 忠
(有) ドッコ／ドッコデザイン研究所
〒151-0072 東京都渋谷区幡ケ谷1-3-1-1110
Tadashi Ishikawa
Docco Design Inc.
Hatagaya Golden Mansion 1110
1-3-1 Hatagaya, Shibuya-ku, Tokyo 151-0072
Tel. 03-3374-4568/4569　Fax. 03-3374-2680
E-mail: docco@ka2.so-net.ne.jp
http://www02.so-net.ne.jp/~docco/

伊藤 紘
伊藤紘制作室
〒108-0014 東京都港区芝5-27-3-504
Hiromu Ito
Hiromu Ito Design Office
5-27-3-504 Shiba, Minato-ku,
Tokyo 108-0014
Tel. 03-3452-4888　Fax. 03-3452-4182

creative house
GROW
岩田 明
クリエイティブハウス グロウ
〒460-0011 愛知県名古屋市中区大須4-9-17
サンパーク上前津203
Akira Iwata
Creative house Grow
4-9-17-203 Osu, Naka-ku,
Nagoya 460-0011
Tel. Fax. 052-264-4636
E-mail: growiwata@msn.com

石橋 政美
(有) 石橋政美デザイン室
〒150-0046 東京都渋谷区松涛1-29-21-603
Masami Ishibashi
Masami Ishibashi Design Inc.
#603, 1-29-21 Shouto, Shibuya-ku,
Tokyo 150-0046
Tel. 03-3477-0484　Fax. 03-3463-5921
E-mail: Masami4033@aol.com

bauhaus
今井 桂子
(株) バウハウス
〒460-0008 愛知県名古屋市中区栄3-19-19
フォルテ栄3階
Keiko Imai
Bauhaus Inc.
Forte-Sakae bldg. 3F 3-19-19 Sakae,
Naka-ku, Nagoya 460-0008
Tel. 052-263-0452 (代)　Fax.052-249-2698

Office Neu Inc.
岩田 幸夫
(株) オフィスニュウ
〒461-0001 愛知県名古屋市東区泉1-15-23
チサンマンション栄リバーパーク405
Yukio Iwata
Office Neu Inc.
1-15-23-405 Izumi,
Higashi-ku, Nagoya 461-0001
Tel. 052-971-8090　Fax. 052-971-7396
E-mail: neu@ngy1.1st.ne.jp

岩本 春彦
(株) コマースデザインセンター
〒160-0022 東京都新宿区新宿2-8-5
東弥ビル3F
Haruhiko Iwamoto
Commerce Design Center Co.,Ltd.
TOYA Bldg. 3F 2-8-5 Shinjuku,
Shinjuku-ku, Tokyo 160-0022
Tel. 03-3356-3731　Fax. 03-3356-5772

大平 敦夫
大平デザイン事務所
〒030-0852 青森県青森市
大野前田74-125 B-101
Atsuo Odaira
Odaira Design Studio
B-101 74-125 Ono, Maeda,
Aomori 030-0852
Tel. 0177-39-6797　Fax. 0177-39-6834

小倉 栄二
オー・グラフィックデザインルーム
〒553-0003 大阪府大阪市福島区福島5-17-40
Eiji Ogura
O'GRAPHIC DESIGN ROOM
5-17-40 Fukushima, Fukushima-ku,
Osaka 553-0003
Tel. Fax. 06-6442-8705
E-mail: ogura@o-graphic.com
http://www.o-graphic.com

海老名 淳
(有) バーヴ
〒154-0001 東京都世田谷区池尻2-35-9
マンション池尻201
Atzshi Evina
Verve Inc.
#201,2-35-9 Ikejiri,
Setagaya-ku, Tokyo 154-0001
Tel. 03-5431-7493　Fax. 03-5431-7489
E-mail: a-ebina@st.rim.or.jp

大谷 四郎
(株) 大谷デザイン研究所
〒153-0051 東京都目黒区上目黒3-8-3
Shiro Ohtani
Ohtani Design Laboratory Co.,Ltd.
3-8-3 Kamimeguro, Meguro-ku,
Tokyo 153-0051
Tel. 03-3791-6181　Fax. 03-3791-6191
E-mail: XLD00074@niftyserve.or.jp

尾崎 克典
尾崎克典デザイン事務所
〒030-0846 青森県青森市青葉3丁目2-18
Katsusuke Ozaki
Ozaki Katsusuke Design Office
3-2-18 Aoba, Aomori 030-0846
Tel. 0177-39-9300　Fax. 0177-39-7781

大石 玲
クリエーティブ・パワー・ユニット (CPU)
〒550-0003 大阪府大阪市西区京町堀1-14-32
セイケンビル3D
Akira Oishi
CPU
Seiken Bldg. #3D 1-14-32 Kyomachibori,
Nishi-ku, Osaka 550-0003
Tel. 06-4803-6090　Fax. 06-4803-6091
E-mail: oishi@c-p-u.co.jp

大庭 三紀
(有) グラフィック・パイ
〒802-0077 福岡県北九州市小倉北区馬借
1-13-29-801
Miki Ohba
GRAPHIC π
1-13-29-801 Bashaku, Kokurakita-ku,
KItakyushu-shi, Fukuoka 802-0077
Tel. Fax. 093-533-1313

小田 勝紀
カラリス
〒173-0026 東京都板橋区中丸町9-1-402
Katsunori Oda
Coloris
9-1-402 Nakamaru-cho,
Itabashi-ku, Tokyo 173-0026
Tel. Fax. 03-5995-2936

大川 栄司
(株) ケイ・クリエイティブ・ファクトリー
〒151-0053 東京都渋谷区代々木2-5-1
羽田ビル703
Eiji Okawa
K-Creative Factory Co., Ltd.
Haneda Bldg. 703 2-5-1 Yoyogi,
Shibuya-ku, Tokyo 151-0053
Tel. 03-5333-7567　Fax. 03-5333-7568
E-mail: ohkawa@kcfactory.co.jp

大町 尚友
ライブクリエイション
〒154-0001 東京都世田谷区池尻2-37-17
ハピネス池尻606号
Shoyu Ohmachi
Live Creation
Happiness Ikejiri 606 2-37-17 Ikejiri,
Setagaya-ku, Tokyo 154-0001
Tel. 03-3795-5302　Fax. 03-3795-5304
E-mail: live-cre@za2.so-net.ne.jp

鬼丸 トシヒロ
(株) グラフィクス アンド デザイニング
〒108-0071 東京都港区白金台3-3-1
G&Dアルケミックハウス
Toshihiro Onimaru
Graphics & Designing Inc.
G & D Alchemic House 3-3-1 Shirokanedai,
Minato-ku, Tokyo 108-0071
Tel. 03-3449-0651　Fax. 03-3449-0653
E-mail: onimaru@QUICHEandTARTE.com

大熊 務
(株) フォーティ・フォー
〒104-0032 東京都中央区八丁堀2-30-17
大岩ビル2F
Tsutomu Okuma
FORTY FOUR Inc.
Oiwa Bldg. 2F 2-30-17 Hacchobori,
Chuo-ku, Tokyo 104-0032
Tel. 03-3552-7946　Fax. 03-3555-0576
E-mail: tsutomu@pis.bekkoame.or.jp.
http://www.bekkoame.ne.jp/~tsutomu/

小川 航司
(株) オフビート
〒104-0041 東京都中央区新富1-7-7
新富センタービル7F
Koshi Ogawa
OFFBEAT
Shintomi Center Bldg. 7F
1-7-7 Shintomi, Chuo-ku, Tokyo 104-0041
Tel. 03-3555-1611　Fax. 03-3555-1622

尾村 匡昭
〒182-0012 東京都調布市深大寺東町6-27-8
Masaaki Omura
6-27-8 Jindaiji-higashicho,
Chofu-shi, Tokyo 182-0012
Tel. 0424-88-8858

太田 徹也
(有) 太田徹也デザイン室
〒107-0062 東京都港区南青山3-14-14
サン南青山303
Tetsuya Ota
Tetsuya Ota Design Studio
SUN Minamiaoyama 303
3-14-14 Minamiaoyama,
Minato-ku, Tokyo 107-0062
Tel. 03-3479-3697　Fax. 03-3479-6434

奥村 昭夫
(株) パッケージングクリエイト
〒540-0012 大阪府大阪市中央区谷町1-2-6
ストライプ7階
Akio Okumura
Packaging Create Inc.
Stripe Bldg. 7F 1-2-6 Tanimachi,
Chuo-ku, Osaka 540-0012
Tel. 06-6941-9618　Fax. 06-6941-9624

TIM GIRVIN DESIGN, INC.
International Brand & Image Management
ティム・ガービン
Tim Girvin
Tim Girvin Design Inc.
5th Floor 1601 2nd Ave. Seattle,
WA 98101-1575 USA
Tel. 206-623-7808　Fax. 206-340-1837
E-mail:tgdjapan@seattle.girvindesign.com
http://www.girvindesign.com/

甲斐 万暢
(株) ノア
〒106-0032 東京都港区六本木4-2-45
高會堂ビル4F
Manyou Kai
NOA
Koukaidou Bldg. 4F 4-2-45 Roppongi,
Minato-ku, Tokyo 106-0032
Tel. 03-3796-3285　Fax. 03-3796-3291

蒲池 文恵
筆工房 K
Fumie Kamachi
Fudekobou K
721 Menlo Ave, Apt E Menlo Park,
CA 94025 U.S.A
E-mail: fudekoubou@aol.com

神田 俊治
K&A office
〒541-0059 大阪府大阪市中央区博労町3-1-8
心斎橋二番館504
Toshiharu Kanda
K & A office
Shinsaibashi Ni-bankan 504 3-1-8
Bakuromachi, Chuo-ku, Osaka 541-0059
Tel. Fax. 06-6252-6118

葛本 茂
(株) ジャパン・アド・クリエイターズ
〒541-0059 大阪府大阪市中央区博労町3-2-3
野村ビル7F
Shigeru Katsumoto
Japan Ad Creators Inc.
Nomura Bldg.7F 3-2-3 Bakuromachi,
Chuo-ku, Osaka 541-0059
Tel. 06-6245-2273　Fax. 06-6245-2148
E-mail: jac@japan-ad.co.jp
http://www.japan-ad.co.jp/

神谷 利男
神谷利男デザイン
〒530-0005 大阪府大阪市北区中之島4丁目2-41
ライオンズマンション中之島506
Toshio Kamitani
Toshio Kamitani Design
4-2-41-506 Nakanoshima, Kita-ku,
Osaka 530-0005
Tel. Fax. 06-6445-8092

神田 浩
神田屋
〒619-0237 京都府精華町光台7-2
Hiroshi Kanda
Kandaya
7-2 Hikaridai, Seika-cho, Kyoto 619-0237
Tel. Fax. 0774-94-5802

加藤 辰二
(株) 並木スタジオ
〒112-0013 東京都文京区音羽2-1-6
トーカン・グランドマンション 1005
Tatsuji Kato
Namiki Studio Co.,Ltd.
Toukan Grand Manshon 1005
2-1-6 Otowa, Bunkyo-ku, Tokyo112-0013
Tel. 03-5940-5055　Fax. 03-5940-5056
E-mail:ekinoue@chive.ocn.ne.jp

河井 義則
(有) カワイデザインステューディオ
〒150-0022 東京都渋谷区恵比寿南1-14-9-301
Yoshinori Kawai
Kawai Design Studio
1-14-9-301 Ebisu-Minami, Shibuya-ku,
Tokyo 150-0022
Tel. 03-3710-6301　Fax. 03-3710-6302
E-mail: kds8387@mail.vinet.or.jp

岸本 一夫
〒901-2300 沖縄県中頭郡北中城村
字石平2153
Kazuo Kishimoto
2153 Aza, Ishihira, Kitanakagusuku-son,
Nakagami-gun, Okinawa 901-2300
Tel. Fax. 098-935-2823

金井 和夫
(有) タイポグラフィックス解
〒182-0012 東京都調布市深大寺東町4-8-40
Kazuo Kanai
Typographics-Kai Inc.
4-8-40 Jindaiji-higashicho,
Chofu-shi, Tokyo 182-0012
Tel. Fax. 0424-42-0504
E-mail: kanai@za2.so-net.ne.jp
http://www03.u-page.so-net.ne.jp/za2/kanai/

川島 周二
(有) イースト
〒530-0043 大阪府大阪市北区天満2-5-4
日本アートビル301
Shuji Kawashima
East
Nippn Art Bldg. 301 2-5-4 Tenma,
Kita-ku, Osaka 530-0043
Tel. 06-6356-0951　Fax. 06-6356-0942
E-mail: estinc95@osk.threewebnet.or.jp

岸本 義弘
岸本デザインオフィス
〒167-0051 東京都杉並区荻窪1-1-6
Yoshihiro Kishimoto
Kishimoto Design Office
1-1-6 Ogikubo, Suginami-ku,
Tokyo 167-0051
Tel. Fax. 03-3391-0367

金井 幸治
K'sデザインスタジオ
〒135-0016 東京都江東区東陽1-28-13
コーポ東陽801
Koji Kanai
K's Design Studio
Corpo Toyo 801 1-28-13 Toyo,
Koto-ku, Tokyo 135-0016
Tel. 03-5690-3969　Fax. 03-5690-3970

河原 英介
(株) 河原宣伝研究所
〒530-0005大阪府大阪市北区中之島3丁目
朝日新聞ビル
Eisuke Kawahara
Kawahara Design Institute
Asahi Shinbun Bldg. 3-chome,
Nakanoshima, Kita-ku, Osaka 530-0005
Tel. 06-6203-4754

北澤 敏彦
(株) ディス・ハウス
〒150-0001 東京都渋谷区神宮前5-1-7
Toshihiko Kitazawa
Dix-House Inc.
5-1-7 Jingumae, Shibuya-ku,
Tokyo 150-0001
Tel. 03-3406-6631　Fax. 03-3486-4940
E-mail: dix-drag@zb3.so-net.ne.jp

蟹瀬 行雄
(株) 蟹瀬デザイン事務所
〒155-0033 東京都世田谷区代田3-5-3
Yukio Kanise
Kanise Design Office Inc.
3-5-3 Daida, Setagaya-ku,
Tokyo 155-0033
Tel. 03-5433-2825　Fax. 03-5433-2826
E-mail: kanise@jade.dti.ne.jp

河村 岳志
オルタ・デザイン アソシエイツ
〒536-0013 大阪府大阪市城東区
鴫野東2-23-15-305
Takeshi Kawamura
Alt. Design Associates
2-23-15-305 Shiginohigashi,
Joto-ku, Osaka 562-0013
Tel. 06-6964-2399　Fax. 06-6964-2398
E-mail: kawamura@alt-design.co.jp
http://www.alt-design.co.jp/

切間 晴美
キリマデザイン事務所
〒530-0036 大阪府大阪市北区与力町1-5
与力町パークビル5F
Harumi Kirima
Kirima Design Office
Yorikimachi Park Bldg. 5F
1-5 Yoriki-machi, Kita-ku, Osaka 530-0036
Tel. 06-6351-7045　Fax. 06-6351-7046

金田一 剛
(有) チーム　T.E.A.M. Design
〒107-0062 東京都港区南青山6-13-2
ブルジョン南青山303
Tsuyoshi Kindaichi
T.E.A.M. Design
6-13-2-303 Minamiaoyama,
Minato-ku, Tokyo 107-0062
Tel. 03-3400-4005　Fax. 03-3400-4205
E-mail: kind@gol.com

倉田 頴作
(株) YAP
〒550-0003 大阪府大阪市西区京町堀1-7-21
薮中ビル2・3F
Eisaku Kurata
Yap Creatives, Inc.
Yabunaka Bldg. 2・3F 1-7-21
Kyomachibori, Nishi-ku, Osaka 550-0003
Tel. 06-6445-2052　Fax. 06-6445-2062

小平 明夫
小平デザイン事務所
〒157-0066 東京都世田谷区成城9-22-12
Akio Kodaira
Kodaira Design Office
9-22-12 Seijo, Setagaya-ku,
Tokyo 157-0066
Tel. 03-3305-9977　Fax. 03-3305-9978

日下部 治朗
(株) アド・クリエイター
〒150-0001 東京都渋谷区神宮前6-33-18
ハイツ原宿102
Jiro Kusakabe
AD. CREATOR Co.,Ltd.
Heights Harajuku 102 6-33-18 Jingumae,
Shibuya-ku, Tokyo 150-0001
Tel. 03-3400-7366　Fax. 03-3400-7027

栗林 孝之
(株) フォルマ
〒153-0043 東京都目黒区東山2-7-5
長谷川アパートメント2B
Takayuki Kuribayashi
Forma Inc.
Hasegawa Apartment 2B 2-7-5 Higashiyama,
Meguro-ku, Tokyo 150-0043
Tel. 03-5723-6537　Fax. 03-5723-6538
E-mail: tk@forma-inc.co.jp

小塚 昌彦
アドビシステムズ (株)
〒141-0032 東京都品川区大崎1-11-2
ゲートシティ大崎イーストタワー
Masahiko Kozuka
Adobe Systems Inc.
Gate City Ohsaki East Tower 1-11-2 Ohsaki,
Shinagawa-ku, Tokyo 141-0032
Tel. 03-5740-2657　Fax. 03-5740-2616
E-mail: mkozuka@adobe.com

工藤 強勝
デザイン実験室
〒107-0062 東京都港区南青山2-22-14
フォンテ青山412
Tsuyokatsu Kudo
Design Laboratory
Fonte Aoyama 412 2-22-14 Minamiaoyama,
Minato-ku, Tokyo 107-0062
Tel. 03-3479-1670　Fax. 03-3479-1850

桑原 孝之
〒206-0803 東京都稲城市向陽台6-11-2-501
Takayuki Kuwahara
6-11-2-501 Koyodai, Inagi-shi,
Tokyo 206-0803
Tel. 042-379-5012　Fax. 042-379-5011
E-mail: ky7t-kwhr@asahi-net.or.jp
http://www.asahi-net.or.jp/~ky7t-kwhr/

後藤 晴彦
(株) Office　HAL
〒107-0062 東京都港区南青山5-1-25
メゾン・ド・ラミア401
Haruhiko Goto
Office HAL Co.,Ltd.
5-1-25-401 Minamiaoyama,
Minato-ku, Tokyo 107-0062
Tel. 03-3409-4895　Fax. 03-3797-3598
E-mail: office-hal@muh.biglobe.ne.jp

工藤 俊之
金沢美術工芸大学 デザイン科 視覚デザイン研究室
〒920-8565 石川県金沢市小立野5-11-1
Toshiyuki Kudo
Kanazawa College of Art Department of Visual Design
5-11-1 Kodatsuno, Kanazawa 920-8565
Tel. Fax. 076-262-3633
E-mail: kudo@kanazawa-bidai.ac.jp

桑山 弥三郎
桑山書体デザイン室
〒201-0012 東京都狛江市中和泉5-40-12
Yasaburo Kuwayama
Kuwayama Design Room
5-40-12 Nakaizumi, Komae-shi,
Tokyo 201-0012
Tel. 03-3488-7717　Fax. 03-3488-7748

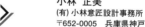
小林 茂二
キースタジオ
〒136-0072 東京都江東区大島3-32-12
東栄ビル303
Shigeji Kobayashi
Key Studio
Toei Bldg. 301 3-32-12 Ohojima,
Koto-ku, Tokyo 136-0072
Tel. 03-3636-1621　Fax. 03-3636-1622
E-mail: key-st@amie.or.jp

熊谷 淳一
(有) ノイエデザイン
〒107-0052 東京都港区赤坂7-6-15
赤坂ロイヤルビル301号
Junichi Kumagai
NOIE DESIGN Inc.
Akasaka Royal Bldg. 301 7-6-15 Akasaka,
Minato-ku, Tokyo 107-0052
Tel. 03-5575-6607　Fax. 03-5575-6609
E-mail: kumagai@j.email.ne.jp
http://www.ne.jp/asahi/noie/kuma/

合田 彰
(株) 博報堂
〒108-0023 東京都港区芝浦3-4-1
グランパークタワー
Akira Goda
HAKUHODO Inc.
Granpark Tower 3-4-1 Shibaura,
Minato-ku, Tokyo 108-0023
Tel. 03-5446-8855　Fax. 03-5446-8907

小林 正美
(有) 小林意匠設計事務所
〒652-0005 　兵庫県神戸市兵庫区矢部町21-5
Masami Kobayashi
Kobayashi Visual Design Office Inc.
21-5 Yabe-cho, Hyogo-ku,
kobe-shi, Hyogo 652-0005
Tel. 078-367-3795　Fax. 078-367-3796

熊野 晃子
クリエイト ASUKA
〒630-0133 奈良県生駒市あすか野南1-3-23
Teruko Kumano
CRETE ASUKA
1-3-23 Asukanominami,
Ikoma-shi, Nara 630-0133
Tel. 0743-79-9939　Fax. 0743-79-5077

古賀 美恵子
(有) エム・シー・シー
〒815-0071 福岡県福岡市南区平和2-6-3
デザインQ-ビル1F
Mieko Koga
M・C・C Inc.
Design-Q Bldg. 1F 2-6-3 Heiwa,
Minami-ku, Fukuoka 815-0071
Tel. 092-523-6449

小宮山 博史
佐藤タイポグラフィ研究所
〒221-0051 神奈川県横浜市神奈川区
幸ケ谷16-6
Hiroshi Komiyama
Sato Institute of Typography
16-6 Kogaya, Kanagawa-ku,
Yokohama-shi, Kanagawa 221-0051
Tel. 045-441-8191　Fax. 045-453-5091

七種 泰史
(株) デザインシグナル
〒150-0011 東京都渋谷区東2-26-16
HANAビル 6F
Yasushi Saikusa
DESIGN SIGNAL INC.
HANA Bldg. 6F 2-26-16 Higashi,
Shibuya-ku, Tokyo 150-0011
Tel. 03-5468-3100　Fax. 03-5468-1616
E-mail: yes-c@wd5.so-net.ne.jp

清水 清
(株) 清水ステュディオ
〒150-0002東京都渋谷区渋谷1-3-18
ビラモデルナB605
Kiyoshi Shimizu
Shimi's Studio Incorporated
Villa Moderna B605 1-3-18 Shibuya,
Shibuya-ku, Tokyo 150-0002
Tel. 03-3498-4231　Fax. 03-3498-4232
http://sente.epfl.ch/shimi/

鈴木 善博
B・BI STUDIO INC.
〒104-0041 東京都中央区新富1-2-13
OXSON 3F
Zempaku Suzuki
B・BI STUDIO INC.
OXSON Bldg. 3F 1-2-13 Shintomi,
Chuo-ku, Tokyo 104-0041
Tel. 03-3552-6960　Fax. 03-3552-6950
E-mail: bbibaby@tky2.3web.ne.jp

坂元 良弘
(株) エージー
〒104-0061 東京都中央区銀座1-6-5
ランディック第二銀座ビル
Yoshihiro Sakamoto
Az Inc.
Landic Daini Ginza Bldg. 1-6-5 Ginza,
Chuo-ku, Tokyo 104-0061
Tel. 03-3562-4917　Fax. 03-3564-2390
E-mail: sakamoto@azinc.co.jp

清水 智子
シミズプランニング
〒461-0002 愛知県名古屋市東区代官町34-20
鳥本ビル4F
Tomoko Shimizu
Shimizu Planning
Torimoto Bldg. 4F 34-20 Daikan-cho,
Higashi-ku, Nagoya 461-0002
Tel. 052-931-4631　Fax. 052-931-4651
E-mail: shimip@pp.iij4u.or.jp

ATELIER KEI
鈴木 正広
アトリエ・ケイ
〒151-0053 東京都渋谷区代々木2-23-1
ニューステートメナー1226号
Masahiro Suzuki
Aterier Kei
2-23-1-1226 Yoyogi,
Shibuya-ku, Tokyo 151-0053
Tel. 03-3375-8167　Fax. 03-3370-8767
E-mail: atelier@wa2.so-net.ne.jp
http://www03.u-page.so-net.ne.jp/wa2/atelier/

佐久間 年春
佐久間デザイン事務所
〒151-0051 東京都渋谷区千駄ヶ谷3-12-10
アピカ原宿セデュー305
Toshiharu Sakuma
Sakuma Design Office
#305 Apica Harajyuku Sedu
3-12-10 Sendagaya, Shibuya-ku,
Tokyo 151-0051
Tel. 03-3479-4406　Fax. 03-3402-8996

SLP DESIGNS
清水 雄介
SLP DESIGNS
〒151-0051 東京都渋谷区千駄ヶ谷4-1-8
桜渓フラット201
Yuuske Simiz
SLP DESIGNS
Ohkei Flat 201 4-1-8 Sendagaya,
Shibuya-ku, Tokyo 151-0051
Tel. Fax. 03-3405-5987
E-mail: slp@wc4.so-net.ne.jp

角 英夫
(株) アングル
〒631-0077 奈良県奈良市富雄川西1丁目17-1
Hideo Sumi
Angle Co.,Ltd.
1-17-1 Tomio, Kawanishi,
Nara 631-0077
Tel. 0742-49-8100　Fax. 0742-49-8101

佐藤 賢治
(株) WINDS
〒103-0016 東京都中央区日本橋小網町3-18
ヤナギホームズビル701・702
Kenji Sato
WINDS
Yanagi Homes Bldg. 701,702 3-18 Nihonbashi-
koamicho, Chuo-ku, Tokyo 103-0016
Tel. 03-3663-8039　Fax. 03-3663-5963
E-mail: k-winds@jb3.so-net.ne.jp

PABLOPRODUCTION
新谷 秀実
(株) パブロ
〒104-0041 東京都中央区新富1-7-3
阪和第2ビル9F
Hidemi Shingai
PABLO PRODUCTION Inc.
Hanwa 2nd. Bldg. 9F 1-7-3 Shintomi,
Chuo-ku, Tokyo 104-0041
Tel. 03-5541-5181　Fax. 03-5541-5183
E-mail: pablo@po.iijnet.or.jp

関 和廣
デザインルーム・アオイ
〒542-0073 大阪府大阪市中央区日本橋2-5-15
クボビル2F
Kazuhiro Seki
Design room Aoi
Kubo bldg. 2F 2-5-15 Nipponbashi,
Chuo-ku, Osaka 542-0073
Tel. 06-6643-5681　Fax. 06-6643-7651
E-mail: aoi00@skyblue.ocn.ne.jp

佐藤 充男
(株) アドテック
〒162-0825 東京都新宿区神楽坂2-22
かつ田ビル2F
Michio Sato
Ad. Tech Co.,Ltd.
Katsuta Bldg. 2F 2-22 Kagurazaka,
Shinjuku-ku, Tokyo 162-0825
Tel. 03-5261-5411　Fax. 03-5261-2004
E-mail: ad-teck@kb3.so-net.ne.jp

菅谷 貞雄
菅谷デザイン室
〒168-0064 東京都杉並区永福2-4-13
Sadao Sugaya
Sugaya Design Office Inc.
2-4-13 Eifuku, Suginami-ku,
Tokyo 168-0064
Tel. Fax. 03-3323-6337

関根 祐司
関根デザイン事務所
〒658-0072 兵庫県神戸市東灘区
岡本7-12-9-303
Yuji Sekine
Sekine Design
7-12-9-303 Okamoto, HIgashinada-ku,
Kobe-shi, Hyogo 658-0072
Tel. 078-452-3459　Fax. 078-452-3469
E-mail: sekined@osk2.3web.ne.jp

篠原 榮太
篠原榮太スタジオ
〒151-0051 東京都渋谷区千駄ケ谷3-5-12
Eita Shinohara
Shinohara Eita Studio
3-5-12 Sendagaya, Shibuya-ku,
Tokyo 151-0051
Tel. 03-3470-2832　Fax. 03-5474-2849

杉崎 真之助
(有) 真之助事務所
〒540-0035 大阪府大阪市中央区釣鐘町2-1-8
都住創釣鐘町602
Shinnoske Sugisaki
Shinnoske Inc.
Tojuso Tsuriganecho 602 2-1-8
Tsuriganecho, Chuo-Ku, Osaka 540-0035
Tel. 06-6943-9077　Fax. 06-6943-9078
E-mail: shinn@shinn.co.jp
http://www.shinn.co.jp/

瀬野 敏春
デザインボックス・セノ
〒358-0002 埼玉県入間市東町3-4-8
Toshiharu Seno
Design Box Seno
3-4-8 Azuma-cho, Iruma-shi,
Saitama 358-0002
Tel. 042-963-2304　Fax. 042-963-9363

園原 稲雄
園原稲雄デザイン室
〒112-0013 東京都文京区音羽2-1-6-1005
Toshio Sonohara
Sonohara Toshio Design Studio
2-1-6-1005 Otowa, Bunkyo-ku,
Tokyo 112-0013
Tel. 03-3944-6466　Fax. 03-5940-5056

高原　宏
高原 宏デザイン事務所
〒107-0062 東京都港区南青山1-15-22
ヴィラ乃木坂305
Hiroshi Takahara
Takahara Hiroshi Design Office Inc.
1-15-22-305 Minamiaoyama,
Minato-ku, Tokyo 107-0062
Tel. 03-3404-9963　Fax. 03-3404-9727
E-mail: YRL03026@niftyserve.or.jp

goi
棚瀬 伸司
グランドキャニオンエンタテインメント (株)
〒500-8237 岐阜県岐阜市切通4-19-3
Shinji Tanase
Grand-Canyon Entertainment
4-19-3 Kiridoshi, Gifu 500-8237
Tel. 058-248-5256　Fax. 058-248-5257
E-mail: geitanase@ma4.justnet.ne.jp

染谷 淳一
(有) ヘッド・バット
〒150-0011 東京都渋谷区東1-27-10
東海ビル4F
Junichi Someya
HEAD BUTT co,.inc.
1-27-10 Higashi, Shibuya-ku,
Tokyo 150-0011
Tel. 03-3409-7397　Fax. 03-3406-5857

滝 政美
滝書体デザイン室
〒196-0031 東京都昭島市福島町3-10-11
Masami Taki
Taki Typeface Design Room
3-10-11 Fukujima-cho, Akishima-shi,
Tokyo 196-0031
Tel. Fax. 042-544-1789

ボナード・チャン
Bernard Chung
HEXA COMMUNICATIONS
7-30 Tongeui - Dong, Chongro - ku,
Seoul, 110 - 040, KOREA
Tel. 82-2-735-7700　Fax. 82-2-735-7705

高田 雄吉
(有) CID研究所
〒540-0026 大阪府大阪市中央区内本町2-4-3-603
Yukichi Takada
CID Lab. Inc.
2-4-3-603 Uchihonmachi, Chuo-ku,
Osaka 540-0026
Tel. 06-6949-0853　Fax. 06-6949-0854
E-mail: cid-lab@gc4.so-net.ne.jp

武士 伸
武士デザイン事務所
〒101-0047 東京都千代田区内神田2-10-3
Shin Takeshi
Takeshi Design Office
2-10-3 Uchikanda, Chiyoda-ku,
Tokyo 101-0011
Tel. 03-3252-6026　Fax. 03-3256-8944

鶴田 栄里
鶴田デザイン事務所
〒640-8355 和歌山県和歌山市北の新地2-21
ワンダーランドPart2　3F
Eri Tsuruta
Tsuruta Design Office
Wonderland Part2. 3F 2-21 kitanoshinchi,
Wakayama 640-8355
Tel. Fax. 073-432-6997
E-mail: tsuruta@gold.ocn.ne.jp

FACE
高橋 健次
(株) フェイス
〒106-0046 東京都港区元麻布3-4-41
麻布台ナショナルコート302号
Kenji Takahashi
Face
Azabudai Nationalcourt 302 3-4-41
Motoazabu, Minato-ku, Tokyo 106-0046
Tel. 03-3405-7622　Fax. 03-3405-7912
E-mail: bm2k-tkhs@asahi-net.or.jp

田島 一夫
(有) もりやけん企画室
〒201-0003 東京都狛江市和泉本町3-35-2
Kazuo Tajima
Moriya Ken Planning Ltd.
3-35-2 Izumihoncho, Komae-shi,
Tokyo 201-0003
Tel. Fax. 03-3480-3088

戸田 武雄
ライオン (株) 広告制作部デザイン室
〒130-0015 東京都墨田区横網1-2-22
Takeo Toda
Lion Corporation Creative Department
1-2-22 Yokoami, Sumida-ku,
Tokyo 130-0015
Tel. 03-3621-6646　Fax. 03-3621-6659
E-mail: todatake@lion.co.jp

高橋 善丸
(株) 広告丸
〒530-0052 大阪府大阪市北区南扇町7-2
ユニ東梅田507
Yoshimaru Takahashi
Koukokumaru Inc.
Uni-higasiumeda 507 7-2 Minamiogimachi,
Kita-ku, Osaka 530-0052
Tel. 06-6314-0881　Fax. 06-6314-0806
E-mail: y-5590@ra2.so-net.ne.jp

gDS
田中 如水
(株) ガルデザインシステム
〒604-8106 京都府京都市中京区御池通堺町670-1
吉岡御池ビル9F
Naomi Tanaka
Gull Design System inc.
Yoshioka Oike Bldg. 9F 670-1 Oikedori,
Sakai-machi, Nakagyo-ku, Kyoto 604-8106
Tel. 075-211-8895　Fax. 075-211-8896
E-mail: gullds@ka2.so-net.ne.jp

Tomo!s
トモ・ヒコ
Tomo!s
〒180-0002 東京都武蔵野市吉祥寺東町2-43-15
Tomo Hiko
Tomo's
2-43-15 Kichijoji-higashicho,
Musashino-shi, Tokyo 180-0002
Tel. Fax. 0422-23-1951
E-mail: tomos@sd5.so-net.ne.jp
http://www08.u-page.so-net.ne.jp/sd5/tomos/

高原 新一
(有) たかデザインプロダクション
〒063-0802 札幌市西区二十四軒2条1-1-57
Shinichi Takahara
Taka Design Production
2-1-1-57 Nijuyonken, Nishi-ku,
Sapporo 063-0802
Tel.011-644-4677　Fax. 011-644-4680

田中 正行
(株) 創美
〒336-0007 埼玉県浦和市仲町4-2-22
Masayuki Tanaka
SOHBI inc.
4-2-22 Naka-cho, Urawa-shi,
Saitama 336-0007
Tel. 048-864-1718　Fax. 048-865-1392
E-mail: image@cml.cyborg.or.jp

豊川 研一
〒553-0001 大阪府大阪市福島区海老江3-8-1
Kenichi Toyokawa
3-8-1 Ebie, Fukushima-ku,
Osaka 553-0001
Tel. Fax. 06-6451-0653

ナガイ 毅
ナガイ毅創作室
〒732-0031 広島県広島市
東区馬木5-1687-10
Tsuyoshi Nagai
Nagai tsuyoshi sousakushitu
5-1687-10 Umaki, Higashi-ku,
Hiroshima 730-0031
Tel. Fax. 082-899-7167
E-mail: nagai@nichibi.co.jp

 中山 泰次郎
(株) スタヂオ・ユニ
〒160-0022 東京都新宿区新宿1-16-10
コスモス御苑ビル4F
Taijiro Nakayama
STUDIO UNI Corporation
Cosmos Gyoen Bldg. 4F 1-16-10 Shinjuku,
Shinjuku-ku, Tokyo 160-0022
Tel. 03-3341-0141   Fax. 03-3341-0145
E-mail: info@stuni.co.jp

 西川 泰司
クリエイティブ コミュニケーションズ キッズ
〒530-0036 大阪府大阪市北区与力町7-11
グランドメゾン与力町501
Taiji Nishikawa
Creative Communications Kids
Grande maison yoriki-machi 501
7-11 Yoriki-machi, Kita-ku, Osaka 530-0036
Tel. 06-6882-0830   Fax. 06-6355-2665
E-mail: kids@osk.3web.ne.jp

 中尾 よしもり
中尾デザイン事務所
〒530-0043 大阪府大阪市北区天満3-12-19
岩井町セブン101・501
Yoshimori Nakao
Nakao Design Room
Iwaicho Seven 501・101 3-12-19 Tenma,
Kita-ku, Osaka 530-0043
Tel. 06-6351-4887   Fax. 06-6351-4648

 成澤 正信
(有) エムズスタジオ
〒150-0031 東京都渋谷区桜丘町14-6
黒松ビル403
Masanobu Narusawa
M's Studio INC.
Koromatsu Bldg. 403 14-6 Sakuragaoka-cho,
Shibuya-ku, Tokyo 150-0031
Tel. 03-5456-8137   Fax. 03-5456-8138
E-mail: narusawa@da2.so-net.ne.jp
http://www02.so-net.ne.jp/˜narusawa/

 西田 一成
デザインソースショップ・カズン
〒151-0064 東京都渋谷区上原3-20-2-C
Kazunari Nishida
Design Source Shop KAZUN
3-20-2-C Uehara,
Shibuya-ku, Tokyo 151-0064
Tel. 03-5465-7177   Fax. 03-5465-7178
E-mail: kazun@ra2.so-net.ne.jp

 中川 憲造
(株) NDCグラフィックス
〒104-0061 東京都中央区銀座1-13-13
Kenzo Nakagawa
NDC Graphics Inc.
1-13-13 Ginza, Chuo-ku, Tokyo 104-0061
Tel. 03-3567-3507   Fax. 03-5250-7364
E-mail: kenzo@gx.ndc.co.jp
http://www.pictor.co.jp/ndc-graphics/

 名和 千明
(有) スペンサー・デザインスタジオ
〒862-0952 熊本県熊本市京塚本町5-13-2F
Chiaki Nawa
Spenser Design Studio Inc.
5-13-2F Kyozuka, Honmachi,
Kumamoto 862-0952
Tel. 096-385-4572   Fax. 096-385-4573
E-mail: spenser@bronze.ocn.ne.jp

 西田 まさを
(株) ユニグラフィック
〒659-0016 兵庫県芦屋市親王塚町13-10
Masao Nishida
Uni Graphic Corporation
13-10 Shinnozuka-cho, Ashiya-shi,
Hyogo 659-0016
Tel. 0797-31-5100   Fax. 0797-31-5105

 中島 安貴輝
アートアンドグラフィック
〒151-0051 東京都渋谷区千駄ケ谷1-3-10
Akiteru Nakajima
Art & Graphic Associates
1-3-10 Sendagaya, Shibuya-ku, Tokyo 151-0051
Tel. 03-3403-5567   Fax. 03-3403-5568
日本大学芸術学部デザイン学科
Tel. 03-5955-8235
E-mail: nakajima@ekoda.art.nihon-u.ac.jp

 南部 俊安
(有) テイスト
〒572-0825 大阪府寝屋川市萱島南町18-10
Toshiyasu Nanbu
Taste Inc.
18-10 Kayashima-minamicho,
Neyagawa-shi, Osaka 572-0825
Tel. 072-824-5538   Fax. 072-824-5583
E-mail: tasteinc@osk.3web.or.jp

西本 和民
(株) ウォーズ
〒150-0012 東京都渋谷区広尾2-3-6
Kazutami Nishimoto
Wars. Inc.
2-3-6 Hiroo, Shibuya-ku, Tokyo 150-0012
Tel. 03-3406-3828   Fax. 03-3406-3254

Polygon ナカノマサオ
(株) ポリゴン
〒158-0092 東京都世田谷区野毛1-7-7
グリーンパレス等々力202
Masao Nakano
Polygon inc.
Greenpalace Todoroki 202
1-7-7 Noge, Setagaya-ku, Tokyo 158-0092
Tel. 03-5758-3073   Fax. 03-5758-3074
E-mail: nakano@polygon.to

仁木 健章
(株) ケイツーアソシエート
〒862-0962 熊本県熊本市田迎4-9-50
Kensho Niki
K・two Associate Co.,Ltd.
4-9-50 Tamukae, Kumamoto 862-0962
Tel. 096-370-1881   Fax. 096-370-1902
E-mail: k-2-idea@inworld.ne.jp

西森 桜子
(有) デュオ
〒606-8393 京都府京都市左京区東竹屋町通
川端東入東竹屋町75-8
Sakurako Nishimori
Duo Inc.
75-8 Higashitakeya-cho, Sakyo-ku,
Kyoto 606-8393
Tel. 075-762-0275   Fax. 075-762-0276

 中野 義三
クリエイティブ オフィス アウリット
〒543-0073 大阪府大阪市天王寺区
生玉寺町4-9-101
Yoshizo Nakano
Creative Office Owlet
4-9-101 Ikutamateramachi, Tennoji-ku,
Osaka 543-0073
Tel. Fax. 06-6773-3006
E-mail: yw2y-nkn@asahi-net.or.jp

 西川 征燿
クレアール デザイン オフィス
〒921-8155 石川県金沢市高尾台2-259-2
Seiyoh Nishikawa
Crear Design Office
2-259-2 Takaodai, Kanazawa 921-8155
Tel. Fax. 076-298-8900

二宮 浩
(株) ヴィッタ
〒810-0022 福岡県福岡市中央区薬院3-12-10
ネオハイツ薬院215
Hiroshi Ninomiya
Vitaa Design Co.,Ltd.
Neo Heights Yakuin 215 3-12-10 Yakuin,
Chuo-ku, Fukuoka 810-0022
Tel. 092-521-9666   Fax. 092-521-9677

野上 周一
(有) 野上デザイン事務所
〒532-0011 大阪府大阪市淀川区西中島5-7-14
大京ビル1F 103
Shuichi Nogami
Nogami Design Office
Daikyo Bldg. 103 5-7-14 Nishinakajima,
Yodogawa-ku, Osaka 532-0011
Tel. 06-6300-1009 Fax. 06-6300-1041
E-mail: ndo@kf6.so-net.ne.jp

 長谷川 眞策
(株) ゼロ
〒106-0042 東京都港区麻布狸穴町47
麻布東急アパート71号
Shinsaku Hasegawa
ZERO Corporation
Azabu Tokyu Apartment 71 47 Mamiana-cho,
Azabu, Minato-ku, Tokyo 106-0042
Tel. 03-3505-6787 Fax. 03-3505-6797
E-mail: zero-co@ja2.so-net.ne.jp

 林 廣行
(株) グラフィクス アンド デザイニング
〒108-0071 東京都港区白金台3-3-1
G&Dアルケミックハウス
Hiroyuki Hayashi
Graphics & Designing Inc.
G & D Alchemic House 3-3-1 Shirokanedai,
Minato-ku, Tokyo 108-0071
Tel. 03-3449-0651 Fax. 03-3449-0653

 延山 博保
(株) NDCグラフィックス
〒104-0061 東京都中央区銀座1-13-13
Hiroyasu Nobuyama
NDC Graphics Inc.
1-13-13 Ginza, Chuo-ku, Tokyo 104-0061
Tel. 03-3567-3508 Fax. 03-5250-7364
http://www.pictor.co.jp/ndc-graphics/

長谷川 純雄
長谷川デザイン研究室
〒169-0051 東京都新宿区西早稲田1-9-13
ダイヤハイツ西早稲田505号
Sumio Hasegawa
Hasegawa Design Room
1-9-13-505 Nishiwaseda, Shinjuku-ku,
Tokyo 169-0051
Tel. Fax. 03-5272-1817

原 征夫
(有) バウハウス
〒840-0806 佐賀県佐賀市神園5-4-9
Yukuo Hara
Bauhaus
5-4-9 Kamizono, Saga 840-0806
Tel. 0952-32-0031 Fax. 0952-33-2284

 野間 卓克
(有) ボックス
〒160-0001 東京都新宿区片町2-4 菱和ビル7F
Takayoshi Noma
BOX Design Co.,Ltd.
2-4 7F Katamachi, Shinjuku-ku,
Tokyo 160-0001
Tel. 03-3341-5428 Fax. 03-3341-5453
E-mail: boxd@mb.infoweb.ne.jp

 畠山 敏
畠山敏デザイン事務所
〒980-0804 宮城県仙台市青葉区大町2-3-12
大町マンション2F
Satoshi Hatakeyama
Satoshi Hatakeyama Design Office
Omachi Bldg. 2F 2-3-12 Omachi,
Sendai-shi, Miyagi 980-0804
Tel. 022-262-1648 Fax. 022-268-7985
E-mail: hata-d@jade.dti.ne.jp

原口 公彦
(有) バウハウス
〒840-0806 佐賀県佐賀市神園5-4-9
Kimihiko Haraguchi
Bauhaus
5-4-9 Kamizono, Saga 840-0806
Tel. 0952-32-0031 Fax. 0952-33-2284

野村 欣司
(株) 日本SPプランニング
〒550-0004 大阪府大阪市西区靭本町2-4-1
靭本町下村ビル3F
Kinji Nomura
NIPPON SP PLANNING CO., LTD.
Utsubo Honmachi Shimomura Bldg. 3F 2-4-1
Utsubo Honmachi, Nishi-ku, Osaka 550-0004
Tel. 06-6444-0863 Fax. 06-6444-9033
E-mail: nspcoltd@mbox.inet-osaka.or.jp

馬場 雄二
(株) ユニ・デザイン
〒108-0073 東京都港区三田5-7-8-501
Yuji Baba
Uni Design Inc.
5-7-8-501 Mita, Minato-ku, Tokyo 108-0073
Tel. 03-3451-5970 Fax. 03-3456-3631
E-mail: babayuji@poplar.ocn.ne.jp

原田 政忠
〒555-0001 大阪府大阪市西淀川区佃5-6-37
Masatada Harada
5-6-37 Tsukuda, Nishiyodogawa-ku,
Osaka 555-0001
Tel. Fax. 06-6477-0332

白子 正人
フロムホワイト
〒565-0853 大阪府吹田市春日4-2-1
緑地公園グランドハイツ407
Masato Hakushi
from White Inc.
Ryokuchi Koen Grand Heights 407
4-2-1 Kasuga, Suita-shi, Osaka 565-0853
Tel. 06-6338-7764 Fax. 06-6338-2932
E-mail: hakushi@alles.or.jp
http://www.hakushi.com/

馬場崎 仁
(株) オブリーク
〒107-0061 東京都港区北青山3-8-8
カーム青山1F
Hitoshi Babasaki
Oblique Inc.
Calm Aoyama 1F 3-8-8 Kitaaoyama,
Minato-ku, Tokyo 107-0061
Tel. 03-5467-8231 Fax. 03-5467-8234

針生 実
ハリウ
〒151-0073 東京都渋谷区笹塚2-38-11-602
Minoru Haryu
Hariu
2-38-11-602 Sasazuka,
Shibuya-ku, Tokyo 151-0073
Tel. 03-3370-7815/03-3378-1519
Fax. 03-3370-7815
E-mail: hariu-m@yc4.so-net.ne.jp

 橋ケ谷 佳正
岡山大学教育学部
〒700-8530 岡山県岡山市津島中3-1-1
Yoshimasa Hashigaya
Okayama University
3-1-1 Tsushima-naka, Okayama 700-8530
Tel. Fax. 086-251-7659
E-mail: h1952712@cc.okayama-u.ac.jp

 早川 さよ子
(有) 栗八商店
〒106-0032 東京都港区六本木3-15-29
Sayoko Hayakawa
Kurihachi Shoten Co.,Ltd.
3-15-29 Roppongi, Minato-ku,
Tokyo 106-0032
Tel. 03-3505-5431 Fax. 03-3505-5433

 治田 育美
(株) ワッチマン
〒530-0044 大阪府大阪市北区東天満2-3-9
Ikumi Haruta
WATCHMAN INC.
2-3-9 Higashitenma,
Kita-ku, Osaka 530-0044
Tel. 06-6353-2944 Fax. 06-6353-3082

樋川 ゆき
アポロスタジオ
〒150-0031 東京都渋谷区桜丘町7-8
ハイツ桜丘305
Yuki Hikawa
apollo studio
Hights Sakuragaoka #305 7-8 Sakuragaoka-cho,
Shibuya-ku, Tokyo 150-0031
Tel. 03-3464-8306　Fax. 03-3464-1970

樋口 清孝
(株) 大広インテレクト
〒105-8533 東京都港区芝公園2-4-1
Kiyotaka Higuchi
DAIKO INTELLECT INC.
2-4-1 Shiba-Koen, Minato-ku,
Tokyo 105-8533
Tel. 03-5400-1423　Fax. 03-3433-3199
E-mail: air@eyelove.org
http://eyelove.org/

樋口 真貴
〒151-0053 東京都渋谷区代々木3-36-5
Maki Higuchi
3-36-5 Yoyogi, Shibuya-ku,
Tokyo 151-0053
Tel. 03-3379-0537　Fax. 03-3370-1723

平田 稔
岡山県立大学 デザイン学部
〒719-1197 岡山県総社市窪木111
Minoru Hirata
Okayama Prefectural University
111 Kuboki, Soja-shi,
Okayama 719-1197
Tel. 0866-94-2111　Fax. 0866-94-2201

平松 多久志
(有) エム・ティー・ティー
〒700-0936 岡山県岡山市富田413-4
プラザビル富田201
Takushi Hiramatsu
MTT Co.,Ltd.
Plaza Bldg. Tomita 201
413-4 Tomita, Okayama 700-0936
Tel. 086-227-4012　Fax. 086-227-4013
E-mail: fons@po.harenet.or.jp

平山 政根
(株) アイドマ 東京事務所
〒150-0001 東京都渋谷区神宮前6-25-8
神宮前コーポラス404
Masamoto Hirayama
Aidma Inc.
6-25-8-404 Jingumae,
Shibuya-ku, Tokyo 150-0001
Tel. 03-3406-0423　Fax. 03-3486-9131
E-mail: hirayams@sepia.ocn.ne.jp

広瀬 憲一
広瀬憲一デザイン事務所
〒175-0082 東京都板橋区高島平3-11-7-1104
Kenichi Hirose
Hirose Kenichi Design Office
3-11-7-1104 Takashimadaira,
Itabashi-ku, Tokyo 175-0082
Tel. 03-3938-6905　Fax. 03-3938-6649

広瀬 弘之
〒563-0123 大阪府豊能郡能勢町
下田尻227-284
Hiroyuki Hirose
227-284 Shimotajiri, Nose-cho,
Toyono-gun, Osaka 563-0123
Tel. Fax. 0727-35-2580

深井 和子
(有) 深井デザイン事務所
〒942-0071 新潟県上越市東雲町2丁目6-39
Kazuko Fukai
Fukai Design Office
2-6-39 Touncho, Joetsu-shi,
Niigata 942-0071
Tel. 0255-44-1991　Fax. 0255-45-1633

深井 宏一
(株) エージー
〒104-0061 東京都中央区銀座1-6-5
ランディック第2ビル
Koichi Fukai
Az Inc.
Landic Daini Ginza Bldg.
1-6-5 Ginza, Chuo-ku, Tokyo 104-0061
Tel. 03-3562-4918　Fax. 03-3564-2390

深野 稔生
(株) 深野プロ
〒980-0021 宮城県仙台市青葉区中央2-9-1
河西ビル3F
Toshio Fukano
Fukano Pro. Co.,LTD.
Kawanishi Bldg. 3F 2-9-1 Chuo,
Aoba-ku, Sendai-shi, Miyagi 980-0021
Tel. 022-262-5974(代)　Fax. 022-265-7839

藤井 陽一郎
Bakery 37.1 藤井陽一郎デザイン事務所
〒150-0001 東京都渋谷区神宮前1-22-1
オークラビル3F
Yoichiro Fujii
Bakery37.1 Yoichirou Fujii Design Studio
Ohkura Bldg. 3F 1-22-1 Jingumae,
Shibuya-ku, Tokyo 150-0001
Tel. 03-3796-6315　Fax. 03-3796-6316

藤田 隆
サントリー (株) デザイン部
〒530-0004 大阪府大阪市北区堂島2-1-5
サントリーアネックス6F
Takashi Fujita
Suntory Limited.
Suntory Annex 6F 2-1-5 Dojima,
Kita-ku, Osaka 530-0004
Tel. 06-6346-1140　Fax. 06-6346-1697
E-mail: takashi_fujita@suntory.co.jp

藤田 努
(株) ウォーク
〒150-0036 東京都渋谷区南平台町4-8
南平台アジアマンション609
Tsutomu Fujita
Walk Inc.
Nanpeidai Asia Mansion 609 4-8
Nanpeidaicho, Shibuya-ku,Tokyo 150-0036
Tel. 03-3476-3570　Fax. 03-3476-1383
E-mail: walk@mtg.biglobe.ne.jp

藤野 真弘
(株) ウェイヴインターナショナル
〒530-0057 大阪府大阪市北区曽根崎2丁目5-10
梅田パシフィックビル11F
Masahiro Fujino
WAVE INTERNATIONAL CO.,LTD.
Umeda Pacific Bldg. 11F 2-5-10 Sonezaki,
Kita-ku ,Osaka 530-0057
Tel. 06-6362-1222 (代)　Fax. 06-6362-1221
E-mail: fujino@mail.wave-int.co.jp

布施 茂
〒351-0036 埼玉県朝霞市北原1-11-28
Shigeru Fuse
1-11-28 Kitahara, Asaka-shi,
Saitama 351-0036
Tel. 048-471-2597　Fax. 048-471-2906
E-mail: fuseruasa@ma4.justnet.ne.jp

細田 ひろし
細田ひろしデザイン事務所
〒468-0054 愛知県名古屋市天白区横町702
天白住宅4-102
Hiroshi Hosoda
Hosoda Hiroshi Design Office
4-102・702 Yokomachi, Tenpaku-ku,
Nagoya 468-0054
Tel. Fax. 052-805-7883

前出 勝人
(株) オフィスクラフト
〒550-0014 大阪府大阪市西区北堀江1-12-9
パークコート北堀江505
Katsuto Maede
Office Craft
Park Court Kitahorie 505
1-12-9 Kitahorie, Nishi-ku, Osaka 550-0014
Tel. 06-6534-1833　Fax. 06-6534-1835
E-mail: craft@pop01.odn.ne.jp

正木 茂
正木デザイン事務所
〒541-0046 大阪府大阪市中央区平野町3-3-7
ニューライフ平野町302
Shigeru Masaki
Masaki Design Office
New Life Hiranomachi 302
3-3-7 Hiranomachi, Chuo-ku, Osaka 541-0046
Tel. 06-6229-1578 Fax. 06-6229-2578
E-mail: masakide@osk.3web.ne.jp

増田 誠二
(株) 岡山毎日広告社
〒700-0824 岡山県岡山市内山下1-3-1
Seiji Masuda
Okayama Mainichi Advertising Inc.
1-3-1 Uchisange, Okayama 700-0824
Tel. 086-231-9031 Fax. 086-226-0952
E-mail: masuda@maico.co.jp

FADIMO
Innovative Visual Communication
松石 博幸
(株) ファディモ
〒807-0822 福岡県北九州市八幡西区
瀬板1-16-1
Hiroyuki Matsuishi
Fadimo Corporation
1-16-1 Seita, Yahatanishi-ku,
Kitakyushu 807-0822
Tel. 093-692-5005 Fax. 093-692-3003
E-mail: matsuishi@fadimo.osk.co.jp

松岡 史郎
大日本印刷 (株)
〒530-0004 大阪府大阪市北区堂島浜2-2-28
堂島アクシスビル10F
Shiro Matsuoka
Dainippon Printing Co.,Ltd.
Dojima AXIS Bldg. 10F 2-2-28 Dojimahama,
Kita-ku, Osaka 530-0004
Tel. 06-6341-1690 Fax. 06-6341-2615
E-mail: matsuoka-s@mail.dnp.co.jp

松木 良介
(株) ネプトーン
〒860-0843 熊本県熊本市草葉町2-28-1201
Ryosuke Matsuki Neptune corporation
2-28-1201 Kusabacho,
Kumamoto 860-0843
Tel. 096-322-7371 Fax. 096-322-7365

松原 邦生
松原邦生デザイン事務所
〒358-0053 埼玉県入間市仏子603-1, 11-101
Kunio Matsubara
Matsubara Kunio Design Office
603-1・11-101 Bushi, Iruma-shi,
Saitama 358-0053
Tel. 0429-32-3712 Fax. 0429-32-6254

松吉 太郎
松吉太郎デザイン事務所
〒107-0062 東京都港区南青山5-17-6
青山グリーンハイツ306号
Taro Matsuyoshi
TARO DESIGN
5-17-6-306 Minamiaoyama, Minato-ku,
Tokyo 107-0062
Tel. 03-5469-5315 Fax. 03-5469-5320

丸山 剛
〒193-0944 東京都八王子市館町486-20
Tsuyoshi Maruyama
486-20 Tatemachi, Hachioji-shi,
Tokyo 193-0944
Tel. 0426-62-5232 Fax. 0426-63-4613
E-mail: maru4837@fa2.so-net.ne.jp

三浦 敏
(株) マクロス
〒983-0852 宮城県仙台市宮城野区
榴岡1-6-3 ホーゲツビル3F
Satoshi Miura
Macros Ltd.
1-6-3-3F Tsutsujigaoka, Miyagino-ku,
Sendai-shi, Miyagi 983-0852
Tel. 022-293-3223 Fax. 022-293-3222
E-mail: m@macros-net.co.jp
http://www.macros-net.co.jp/

三木 健
三木健デザイン事務所
〒530-0041 大阪府大阪市北区天神橋1丁目3-4
中之島フラッツ601・602
Ken Miki
Ken Miki & Associates
Nakanoshima Flats 601・602
1-3-4 Tenjinbashi, Kita-ku, Osaka 530-0041
Tel. 06-6358-5270 Fax. 06-6358-1785
E-mail: ken-miki@pop11.odn.jp

水井 正
水井正デザイン室
〒358-0011 埼玉県入間市下藤沢1314-3
ダイアパレス武蔵藤沢604号室
Tadashi Mizui
Mizui Tadashi Design Room
1314-3-604 Shimofujisawa,
Iruma-shi, Saitama 358-0011
Tel. 042-965-0926 Fax. 042-962-4540

道吉 剛
(株) 道吉デザイン研究室
〒150-0002 東京都渋谷区渋谷1-1-3
三河屋青山ビル7F
Gow Michiyoshi
Michiyoshi Design Laboratory Inc.
Mikawaya Aoyama Bldg. 7F
1-1-3 Shibuya, Shibuya-ku, Tokyo 150-0002
Tel. 03-3409-5955・5956 Fax. 03-3409-5824
E-mail: mitiyosi@cc.mbn.or.jp

峰尾 裕己
(株) マゼンタ
〒150-0022 東京都渋谷区恵比寿南3-10-12
渋谷原町アビタシオン502
Hiroshi Mineo
Magenta Inc.
502 Shibuya Haramachi Habitation 3-10-12
Ebisu-Minami, Shibuya-ku, Tokyo 150-0022
Tel. 03-5721-8371 Fax. 03-5721-8377

MIYAKE
三宅 康文
(有) ティーディーアイ
〒162-0827 東京都新宿区若宮町31-2
市ケ谷若宮町ロイヤルコーポ107・108
Yasubumi Miyake
TDI Inc.
31-2-107・108 Wakamiyacho,
Sinjuku-ku, Tokyo 162-0827
Tel. 03-3267-6521 Fax. 03-3267-6685

宮坂 克己
(有) ケイアタック
〒106-0031 東京都港区西麻布1-8-20
エメロード西麻布3F
Katsumi Miyasaka
K-Attack Inc.
Emeraude Nishiazabu 3F 1-8-20 Nishiazabu,
Minato-ku, Tokyo 106-0031
Tel. 03-3408-1737 Fax. 03-5413-6551
E-mail: katsumiy@mx2.alpha-web.ne.jp

宮崎 利一
(有) スタジオM42
〒542-0081 大阪府大阪市中央区南船場4-10-21
大阪屋エコービル408
Toshikazu Miyazaki
Studio M42 Inc.
Osakaya Eko Bldg. 408 4-10-21
Minamisemba, Chuo-ku, Osaka 541-0081
Tel. 06-6244-0260 Fax. 06-6244-0460
E-mail: m42@osk2.3web.ne.jp

宮野 一男
(株) ピービー・グラフィックス
〒980-0804 宮城県仙台市青葉区大町2-3-12
大町ビル2F
Kazuo Miyano
P・B Graphics
Ohmachi Bldg. 2F 2-3-12 Ohmachi,
Aoba-ku, Sendai-shi, Miyagi 980-0804
Tel. 022-711-4566 Fax. 022-711-4560
E-mail: miya@nn.iij4u.or.jp

MIYOSHI
DESIGN
OFFICE
三吉 隆
三吉デザイン室
〒570-0015 大阪府守口市梶町3-57-1-110
Takashi Miyoshi
Miyoshi Design Office
3-57-1-110 Kajimachi, Moriguchi-shi,
Osaka 570-0015
Tel. Fax. 06-6904-5990

ART SYSTEM
武藤 正彦
(株) アートシステム
〒010-0921 秋田県秋田市大町4-4-15
農業会館別館1階
Masahiko Muto
Art System Co.,Ltd.
Agriculture-hall Annex. 1F
4-4-15 Ohmachi, Akita 010-0921
Tel. 018-863-2652　Fax. 018-865-4078

 YAGI CREATION
八木 是和
(株) ヤギクリエーション
〒537-0025 大阪府大阪市東成区中道4-11-19
Yoshikazu Yagi
Yagi Creation Co.,Ltd.
4-11-9 Nakamichi,
Higashinari-ku, Osaka 537-0025
Tel. 06-6977-1571 (代)　Fax. 06-6977-1573
E-mail: yagi-cr@msc.biglobe.ne.jp

YDR
山田 米英
(有) 山田デザイン室
〒215-0027 神奈川県川崎市麻生区岡上10
カリヨンカネカ102
Yonefusa Yamada
Yamada Design Room
Kariyonkaneka 102 10 Okagami,
Aso-ku, Kawasaki 215-0027
Tel. Fax. 044-987-7572

STUFF
村上 三千朗
(有) スタッフ
〒030-0852 青森県青森市大野字若宮110-11
Michiro Murakami
Stuff Ltd.
110-11 Wakamiya Aza, Ono, Aomori 030-0852
Tel. 0177-29-4671　Fax. 0177-29-4641

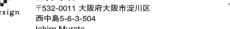
山口 至剛
(有) 山口至剛デザイン室
〒150-0002 東京都渋谷区渋谷4-3-13
常磐松葵マンション906号
Shigo Yamaguchi
Shigo Yamaguchi Design Room Co.,Ltd.
Tokiwamatsu Aoi Bldg. 906 4-3-13 Shibuya,
Shibuya-ku, Tokyo 150-0002
Tel. 03-3486-1052　Fax. 03-3486-1053

山本 敦
(有) ネオス
〒940-0033 新潟県長岡市今朝白3-16-23
Atsushi Yamamoto
NEOS
3-16-23 Kesajiro, Nagaoka-shi,
Niigata 904-0033
Tel. 0258-33-8836　Fax. 0258-33-8837
E-mail: neosdesign@mail.mynet.or.jp

 u:design
村田 一郎
ユウデザイン
〒532-0011 大阪府大阪市淀川区
西中島5-6-3-504
Ichiro Murata
Yu Design
5-6-3-504 Nishinakajima,
Yodogawa-ku, Osaka 532-0011
Tel. 06-6304-3054　Fax. 06-6304-3064
E-mail: udesign@osk3.3web.ne.jp

NICK CREATIVE GROUP
山口 哲雄
(株) デザインスタジオ ニック
〒102-0085 東京都千代田区六番町3-20
佐藤ビル1.2.3.F
Tetsuo Yamaguchi
Design Studio NICK Inc.
Sato Bldg. 2F 3-20 Rokuban-cho, Chiyoda-ku,
Tokyo 102-0085
Tel. 03-3234-2229 (代)　Fax. 03-3237-1299 (代)
E-mail: nick-co@ra2.so-net.ne.jp

山本 洋司
(株) 日本デザインセンター
〒104-0061 東京都中央区銀座1-13-13
中央大和ビル
Yoji Yamamoto
Nippon Design Center
Chuo Daiwa Bldg. 1-13-13 Ginza,
Chuo-ku, Tokyo 104-0061
Tel. 03-3567-3542　Fax. 03-3564-9445
E-mail: yamamoto@ndc.co.jp

MZ GRAPHIC
村田 満
エムズグラフィック
〒862-0975 熊本県熊本市新屋敷3-1-9
フローラル新屋敷202
Mitsuru Murata
MZ GRAPHIC
3-1-9-202 Shinyashiki,
Kumamoto 862-0975
Tel. 096-372-4346　Fax. 096-372-4347
E-mail: mzg@try-net.or.jp

山口 信博
山口デザイン事務所
〒107-0062 東京都港区南青山4-17-12
クレセント青山206
Nobuhiro Yamaguchi
Yamaguchi Design Office
206 Crescent Aoyama 4-17-12 Minamiaoyama,
Minato-ku, Tokyo 107-0062
Tel. 03-3405-8480　Fax. 03-3405-8281

吉田 修一
(有) アルファ
〒102-0074 東京都千代田区九段南3-9-4
エルハイム麹町704
Shuichi Yoshida
ALFA INC.
L Heim Kojimachi 704 3-9-4 Kudan-minami,
Chiyoda-ku, Tokyo 102-0074
Tel. 03-3261-2655　Fax. 03-3261-2667
E-mail: alfashu@ta2.so-net.ne.jp

Japan Art Publicity
森相 文宏
(株) ジャパン・アート・パブリシティ
〒107-0062 東京都港区南青山5-12-24
シャトー東洋南青山610号／302号
Fumihiro Moriai
Japan Art Publicity Inc.
Syato Toyo Minamiaoyama 610・502
5-12-24 Minamiaoyama, Minato-ku,
Tokyo 107-0062
Tel. 03-3498-9245　Fax. 03-3498-9246

 DESIGN BOX
山田 正彦
DESIGN BOX
〒464-0858 愛知県名古屋市千種区
千種3-11-2-402
Masahiko Yamada
DESIGN BOX
3-11-2-402 Chikusa, Chikusa-ku,
Nagoya 464-0858
Tel. Fax. 052-732-8710
E-mail: seigen@bd5.so-net.ne.jp

吉田 哲
(有) 吉田デザイン事務所
〒104-0045 東京都中央区築地1-4-8
築地ホワイトビル703号
Tetsu Yoshida
Yoshida Design Office Co.,Ltd.
Tsukiji White Bldg. 7F
1-4-8 Tsukiji, Chuo-ku, Tokyo 104-0045
Tel. 03-3542-3337　Fax. 03-3542-3338

八木 健夫
(株) オフィス・ピーアンドシー
〒150-0011 東京都渋谷区東1-3-1
常盤松ロイアルハイツ601
Tateo Yagi
Office P&C Inc.
Tokiwamatsu Royal Heights 601
1-3-1 Higashi, Shibuya-ku, Tokyo 150-0011
Tel. 03-3406-0191　Fax. 03-3406-1084

山田 佳明
山田佳明デザイン事務所
〒526-0041 滋賀県長浜市四ツ塚町182-8
ランドマークビル
Yoshiaki Yamada
YAMADA yoshiaki DESIGN OFFICE
Landmark bldg. 182-8 Yotsuzuka-cho,
Nagahama-shi, Shiga 526-0041
Tel. 0749-65-2340　Fax. 0749-64-1899
E-mail: yoshiaki@pop.biwako.ne.jp

 YOSHIDA VISUAL DESIGN OFFICE
吉田 佳広
(有) ヨシダデザインオフィス
〒162-0065 東京都新宿区住吉町1-23
サンメゾン大谷303
Yoshihiro Yoshida
Yoshida Visual Design Office
San Maison Otani 303 1-23 Sumiyoshicho,
Shinjyuku-ku, Tokyo 162-0065
Tel. 03-3353-6300　Fax. 03-5363-7526
E-mail: yodesign@ask.or.jp

吉津 孝彦
イグレック・イデア
〒542-0083 大阪府大阪市中央区
東心斎橋1-11-13 グランドメゾン心斎橋903
Takahiko Yoshizu
Igrek idea
#903 1-11-13 Higashi-Shinsaibashi,
Chuo-ku, Osaka 542-0083
Tel. 06-6253-1143　Fax. 06-6253-1183
E-mail: yoshidzu@netplus.or.jp

吉延 高明
(株) ヨシノブデザイン
〒150-0031 東京都渋谷区桜丘町4-17-103
Takaaki Yoshinobu
Yoshinobu Design Inc.
4-17-103 Sakuragaoka-cho,
Shibuya-ku, Tokyo 150-0031
Tel. 03-3462-6439　Fax. 03-3462-6438
E-mail: yosinobu@fa2.so-net.ne.jp

饒平名 克郎
Y工房
〒658-0037 兵庫県神戸市東灘区西岡本4-3-13
アンビエンテ屋敷本101
Katsuro Yohena
Y KOBO
4-3-13-101 Nishiokamoto, Higashinada-ku,
Kobe-shi Hyogo 658-0037
Tel. 078-436-2622　Fax. 078-451-7514

バーンド F. ランガー
(株) コンセプトインターナショナル
〒100-0006 東京都千代田区有楽町1-7-1
有楽町電気ビル南館12階
Bernd F. Langer
Concept International Co.,Ltd.
Yurakucho Denki Bldg., South Tower 12F
1-7-1 Yurakucho, Chiyoda-ku, Tokyo 100-0006
Tel. 03-3287-1521　Fax. 03-3287-1522
E-mail: concept@cyborg.or.jp

利 絵
(株) プラグ
〒540-0036 大阪府大阪市中央区船越町2-4-1
三浦ビル2F
lie
PLUG CO.,LTD.
Miura Bldg. 2F 2-4-1 Funakoshicho,
Chuo-ku, Osaka 540-0036
Tel. 06-6944-1123　Fax. 06-6944-1117
E-mail: liedebut@mx5.nisiq.net

渡邉 勝則
(株) バウハウス
〒460-0008 愛知県名古屋市中区栄3-19-19
フォルテ栄3階
Katsunori Watanabe
Bauhaus Inc.
Forte-Sakae bldg. 3F 3-19-19 Sakae,
Naka-ku, Nagoya 460-0008
Tel. 052-263-0452 (代)　Fax. 052-249-2698
E-mail: katsu@bauhaus-dessau.co.jp
http://www.bauhaus-dessau.co.jp/

渡邊 邦雄
アドハウス (株)
〒103-0013 東京都中央区日本橋人形町3-3-15
Kunio Watanebe
AD HOUSE
3-3-15 Nihonbashi-ningyocho,
Chuo-ku, Tokyo 103-0013
Tel. 03-3666-6545　Fax. 03-3666-2275
E-mail: ad-house@sb-net.or.jp

渡部 孝一
(株) 渡部デザイン事務所
〒151-0072 東京都渋谷区幡ケ谷1-3-1
幡ケ谷ゴールデンマンション1009
Koichi Watanabe
Watanabe Design Office Inc.
1009 Hatagaya Golden Mansion
1-3-1 Hatagaya, Shibuya-ku, Tokyo 151-0072
Tel. 03-3320-5166　Fax. 03-3320-5161

渡辺 富男
(有) ウェーヴクリエーション
〒104-0032 東京都中央区八丁堀3-3-2
井田八丁堀ビル6F
Tomio Watanabe
WAVE CREATION
Ida Hatchobori Bldg. 6F 3-3-2 Hatchobori,
Chuo-ku, Tokyo 104-0032
Tel. 03-5541-5005　Fax. 03-5541-7592
E-mail: wave@kt.rim.or.jp

OB会員　奥泉 元晟
〒369-1411 埼玉県秩父郡皆野町
三沢4020-24
Motoaki Okuizumi
4020-24 Misawa, Minanomachi,
Titibugun, Saitama 369-1411
Tel. Fax. 0494-65-0175

OB会員　中林 基
〒569-1029 大阪府高槻市安岡寺町3-9-5
Osamu Nakabayashi
3-9-5 Ankoji-cho, Takatsuki-shi,
Osaka 569-1029
Tel. Fax. 0726-87-2213

Arjo Wiggins アルジョウィギンズ・ファインペーパー社
(株)ヤマト海外室　大内　容美
〒104-0041東京都中央区新富1-13-21
Arjo Wiggins Fine Papers Limited
PO Box 88 Gateway House,　Basingstoke
Hampshire　RG21　4EE　England
Hiromi Ohuchi
1-13-21Shintomi, Chuo-ku ,Tokyo 104-0041

 株式会社 視覚デザイン研究所
葛本　京子
〒541-0059 大阪府大阪市中央区博労町3-2-3
野村ビル 7F
VISUAL DESIGN LABORATORY INC.
Kyoko Katsumoto
Nomura Bldg. 7F 3-2-3 Bakuromachi,
Chuo-ku, Osaka 541-0059
Tel. 06-6245-7745　Fax. 06-6258-6636
E-mail: vdl@vdl.co.jp
http://www.vdl.co.jp/

王子製紙株式会社
鈴木　満雄
〒104-0061 東京都中央区銀座5-12-8
王子製紙1号館
OJI PAPER CO.,LTD.
Mitsuo Suzuki
5-12-8 Ginza, Chuo-ku, Tokyo 104-0061
Tel. 03-5550-3090　Fax. 03-5550-2955
http://www.ojipaper.co.jp/

shaken 株式会社 写研
平賀　隆二
〒170-0005 東京都豊島区南大塚2-26-13
SHA-KEN CO.,LTD.
Ryuji Hiraga
2-26-13 Minamiohtuka, Toshima-ku,
Tokyo 170-0005
Tel. 03-3942-2211　Fax. 03-3942-2301

Canon キヤノン株式会社
渋谷　薫
〒146-8501 東京都大田区下丸子3-30-2
CANON Inc.
Kaoru Shibuya
3-30-2 Shimomaruko, Ota-ku,
Tokyo 146-8501
Tel. 03-5482-8638　Fax. 03-3758-3521
E-mail: shibuya@drc.canon.co.jp
http://www.canon.co.jp/

EPSON セイコーエプソン株式会社
丸山　佳弘
〒399-0785 長野県塩尻市広丘原新田80
SEIKO EPSON CORPORATION
Yoshihiro Maruyama
80 Harashinden, Hirooka,
Shiojiri-shi, Nagano 399-0785
Tel. 0263-54-1894　Fax. 0263-52-9217
E-mail:Maruyama.Yoshihiro.exc.epson.co.jp
http://www.epson.co.jp/

株式会社 コムカット
田邊　浩
〒130-0002 東京都墨田区業平5-11-3
イトミックビル 2F
COMCUT CO.,LTD.
Hiroshi Tanabe
5-11-3 Narihira, Sumida-ku,
Tokyo 130-0002
Tel. 03-3623-6041　Fax. 03-3623-6540

SONY ソニー株式会社
尾村　匡明
〒141-0001 東京都品川区北品川6-7-35
Sony Corporation Corporare Design Center
Masaaki Omura
6-7-35 Kitashinagawa, Shinagawa-ku,
Tokyo 141-0001
Tel. 03-5448-3369　Fax. 03-5448-7822
E-mail: omura@dc.sony.co.jp
http://www.sony.co.jp/

THE
DESIGN
ASSOCIATES 株式会社 ザ・デザイン・アソシエイツ
佐藤　忠敏
〒106-0046 東京都港区元麻布3-2-9
THE DESIGN ASSOCIATES
Tadatoshi Sato
3-2-9 Motoazabu, Minato-ku,
Tokyo 106-0046
Tel. 03-3404-0328　Fax. 03-3404-0254
E-mail: tda@gol.com

B 株式会社 タイプバンク
林　久美子
〒160-0015 東京都新宿区大京町29番地
御苑プラザビル302
TypeBank Co.,Ltd.
Kumiko Hayashi
Gyoen Plaza Bidg. 302 29 Daikyo-cho,
Shinjyuki-ku, Tokyo 160-0015
Tel. 03-3359-6013　Fax. 03-3359-6016
E-mail: info@typebank.co.jp
http://www.typebank.co.jp/

C&G
character and graphics 株式会社 シー アンドジイ
鈴木　竹治
〒162-0801 東京都新宿区山吹町263-2-1104
C&G Inc.
Takeharu Suzuki
No.1104 263-2 Yamabuki-cho,
Shinjuku-ku, Tokyo 162-0801
Tel. 03-5261-3591　Fax. 03-5261-3593

 株式会社 竹尾
林　治雄
〒101-0054 東京都千代田区神田錦町3-12-6
TAKEO COMPANY LIMITED
Haruo Hayashi
3-12-6 Kanda, Nishiki-cho, Chiyoda-ku,
Tokyo 101-0054
Tel. 03-3292-3619　Fax. 03-3219-9060
E-mail: info@takeo.co.jp
http://www.takeo.co.jp/

株式会社 中川ケミカル
桶谷 尚夫
〒103-0004 東京都中央区東日本橋3-7-13
相良ビル 4F
NAKAGAWA CHEMICAL INC.
Masao Oketani
Sagara Bldg. 4F 3-7-13 Higashinihonbashi,
Chuo-ku, Tokyo 103-0004
Tel. 03-3668-8141　Fax. 03-3668-5705
http://www.cs-nakagawa.com/

ムーサ株式会社
山鹿 正隆
〒577-0013 大阪府大阪市東大阪市長田中3-1-3
MUSA CO., LTD.
Masataka Yamaga
3-1-3 Nagatanaka, Higashiosaka-shi,
Osaka 577-0013
Tel. 06-6743-0331　Fax. 06-6743-0333

株式会社 ニィス
伊藤 晃
〒112-0002 東京都文京区小石川5-4-4
すみれビル 3F
NIS Corporation
Hikaru Ito
Sumire Bldg. 3F 5-4-4 Koishikawa,
Bunkyo-ku, Tokyo 112-0002
Tel. 03-3814-3201　Fax. 03-3814-3206
E-mail: nischan@magical.egg.or.jp
http://www.nisfont.co.jp/

MOTOYA 株式会社 モトヤ
大本 義秀
〒542-0081 大阪府大阪市中央区南船場1-10-25
MOTOYA CO.,LTD.
Yoshihide Omoto
1-10-25 Minamisenba, Chuo-ku,
Osaka 542-0081
Tel. 06-6261-2413　Fax. 06-6261-1930
E-mail: mtyfont@ra2.so-net.ne.jp
http://www.motoya.co.jp/

株式会社 日本ソフトウェアサービス
日高 通
〒336-0017 埼玉県浦和市南浦和2丁目38-8
ケーアイビル 3F
NIHON SOFTWARE SERVICE Co.,Ltd.
Toru Hidaka
KI Bldg. 3F 2-38-8 Minamiurawa,
Urawa-shi, Saitama 336-0017
Tel. 048-883-8451　Fax. 048-883-8458

モリサワ 株式会社 モリサワ
冨田 信雄
〒556-0012 大阪府大阪市浪速区敷津東2-6-25
Morisawa & Company Ltd.
Nobuo Tomita
2-6-25 Shikizuhigashi, Naniwa-ku,
Osaka 556-0012
Tel. 06-6649-2151
E-mail: tomita@morisawa.co.jp
http://www.morisawa.co.jp/

BIKOHSHA
INC
株式会社 びこう社
永山 隆久
〒107-0062 東京都港区南青山4-15-5
BIKOHSHA INC
Takahisa Nagayama
4-15-5 Minamiaoyama, Minato-ku,
Tokyo 107-0062
Tel. 03-3796-0737　Fax. 03-3403-4475

株式会社ヤマト
株式会社 ヤマト
東出 昭夫
〒104-0041 東京都中央区新富1-13-21
YAMATO INC.
Akio Higashide
1-13-21 Shintomi, Chuo-ku,
Tokyo 104-0041
Tel. 03-3551-8286(代)　Fax. 03-3553-9334

FONTWORKS
株式会社 フォントワークスジャパン
藤田 重信
〒810-0001 福岡県福岡市中央区
天神3丁目9-25 東晴天神ビル 4F
Fontwoks Japan, Inc.
Shigenobu Fujita
Tosei Tenjin Bldg. 3-9-25 Tenjin,
Chuo-ku, Fukuoka 810-0001
Tel. 092-722-5558　Fax. 092-722-5559
E-mail: sfujita@fontworks.co.jp
http://www.fontworks.co.jp/

RYOBI リョービイマジクス株式会社
吉田 俊一
〒101-0044 東京都千代田区神田鍛冶町2-10-11
リョービイマジクスビル6F
RYOBI IMAGIX Co.,
Shunichi Yoshida
Ryobi Imagix Bidg. 6F 2-10-11 Kajicho,
Kanda, Chiyoda-ku, Tokyo 101-0044
Tel. 03-3257-1260　Fax. 03-3257-1237
E-mail: rimagix@blue.ocn.ne.jp
http://www.ryobi-group.co.jp/imagix/font

brother ブラザー工業株式会社
森下 眞行
〒467-8562 愛知県名古屋市瑞穂区河岸1-1-1
Brother Industries, LTD.
Masayuki Morishita
1-1-1 Kawagishi, Mizuho-ku, Nagoya 467-8562
Tel. 052-824-2452　Fax. 052-811-4110
E-mail: masayuki.morishita@brother.co.jp
http://www.brother.co.jp/

作品募集のご案内

[日本タイポグラフィ年鑑]では毎年作品の募集を行
なっております。次号も作品募集のご案内をできる限
り多くの方々にお配りしたいと思います。ご希望が
ありましたら郵便はがきで、随時お申し込みください。
募集が始まり次第、一斉にお送り致します。

募集要項のお申し込みは
[日本タイポグラフィ年鑑]作品募集要項希望と記し
て、はがきで下記へ

〒102-0073 東京都千代田区九段北1-9-12
グラフィック社［日本タイポグラフィ年鑑］係

本号へご応募された後、住所を変更された方もご一
報ください。

造本設計データ

判　型	天地297mm x 左右210mm（A4判）
製　本	上製本、ホロウバック、糸かがり綴じ、角背、厚表紙、みぞつき
カバー	オフメタル銀四六判130kg（王子製紙）
表　紙	オフメタル銀四六判130kg（王子製紙）
見返し	キクラシャ黒 69.5kg（日清紡績）
本　文	OKロイヤルコート菊判76.5kg（王子製紙）
後付け一色頁	Aプランピュアホワイト菊判 71.5kg（王子製紙）
書　体	見出ゴシックMB101ボールド
	見出ゴシックMB31
	太ゴシックB101
	中ゴシックBBB
	見出ミンMA31
	B太MA101
	ヘルベチカ
	ヘルベチカボールド
	フーツラヘビー
	フーツラブック
	フーツラボールド
	タイムスボールド

日本タイポグラフィ年鑑 2000

2000年5月25日　初版第1刷発行

編　者	日本タイポグラフィ協会
発行者	菅谷誠一
印　刷	錦明印刷株式会社
製　本	錦明印刷株式会社
発行所	株式会社グラフィック社
	102-0073 東京都千代田区九段北1-9-12
	Tel. 03-3263-4318 Fax.03-3263-5297
	振替 00130-6-114345
	http://www.graphicsha.co.jp

乱丁・落丁はお取り替え致します。
ISBN4-7661-1157-5 C3070
本書の無断転載、引用等を禁じます。